MW01147655

RIGHTING WRITING

by Michael Bailey

Cover and interior design by Michael Bailey

Published by Written Backwards
www.nettirw.com

ISBN: 978-1-7355981-9-2 / Paperback Edition
ISBN: 979-8-9867488-3-2 / eBook Edition

for those who ~~want~~ need to write

RIGHTING WRITING

CONTENTS

Where to find everything.

INTRODUCTION

Need vs. want and the sickness that is writing.

> "You don't start out writing good stuff. You start out writing crap and thinking it's good stuff, and then gradually you get better at it."
> - Octavia E. Butler

Writing is a disease without a cure. Once infected, the virus is in the host for good, until death. Something first sparked creative curiosity to write, though, so what was it? Hopefully, the answer is a book, or a short story, a poem, or any other form of writing. Maybe *this* book, eventually. Whatever it may be, there are three rules to follow.

WRITERS READ

To have the passion to *write*, there must first be a passion to *read*. Reading should always be the reason someone has the yearning to say, "I want to write a book." Books take dedication, and while reading a book can take months, weeks, or a single day, writing a book can take years, or, if a fire is burning inside, a first draft can take a month.

In order for the writerly disease to spread, one must read regularly, and not from a single or favorite genre but across the spectrum: fiction, nonfiction, poetry, anything and everything word-related. If only ever reading one type of story, a writer will only be capable of producing one type of story. They will become a copycat, unable to develop their own literary voice, their own style, their own brand.

A wise writer once said, "Read a thousand books before ever writing one," then, "read a few hundred books between writing any others." Dallas Mayr, who went by the pseudonym Jack Ketchum, knew what he was talking about.

Do I enjoy reading? Do I read diversely? Do I read regularly? If the answer to any of those questions is "no" or there is the slightest of hesitations, do not write. The disease is not there. Close this book. Move on. Watch television instead, although *all* forms of film first start with words by way of an original script or adapted story.

Writers need to read, and writers needs to *love* reading, or they cannot be writers.

A common answer many editors hear while helping new writers after asking the question "What do you read?" is "Oh, not much" or "I don't really like to read." This is not a healthy mindset for a writer. Writers read diversely until ready, and only then do they put words to paper.

WRITERS WRITE

Ask those same three questions, but centered around writing: *Do I enjoy writing? Do I write diversely? Do I write regularly?* If the answer to any of those questions is also "no" or there's a hesitation, then ask the most important question all writers should ask themselves: "Do I *want* to write, or do I *need* to write?" A writer *needs* to write.

"Write at least three full-length manuscripts before attempting to publish" is not the advice an ambitious writer wants to hear, yet it is healthy to write hundreds of thousands of words as practice. One can hit the ground running and be successful with their first book, theoretically, but there will be stumbling and future regret.

A "trunk" manuscript is an unpublished draft that

should be hidden in a trunk lest it fester and corrupt or become a burden. Consider writing one minimum, although three is highly suggested. They can be revisited and revised later but keep them out of sight and work on the next project, always finding ways to improve the craft.

Write hundreds of thousands of words well before publishing a book that might represent undeveloped talent. Get unhealthy habits out of the system. Write them out. Read them out. Develop the talent. Otherwise, that first book will forever be out there for readers to find, and a pseudonym might be necessary for a second attempt at being a writer.

Josh Malerman, *New York Times* best-selling author of the post-apocalyptic novel *Bird Box*, is a prime example of how to do it right. *Bird Box* may have been his first published novel, and an enormous success (book and later film), but he wrote more than a dozen full-length manuscripts prior to that one, a million or more words. The first draft of his "debut" was single-spaced, no tabs, *all* the text italicized. Considered artful at the time of creation, he envisioned publishing the book in that format because his talent had not fully developed. If he had published the book that way, it might have stained him as a writer.

Words in the past mean better words in the future, which applies to both reading *and* writing.

WRITERS ACT PROFESSIONALLY

Publishing has changed. It is easier not only to write a book, but to "publish" a book. Publish is in quotes because of the ability to self-publish and print a book without any editor or professional involvement. Now, a story can simply be published online for all the world to see. And yes, once it is online, it is published, and will be quite difficult to sell traditionally.

Each manuscript needs to go through a first draft, but also a second and third (minimum), and a rewrite if necessary. It needs to be professionally edited, copyedited, proofread, and so on, whether done the old-fashioned way with traditional publishing, or through third-party services. A book needs to go through hell before ever becoming a book, so always work professionally and use such services whether paid out of pocket or not.

Published work is a writer's resume, so only ever put the best stuff out there.

A successful writer needs to dedicate thousands upon thousands of hours to the craft. Years and years of letting the disease spread. A novice writer without experience cannot crank out a book and instantly become successful, the same way a novice driver cannot crank over an engine and become a perfect driver without having experience behind the wheel.

Righting Writing is designed to shape aspiring writers into professional writers and to further shape professional writers into better professional writers, offering advice all should know *before*, *while*, and *after* putting words on the page.

As multiple Hugo and Nebula award-winning author Octavia E. Butler says in that opening quote, no one ever starts out writing the good stuff, but crap that is thought of as good. The key is righting writing until the crap is gone.

Welcome to the sickness.

PART 1: THE BEGINNING

A few things before / while writing.

"In the beginning was the Word, and the Word was with God, and the Word was God." - John 1:1

A writer is the creator of their story, so it might work well to swap 'God' for 'The Writer' for *Book 1:1* (a placeholder title for the eventual book). The line would then read: "In the beginning was the Word, and the Word was with The Writer, and the Word was The Writer."

WRITER / AUTHOR

Authoring a book starts with a single word, an insignificant one like 'The' or one more important such as a character name or location or the start of an important event that pushes the story into action. It might also be the first word of the book's title. Whatever that first word may be, and while important, it is not going to last. So write.

Any word will do to start a manuscript, so do not fret too long and just get it over with already. The entire first page might not even make it through the editing and revision stages that will inevitably follow, or even the first ten pages or entire chapter(s), but a story must start with a single word from the story's god.

A book never *wants* to be written; it *needs* to be written. Words eventually spill out with reckless abandon, character, dialogue, voice, and plotlines taking over, the book writing itself at times, conflict stacking, themes evolving, an imagined setting taking on an impossible shape in the mind and then onto the page. An author is someone who has published their work. A writer is someone who writes, whether or not their work is published. Avoid taking on the "author" title, which could be a temporary thing (anyone can write and publish a book); instead, be a *writer*. As writing mentor Thomas F. Monteleone is noted as saying, "You're an entertainer. You're a writer. You *write*. You're no *author*. You don't 'auth' anything . . . whatever that means."

Every idea for a book starts small: a *what if?* moment, an *idea*, a *feeling*. What is important is to take that small thing, whatever it may be, and explore the potential. Write it down.

This is the beginning, and—

"In the beginning was the Word . . ."

Writing is magic, as is all creation, the ability to create something from nothing. The fire is there, perhaps hiding in the writer, wanting to spread, but . . . nothing happens at first—a white page and nothing more.

This dreamy state, this *not*-writing, is part of the process. It is not writer's block, although sometimes seen that way. A writer must stare at a blank page, or a blank screen, or a wall, or be in one's head without writing any words at all, everyone around them wondering if something is wrong, the writer wondering as well. It is also equally important not to stay in that dreamy, not-writing state too long. It is important, but so is knowing when it must end, otherwise it becomes a trap and the book will never be written.

A story is never started with words, but emotions that turn into words. It is crucial to respect that blank stare, and likewise important for creatives and others around them not to think of those bland moments as downtime but as a part of story development. Writing is often doing nothing, and a single interruption can destroy that magic. Isolation is sometimes necessary for those quiet moments to turn into sounds of pens scribbling or keys tapping.

Once the words start flowing, then maybe it is time for an elevator pitch. This is the phrase used to describe a book in as few words as possible, as one might explain to another while riding in an elevator. And it is okay to have this well before the writing process begins. Having an elevator pitch, which can change over time, keeps a writer in check for that "What's your book about?" question. Have the answer ready or prepare to stumble over the unwritten words.

"*The book is about, uh, well, there's this character who, sort of, has this problem dealing with tricky situations, and, you see, there's this woman in the story who—*" and so on. Pitches can seem to last lifetimes with nothing said about a story at all. A writer should be prepared to rattle off what their book is about and to keep it succinct.

The Sixth Sense, an Academy Award-winning screenplay by M. Night Shayamalan, could be simplified to: "A troubled, isolated young boy who communicates with the dead seeks help from a disheartened child psychologist to unravel a murder mystery." Those twenty-two words summarize the script, and while not giving anything away, it is intriguing.

Who is this boy and why is he troubled? What's his name? Wait, he can communicate with the dead? Does he see them, or can he only hear or sense them? Someone was murdered? Who? More than one? Why is the child psychologist disheartened? That is twice as many words to describe the intrigue created by half as many.

Fifty words or fewer for an elevator pitch is ideal. This, of course, might lead to other questions about the characters, the plot, etc., which should be easier to explain than summarizing an entire book within so many words.

In her article for the *BookBub Partners Blog*, Jennie Nash says that with a good elevator pitch "it's much easier to answer when people ask, 'So what's your book about?'"[1]

The elevator pitch is the first hook used to gain reader interest. If fiction, creative nonfiction, or a memoir, it should briefly summarize what the story is about and include main characters. If nonfiction, it should include the main topic, and what readers might learn, even if that is in the form of a question. With all books, readers want to be immersed, so offer what is expected in terms of location, timeline, context of issues explored, all the basics.

Why should readers care about the book, what should they feel, and what is the point?

It may be handy to create character sketches. Some writers use this method; some do not. These are lists of traits that create a strong mental image of characters, along with a quick backstory, wants and needs, personalities, beliefs, how they might act, talk, think, strengths and flaws, how they change throughout the story—the most important part of their arc—and physical descriptions, if important. The more the writer knows about a character, the less needs to be written about them in the narrative, letting the details form naturally in the reader's mind instead.

Some writers outline; some do not. Consider early on if outlining might be useful (or necessary) to help the story along, or if the story will survive without one. If stuck, a writer can always create an outline later to help get unstuck. All it takes is a few sentences about each chapter, a rough framework for the book, or bullet points. The less written in a chapter-by-chapter outline, the more freedom there is to let the characters take over the storytelling.

Another piece of writing that might be useful is a book synopsis. This can be a single page or however many pages are needed to summarize the book in full detail. A synopsis does not tease the book but reveals everything that happens with spoilers. Agents often request synopses, typically in the three-, five-, and seven-page variety, depending on the publishers they seek, and can be useful to bring editors quickly up to speed, thus helping *them* help *you*. Editors and agents and publishers do not care about spoilers. They, like the writer, need to know all the secrets: beginning, middle, and end.

The beginning—that is where to start. The middle or end might be known but start at the beginning if new to writing. Do not try nonlinear, not at first. Starting elsewhere typically leads to passive voice.

Start with Chapter 1, Scene 1.

Those first pages need to establish character and create conflict, atmosphere, intrigue. They need to hook the reader, so start at the beginning of the story, not somewhere later, and do not rely on excessive description. What is the immediate narrative moment? Let that moment pop with tension, imagery, vividness . . .

And avoid prologues whenever possible. A prologue is the past, and backstory a difficult means of propelling readers forward. Start at the end and rewind, if necessary, but do not start at the beginning by first rewinding. Also avoid dreams, flashbacks, and backstory, as these are interjections from the story timeline, or distractions.

Always move the story forward.

Don't be an "author," having written and published; be a writer who never stops writing and improving.

IMPOSTOR SYNDROME & OTHER MISTRUTHS

Everyone is an impostor, so get over it.

"I am not a writer. I've been fooling myself and other people."
- John Steinbeck

Every writer has impostor syndrome. Also known as *impostor phenomenon*, impostor syndrome is a psychological pattern in which a person doubts a certain skill, talent, or even accomplishment and experiences an overwhelming and persistent fear of being called a fraud. It is not an actual disorder.

Clinical psychologists Pauline Clance and Suzanne Imes coined the term "impostor phenomenon" in the 1970s, with Imes stating, "There can be a lot of confusion between approval and love and worthiness. Self-worth becomes contingent on achieving." [2]

According to the American Psychological Association (APA), 70% of all people have impostor syndrome in some form or another [3] but for writers, and creators in general, the number is much higher. 100%.

To help avoid impostor syndrome, write for the self first, the audience second. Do not worry about the *image* of the writer; worry about the writing itself, putting words on the page primarily and later making sure they are right.

Am I good enough? Will I ever be good enough? Is my writing terrible?

"Maybe" is an answer to any of those questions, but so what (not a question). The goal of a writer is to write and to constantly improve their writing. "Writing is never finished, only abandoned" — someone famous said that.

Anxiety, however, is real and a normal and often healthy emotion, so the goal of a writer is to never give up but to listen to their anxiety. Stop asking "Is anyone ever going to read this?" and "Should I just give up?" because the answer to the first question should always be "It doesn't matter" and the answer to the second a resounding "No."

What gives a person the right to write? Nothing. Anyone can write.

Nonfiction writers are professional truth tellers, and fiction writers are professional liars, and poets tell both truths and lies through verse and imagery. *All* writers are frauds, in terms of achievement, but only if they *believe* they are frauds. The secret is to shake off thoughts of "not good enough" as early as possible, to face fear head-on and shrug off the nerves because impostor syndrome itself is a fraud.

Every writer starts with a blank page, whether the first attempt or thousandth. It's not until a writer completely finishes what they are working on, until their work has gone through multiple drafts, revisions, is self-edited, beta-read, has gone through rounds upon rounds of edits, is copy-edited, and finally proofread, not until the writing is in print and in the past, that a writer can ever look beyond being an impostor (for *that* particular work); and even *then* they will remain "a fraud" until putting that nonsense to rest.

It is completely normal to feel like an impostor; it is a part of all creation.

Social media has much to do with an underwhelming sense of achievement, with a constant societal pressure for a digital representation of the self to reflect an over-whelming sense of achievement. What is shared are mostly lies: forced smiles, digitally enhanced and/or manipulated. Photos shared on social media are filtered—words filtered just the same—and presented "better" than the original before judged publicly or non-publicly for clout.

Online feedback for books, or *anything*, for that matter, can be just as cruel, with most reviews left from opposite extremes: "Best ever!" to "Worst ever!" and seldom anything in between. Worrying over image is cancerous.

Write what *needs* to be written, good or bad. Get words onto the page, then keep working at it, one word at a time. The first draft will not be perfect, not by a long shot. Prepare to spend countless grueling hours homing in on the craft and learning what is necessary to make the writing the best it can be. Do not worry about image, otherwise impostor syndrome will reveal itself. And it will, at some point, even though it is all in the head.

Metacognition is the awareness and understanding of one's own thought processes, which could be part of the problem: "thinking about thinking," or "cognition about cognition," a person *over*thinking. But it can also improve one's writing if metacognitive ability is used to improve the learning of what it takes to become a better writer.

Like any talent or skill, writing takes time and practice. It takes passion. And reading, wherein the more words read makes for a better *reader*, the more words written makes for a better *writer*.

> "Better to write for yourself and have no public, than to write for the public and have no self."
> - Cyril Connolly

A comprehensive list of ways to forever stay an impostor and never become a writer:

Never read.
Never write.
Never focus on improving.
Never accept constructive criticism / feedback.
Never think writing is hard.
Never think editing is hard.
Never sacrifice words.
Never read / write diversely.
Never read aloud.

Remove the word "never" and it becomes a list of how to become a professional writer: *read, write, focus on improving, accept constructive criticism / feedback, think writing is hard*, that *editing is hard, sacrifice words, read / write diversely*, and *read aloud.*

Dr. Valerie Young, author of *The Secret Thoughts of Successful Women: Why Capable People Suffer from the Impostor Syndrome and How to Thrive in Spite of It*, through much research over the last few decades, has broken impostor syndrome down into five different "competence types." [4] To help get over the feeling of fraud, consider the following, but in terms of the writer.

THE PERFECTIONIST

"If it's not done right, it shouldn't be done at all."

The writing perfectionist tends to set extremely ambitious goals, and when not reaching those goals experiences self-doubt. These are the "control freaks" who take on all responsibilities themselves to do things "right." The work must be perfect, which leads to work never getting finished.

Perfectionists hold a belief that their writing will never be completely flawless, and so they have the tendency to fall into endless editing loops striving for that unattainable perfection. If a work is not perfect it can never be published. But writing is never finished, only abandoned, so a perfectionist must eventually accept that fate and move on.

THE SUPERWOMAN / MAN

"I can do everything myself, just you watch."

These are the "pushers," those who constantly push themselves to work harder, to do better, and to be a better writer than they can become by taking the time to learn the many skills necessary to improve their craft. They wake up early and stay up late, often setting aside life to put words on the page, no matter the cost, all downtime considered wasteful, including sleep, including time spent with family and friends.

For the superwoman / superman, criticism is typically taken as insult, not to improve. Young implies that "imposter workaholics" are addicted to work validation, not the actual work, and so they must train themselves over time not to require such validation.

THE NATURAL GENIUS

"I should be better than this."

Like perfectionists, the natural genius sets their bar(s) too high, with a false belief that they need to be a "natural," and so they often judge their writing based on speed and ease rather than effort. Shame is often experienced when proficiency is not accomplished easily, and without spending the time to learn what is necessary to improve their craft. They should be able to get it right the very first try, their first draft flawless.

Natural geniuses should not need editors, for example, and so constructive criticism is taken as failure, not an area of improvement, and feedback is pushed aside. But to become a great writer, it takes skill-building, accepting that a writer is not born with a natural ability to write.

THE SOLOIST

"I don't need *anyone's* help."

These are the independent types, those who believe that asking for any type of help reveals the impostor. They tend to refuse advice or aid to prove their worth as writers. The soloist can do everything themselves, like the superwoman / man, but struggle when having to reach out for help because then it will not just be *them* tooting their own horn.

Writing is a lonely profession, but it does not have to be. There is a reason editors exist, and beta-readers, and writing support groups, and writing mentors, and books designed to teach the art of writing. A symphony takes many instruments, not one.

THE EXPERT

"I need to know *everything*,
or I can't possibly write about this."

Confidence is measured, by the expert, as how much or what is known firsthand, the belief that if they do not know enough about a certain subject, they cannot write about it. They spend more time researching than writing, and often get sucked down the information rabbit hole. One article leads to another, leads to another, leads to another . . . The expert needs to understand that eventually they will have to stop researching and start writing.

No matter the writer type, words need to go on the page. Writers may need to recognize what kind of writer they are in order to tell their story, but in all cases impostor syndrome needs to be recognized as acceptable and be pushed aside so they can get to work.

A writer is never perfect, yet strives for perfection.

A writer is not born with a special talent to write but can develop their skill and become a better writer.

A writer cannot do it alone, and never should.

A writer does not have to know absolutely everything there is to know about a subject, just *enough.*

Am I good enough? Practice reading and writing often, and the answer will be yes. *Will I ever be good enough?* Yes. *Is my writing terrible?* It might be at the start, but not at the end.

Successful writers start without any words on the page, and then some terrible words, and then better ones, and then, after spending time developing their craft, hacking and slashing at those words, always seeking perfection, they eventually start looking like they know what they are doing and manage to publish a book.

Every writer is an impostor, so get over it. Tell the story that needs to be told.

THE WRITER LIFE

Hard work and dedication.

"Write.

"Write more.

"Write even more.

"Write even more than that.

"Write when you don't want to.

"Write when you do.

"Write when you have something to say.

"Write when you don't.

"Write every day.

"Keep writing."

- Brian Clark

Successful writers have one thing in common: *routine*. They get up every day with a mug of coffee or a cup of tea and they tap on keys—by typewriter or computer—and get the ugly words out before the good ones start flowing. They pick up a pen or pencil and handwrite, or they record their words by some other means. They sit and they write.

Routine is a sequence of actions regularly followed. Part of the writing routine can be as simple as wearing the same hat every day, or scarf, or drinking out of a favorite mug or cup, or using the same pen, or beginning each day reading what was written the day before prior to starting anew. Whatever the routine, it needs to be an organized event carried out on a regular basis but will need to include actual writing.

Putting a certain number of words on the page each day or each week is a requirement, or, like a select few, cranking out tens of thousands over the span of a few days. Aim for a certain word count, then aim a little higher.

Kenra Cherry in her article "The Importance of Maintaining Structure and Routine During Stressful Times" for *Verywell Mind* writes that routine can be helpful when establishing healthy habits, especially when feeling uncertain. [5]

A rhetorical question: How many novice writers are uncertain about writing their first book?

Implementing structure is helpful when times are difficult, unpredictable, or when stressed. It can offer a writer organization, productivity, and a sense of control. And structure, by way of routine, can help accomplish tasks that must be completed and help with depression, so make writing a priority because it can be therapeutic.

The first step is to decide which approach to take: *plotter* or *pantser*. Writers are typically one or the other, or a strange mix of the two: *plantser*.

A plotter plans out their book before writing it, plotting each event beforehand, perhaps coming up with an outline or synopsis to figure out how the book will play out; whereas a pantser "flies by the seat of their pants," not planning anything, or plotting very little, and letting the process of writing and the characters help map out the book along the way; and the plantser is a little of both, typically leaning more toward one method over the other.

PLOTTER

When planning a book from beginning to middle to end, chapter by chapter, plot point by plot point, and/or mapping out story arcs for characters, plotters know exactly what is going to happen. Outlining can consist of bullet points or paragraph summaries of each scene, or an in-depth breakdown of each chapter, or an array of Post-It notes stuck to the wall. This takes the "unknown" out of the equation.

Plotters would argue that planning and plotting and character sketches make the writing process easier, and faster, although pantsers would argue that all the planning on the frontend is a waste of time.

A downside of the plotter approach is that it can become confining. If changes need to be made during the writing process, it could mean having to redo part or all of the outline created, but it could also simply mean shifting things around to make room for new developments and not necessarily take up a lot of time.

Some plotters create a synopsis before they begin, which is a summary of the book, and can run anywhere from a single page to three, five, seven, or nine. Publishers tend to ask for synopses before considering reading a manuscript, so this could also entail having to rewrite the synopsis—or multiple synopses—to better fit the book after it is written.

PANTSER

The "unknown" drives the pantser. No planning involved. No plotting. No outline. No character sketches. They might understand what needs to happen overall, or know the climax, or have certain scenes in mind or an understanding of what needs to happen to characters, but otherwise the writer is along for the ride.

Pantsers let the story and characters take them any direction desired or undesired. They do not follow an outline and can drive off the map or color outside the lines. They might argue that all the preplanning involved with plotting takes away the fun of the creative writing process, that knowing how the book ends kills motivation to get there.

Writing without a plan can make it easier to get stuck, though, having to find a way to write out of a corner, or having to fill a gap in the plot not previously considered.

Despite the flexibility and having the ability to change characters on a whim, or kill them off if unlikeable or too difficult to work with, or to change the plot if not to their liking, it's no easy task creating a book without planning, which is why it's common for pantsers to abandon one project for another.

PLANTSER

As the combined name implies, a planster is a mix of plotter and pantser with the pros and cons of each. They are typically one more than the other, using the joint approach when stuck. They might compose a quick outline to help figure out how to get unstuck, or create character sketches to better understand them.

A plantser might start off with an outline, everything detailed along the way, and then start flying by the seat of their pants for the rest of the book, but checking in every once in a while on their original plan.

However one writes, a healthy writing routine must be established. A pattern. It is different for everyone. Whether the routine is a daily word count, a binge-writing session on weekends, or a mix of the two, writing needs to be a regular occurrence of bleeding one's heart onto the page.

What is needed to establish routine?

Goals. Consistency.

Every writer writes at a different pace, so first determine what needs to be written and what ultimate word count goal that entails, and then figure out how to get there:

Calendar time. Block out an hour each day of uninterrupted "I'm unavailable for anything else" time, or a few hours, or an entire day to work on the book. This could be outlining, creating character sketches, writing out the crap to get to the good stuff. Anything that serves the book. The goal is word count, and ideas flow once the words flow.

Set reminders. Rise an hour earlier each day. Break the normal routine and reutilize time otherwise spent sleeping. Sacrificing sleep is suffering, is passion. Have an alarm go off as a reminder to write. If time in the morning cannot be spared, stay up an hour later and write by night. Creativity works differently at both ends of the clock.

Set timers. Since the hands of the clock are always ticking, why not let time be the one to hold the writer accountable? A timer can be a wonderful way to make sure an entire hour or longer is spent researching or writing, and a reminder to stop when a break is needed, or when life or duty calls.

Set expectations. Set a goal of 1,000 words, or three pages, or write until a chapter is finished, or whatever it may be. Do not do anything else until that happens.

Leave work unfinished. Leave a sentence unfinished at the end of a writing session. Before starting the next writing session, read what was previously written; seeing that unfinished sentence or paragraph will inspire a writer to finish it, getting the creative juices flowing again.

Eliminate distraction. The internet is the biggest time-suck for a writer. Close web browsers or unplug from any and all technology, or use internet blocking software. Silence cell phones or put them in another room entirely. Every time a computer dings, or a phone buzzes with a notification, it kills the creative moment, and getting back in "the zone" could take hours. Kill the habit of distraction.

Schedule binge-writing. Every so often, set up a large block of time to focus on the book, preferably an entire day, or weekend. Remember to eat and drink and sleep, but marathon it occasionally. Aim high: 5,000 words a day, or 10,000 words a weekend. Push hard, but do not push hard too often or risk burnout.

Reward milestones. Have a favorite food or drink, a favorite treat, edible or otherwise? Celebrate every 10,000 words, or at the halfway point, and especially when finished.

Once routine is established or at least *planned*, whatever that entails, word or page count goals must be determined. For novice writers, start small, maybe a few hundred words each day, or a couple pages.

The average printed page runs 250 words when formatted, depending on layout. Those bulleted points above add up to little over 400. Consider an initial goal of 500 words per day (two pages if double-spaced manuscript) and work up from there. It is not much, but words add up quickly when sticking to a routine. 500 words per day is 2,500 words per week, if only writing Monday through Friday, or 130,000 words per year (two full-length books).

> "You can't wait for inspiration. You have to go after it with a club."
> - Jack London

Jack London (1876 - 1916) is the author of such classics as *White Fang* and *The Call of the Wild*. Although he died young, he was one of the most prolific and successful writers of his time. In terms of modern writers, his output would be comparable to that of Stephen King.

According to "100 Years After Jack London's Death, Hearing His Call" by Juan Vidal for *NPR's Book News & Features*, he was "the first American author to earn a million dollars in his lifetime." And that was in the early 1900s. [6]

London did not find fame until the age of twenty-seven (1903) and died thirteen years later, but he published more than fifty books in his last sixteen years of life. That is just over three books per year, or 150,000 to 250,000 words per year. If he had lived as long as Stephen King, he could have published anywhere from 160 to 180 books, depending on length. What should also be noted is that those numbers only include *published* work.

Seven days a week, for his entire writing life, he wrote 1,000 words per day. Most of this was on typewriter, some longhand. At that rate, he could have written 365,000 words per year, netting over 5.8 million words in sixteen years.

A little adds up to a lot, in other words, figuring a daily

1,000-word goal is only four pages of double-spaced manuscript. This section so far on establishing routine and setting goals is about 2,000 words for comparison. It is not much.

Relentless routine and word count goals make a writer. It takes dedication and time. To do it right, set a daily word count goal, or a weekly word count goal. 1,000 words per day, or 5,000 words per week. Three months of this is novel-length material.

No matter what, avoid burnout.

Between writing sessions, take a break. Go for a walk, breathe fresh air, get the body moving. Exercise releases endorphins, which are powerful chemicals in the brain that energize the mind, motivating productivity and spurring creativity, which can help when stuck or in what some refer to as "writer's block."

There's no need for the work to be perfect from the start, so get words onto the page by any means necessary, however ugly, and don't get caught in revision loops. Word count goals should be in terms of "rough" manuscript.

Look forward, never back. There will be time later to revise and present the work professionally. Writing will *never* be perfect right out the gate. Plan for it to be cringeworthy, to be highly overwritten and terrible, for an editor to slash the hell out of it. All writing starts ugly. Have faith it will eventually improve.

Routine can also include time spent researching material for the book, or improving one's skills with writing fundamentals: *character, dialogue, voice, plot, conflict, theme, setting,* etc. Only with dedication and passion for learning these core components will a writer ever have the potential to become any better.

OUTLINES

Is there a need to outline before writing a book? Some writers feel there is a need to setup a skeletal framework prior to starting a new manuscript, others do not, and some outline only after writing themselves into a corner. If outlining, it is best to keep it short: a few sentences or paragraphs about each chapter, story beats, major plot points, sub-plot points, a few lines of dialogue or action items that *must* make it onto the page. The less written in the outline, the more magic can happen naturally.

Flip to the Table of Contents for *Righting Writing*. Each chapter title listed could start the framework for an outline of this book if adding a few lines highlighting what will go into the individual chapters. Three parts: *beginning*, *middle*, and *end* (a three-act structure), and nine chapters for each of those parts. Flip to the chapter title page for any of the chapters within this book and the main takeaways for each chapter are listed on those pages, which could further develop the outline. And finally, flip ahead to the next chapter and skim the headers and sub-headers, which could be topics and sub-topics included in an outline. This is all that is needed to get started on an outline prior to working on a manuscript, or if needing to build one later.

An outline was not originally created for this book (the author is a *pantser*), but one took shape after noticing interruptions in chapter flow (and sometimes a *plantser*), and that very loose outline eventually became the Table of Contents. Outlines can be incredibly useful to keep a writer on track, but it is up to the writer to determine if outlining is a part of their character.

CHARACTER

The most important part of any book.

"Dreams are the touchstones of our characters." - Henry David Thoreau

The most important writing fundamental is developing the character of the people in the story. Whether they exist in real life or in the imagination, they need to hold truth. They must be likeable or hateable. They must act, and more importantly *react*. They must have an arc, changing over the course of a narrative. And they must come alive.

With nonfiction, characters are real, but that does not mean they are any easier to write. Change any fact, and the nonfiction becomes fiction. This is true for both nonfiction and creative nonfiction. Every word of dialogue needs to be "as remembered," otherwise there are ramifications of misquoting. It needs to sound like something the speaker would have said based on the memory, as real to the reader as it was to the character.

In "Craft True-to-Life Nonfiction Characters," an article written by Bill Roorbach and Kristen Keckler for *Writer's Digest*, "Characters are the soul of what's come to be called creative nonfiction, an umbrella term that covers memoir, the personal essay and literary journalism, among others. But characters in nonfiction present special problems: While characters in fiction are often based on real people, there's still that screen. In nonfiction, by contrast, the writer is telling the reader: *These people I'm bringing to you are real*." [7]

Whether writing fiction or nonfiction, the same rules apply for building believable characters. Each characteristic needs to be vivid in the reader's mind. This can be done through traits, mannerisms, dialogue, thoughts, emotions, or how they react to conflict. To really understand a character, throw an obstacle their way, something difficult. How do they act / react? What do they say? How does it make them feel? Some would argue that all fiction is autobiographical, and that has much to do with the adage "write what you know." To write autobiographical fiction, a writer does not need to be the *character*, the character needs to be *the writer*, through one or preferably all of three ways:

Knowledge. Everyone has a specialty (knowledge on a certain subject), something they are good at, a unique insight or talent. "Write what you know" in this case means putting that on the page. Writing about a specialty will give the book authority and merit because it will be from a reliable source: the author. The key is to never believe a specialty is not enough. Exceptional at underwater basket weaving? Have a passion for Frisbee golf and know strategies for the sport? Not many readers will have that knowledge, or have developed those talents, so what is shared will be interesting, even if it seems boring—or not good enough—to the writer.

Experience. The senses are a powerful way for writers to connect with readers. Think in terms of fragments of the past. Fictional characters go through a number of ordeals or challenges. They suffer and overcome. They learn and develop. They become better or worse. All creativity is based on another's creativity, so why not "write what you know" by pulling from past experiences? Do not simply copy a personal story and change names but use fragments of such stories and incorporate them into the characters: the first time holding a love interest's hand, emotions felt watching the family home burn to the ground, the scent of the ocean and taste of saltwater taffy, the sound of mud pots bubbling in Yellowstone.

Emotional truths. Emotional truth is expressing oneself through the voice of the heart. No one can take another's feelings. Feelings are personal and real, and cannot be categorized as either fact or truth, and so how a person *feels* an incident from the past does not necessarily have anything to do with fact. Siblings can share the same experience as children, from two entirely separate perspectives, and both remember them as entirely different. "How did this happen to me, and how did I see it?" Share truths, not what others might want to read as truths. Express how the beliefs or experiences are remembered.

Outside a writer's knowledge, and/or experience, and/or emotional truths, characters are defined by their *roles*, their *types*, and their *archetypes*, according to MasterClass. In their article "Writing 101: All the Different Types of Characters in Literature - 2020," they break down these building blocks of character, such as with more roles than the widely known protagonist and antagonist, and the different types of characters based on how they "change" throughout a narrative, as well as a multitude of archetypes. [8]

ROLES

There are seven roles of a character, whether that is a *protagonist*, an *antagonist*, or any number of secondary characters (supporting cast) who are sometimes but not always necessary to move the plot forward, positively or negatively. Readers might develop passing attachments and sympathize with these characters, but not as deeply as with the protagonist or main antagonist.

Each of the roles, broken down:

PROTAGONISTS

These are the main characters, sometimes referred to as the heroes at the center of the story. Every story needs a protagonist, a hero or an anti-hero (a character lacking conventional heroic attributes, such as Walter White from *Breaking Bad*, Maya Miller from *Ozark*, Thelma & Louise, Deadpool). The protagonist makes key decisions, experiences the consequences of those decisions, and is the primary agent propelling the plot forward. The protagonist faces the most significant obstacles and is the one rooted for by the reader, good or bad. Put into *Harry Potter* terms, this would be Harry Potter. Without a protagonist, there is no plot, as there would be no conflict and no story. Consider the following four types:

The ordinary is the most common. They are regulars going about their business, suddenly finding themselves in the middle of a disaster or mess, or at the beginning or end of a love story. Some call this type "the man from the crowd," since he's a regular ol' Joe just going about his day, his life relatable and only changed at the end and by what happens. Such characters quickly gain trust because most readers consider themselves "normal," and could imagine empathetically falling into similar situations. The downside is that "the ordinary" tend to have average personalities, so readers might not find them interesting enough.

The underdog is easy to root for, and easily loved by readers. Who *does not* root for the underdog? They start as nobodies and work their way through any number of obstacles or roadblocks on their journeys to becoming somebodies. The world is cruel, and only the bravest can survive. The underdog is regular ol' Joe walking through a forest, lost, the trail gone because he was staring up into the trees, and he is hungry, has no water, and it is getting dark. *He's gonna make it, right?*

The lost soul takes the underdog type one giant step further. They are lost to society, having crossed over from bad to good at some point and no longer considered unlawful or immoral. This is regular ol' Joe after serving his time in prison for embezzlement, now out and helping the law track down similar criminals, but still *seen* as a criminal by those he knew, those family and friends and coworkers he lost over the years for what he's done to them. The only way to gain sympathy of others—as well as the reader—is if this poor lost soul fights the bigger fight, never wholly redeemed, but always *trying* to be better.

The idol is a true hero. While not perfect, most traits are admirable by all but the antagonists. They are typically attractive, well-built, intelligent, problem-solvers, the person everyone wants to be. They are detectives solving crimes, doctors performing life-saving surgeries, superheroes saving the world. This is no ordinary Joe, and he is not an underdog, and his soul is not lost. He is all but perfect. The *but* is important. The idol *cannot* be perfect; the idol must have at least one flaw.

ANTAGONISTS

These are characters presented as foes of the protagonist, sometimes the villain. The antagonist is the one who opposes, struggles against, or competes with the protagonist, and considered an opponent or adversary. Antagonism is crucial to all storytelling; plot does not move without conflict, and conflict is created by antagonizing the protagonist. Therefore, antagonists should always be as equally developed as protagonists. Opposite to Harry Potter, this would be Voldemort, his archnemesis. Antagonists can be a single character or a group of characters, as long as they work *against* the protagonist. Antagonists in the *Harry Potter* series include Draco Malfoy, Snape, his foster parents, and a multitude of others. Consider the following four types:

Villains are the typical "bad guys" in the narrative, often working to destroy the hero. There can be villainous protagonists, but villains are strictly antagonists when they are not the central character to the story and work in opposition to the protagonist. And there are multiple levels of villainy:

> *Anti-villain* - evil characters with sympathetic and/or appealing characteristics, considered "bad for the greater good" and at the forefront of the narrative, and rooted for, or even written as the protagonist (Hannibal Lector in *The Silence of the Lambs*).

Supervillain / Mastermind - the villain at the top of the foe pyramid with a diabolical plan; popular in thrillers and mysteries, and not necessarily in direct opposition to the protagonist (typical *James Bond* villains, or Lex Luthor from *Superman*).

Subordinate - the henchmen or "muscle" working for villains higher up, often expendable.

Equal / Equivalent - a villain with the same skill set or knowledge as the protagonist but an opposing view of ethics or morality (Spider-Man vs. Venom).

Femme Fatale - a classic trope villain who clashes with the protagonist and is often seductive; common in thrillers and noir (*Basic Instinct*, *Fatal Attraction*), and often works both sides of the conflict or interacts with both protagonists and antagonists.

Authority Figure - a character who represents opposition to the free will of the main characters; often seen as "evil" by the protagonist, but not necessarily so (military leaders, trainers, school principals).

Corrupt / Criminal - a once "good" character who has changed sides, so to speak, becoming "bad" (Jack Torrance in *The Shining*, corrupted cops or politicians or those who break the law).

Tormentor - one who works against the protagonist without psychological reasoning and/or explanation, such as a bully often experiencing a lack of ethics or moral values; mean for the sake of mean.

Damaged / Disturbed - characters with psychological and/or personality disorders; often violent or unpredictable, but can show sympathy or empathy (Annie Wilkes from *Misery*).

Beast - a stumbled-upon or unleashed being (natural or extraterrestrial) with ill-intent, preying upon the protagonist or other characters; common in horror, science fiction, and thrillers (the alien in *Alien*).

Paranormal - beings that bend the rules of the natural; also common in horror and science-fiction (Freddy Kreuger from *A Nightmare on Elm Street*, demons, ghosts, other inhuman entities).

Machine / Technology - a lifeless, emotionless entity incapable of expressing fear or feeling pain; popular in science-fiction (HAL 9000 from *2001: A Space Odyssey*, the *Terminator*, *The Matrix*).

Evil Personified - pure evil, plain and simple, with no need for explanation, motive, or backstory (Sauron in *The Lord of the Rings*).

Nature Personified - the all-powerful, unstoppable and unforgiving Mother Nature / Gaia / Earth; protagonists can only attempt to survive (earthquakes, floods, famine, wildfires, hurricanes, viruses, etc.).

Conflict-creators are characters whose goals and motives directly conflict with those of the protagonist. They do not necessarily need to be "bad" characters, but their actions clash with those of the protagonist.

Inanimate forces can work against protagonists by more natural means, such as with setting: violent waves during a sea voyage, wind spreading fire, the sky during a hot air balloon ride mishap, or the passing of time.

The protagonist is considered an antagonist when the conflict comes from within, such as with insecurities, obsessions, or other inner conflicts. One's own worst enemy is oftentimes the self.

TERTIARY / SUPPORTING CHARACTERS

Tertiary characters are the *third* most important of all the characters, often popping in for only a scene or two, but this does not mean they are not important. There are also a number of other supporting characters:

Deuteragonists are the sidekicks, to put it simply. They are closely attached to the main character, although their own story arc does not correspond with that of the protagonist's. Some stories have a group of deuteragonists collaborating with the protagonist. To return to the *Harry Potter* example, this would include Ron, Hermione, and any other number of supporting characters he runs with. Samwise Gamgee from *The Lord of the Rings* is another prime example. They can be confidants or not to the protagonist, or even arch-enemies, but all add heart to a story, and sometimes liked by readers more so than the main character.

Confidants are characters closet to the main character, those with whom they express their most personal thoughts and feelings and emotions. Samwise Gamgee, for example, would be both a deuteragonist and confidant to Frodo Baggins during his journey. Confidants can be mentors, best friends, or even love interests.

Love interests are characters physically or emotionally desired by the protagonist, or characters who desire the protagonist. They are often one of the deuteragonists or confidants, close enough to show interest in a more intimate relationship.

Tertiaries are the minor characters who serve smaller roles, those who live on the pages but are not linked directly to the main plot. In terms of *Harry Potter*, this could be any number of not-so-important classmates or teachers.

Foils are characters whose personalities, moral, or ethical values clash with those of the main character, thus highlighting main character strengths. The foil's personality or values are often the exact opposites of the protagonist.

No matter what role ends up on the page, whether it is a protagonist, antagonist, deuteragonist, confidant, love interest, tertiary, or foil, there are many classifications of character and twelve common *archetypes*.

TYPES

Dynamic characters change who they are and/or what they believe along their journey, or at least by the end of the narrative, which is why they often make ideal protagonists. They have a clear beginning, middle, and end.

Round characters play major roles and their ability to change is clear from the start, but typically they do not change who they are and/or what they believe until conflict forces that change upon them.

Static characters noticeably change during their journey but seem tertiary and are flat to the reader. Who they were yesterday is not so different than who they will become in the foreseeable future.

Stock characters have fixed personality traits. Simply put, they are who they are.

Symbolic characters represent something of a larger scale, existing to sway the reader's thoughts to broader concepts.

ARCHETYPES

Along with character *types*, there are also character *archetypes* to consider. In ancient Greek, the word *archetype* translates to "original pattern," a typical example or "template" of what makes a person. Carl Gustav Jung was considered unorthodox in his study of classic psychoanalysis, going against the norm of Freudian ideas, and he instead studied the collective unconscious. What he produced while dissecting ancestral roots was twelve universal archetypes that represent human motivation, now referred to as the 12 Jungian Archetypes. [9] A quick breakdown of each:

The Caregiver wants to serve, to protect others from harm. They would rather avoid danger and risk for the sake of the happiness of others but can turn into martyrs for their sacrifices. They are compassionate.

The Ruler wants control, or to lead, and wants nothing but excellence and for everyone to follow them as they concentrate their efforts on power, but they can turn into tyrants.

The Creator / Artist wants innovation on their quest for freedom. They are nonconformists, clever, and work independently. They are highly imaginative but lost in thought.

The Innocent wants safety and are always optimistic in their never-ending quest for happiness. They see the good in the bad and want to please the world and know they belong as they do what is right.

The Sage wants knowledge and understanding. They are free-thinkers, and their essence relies on their intelligence and ability to analyze as they try to understand their place in the world.

The Explorer wants freedom and to travel the world, always on the lookout for new adventures because of their love of discovery and learning who they are: perfectionists.

The Outlaw / Rebel wants liberation, which is the freedom from having limits on thought or behavior. They do not tend to care about opinions of those around them, often provoke, and are self-centered and not easily influenced, but they can also self-destruct.

The Magician (not necessarily "a magician") is a character who wants power, always trying to make things happen, to understand the world around them on their quest to make their dreams come true, but they can become manipulative to other characters.

The Hero wants understanding of all life throws at them in their overly ambitious fight for power, and they often have enduring vitality, willing to push their limits to win. They never lose because the fight is never over.

The Lover wants intimacy. Their hearts are full, yet sensitive, and they not only want to love others but want the love of others, valuing beauty. They are often led by the heart through humanism and conviction.

The Jester wants pleasure and enjoyment and, of course, to laugh, both at others and at themselves. Life is not often taken seriously but highly enjoyed, and so this can make them greedy and lewd.

The Everyman / Orphan wants nothing more than to belong. Everyone is created equal, so why were they not? They are realists, and empaths, and tend to lose themselves while trying to blend in.

Each archetype fits within four cardinal orientations: *order* (provides structure), *freedom* (yearns for spiritual journey), *ego* (likes to leave a mark), or *social* (needs to connect with others).

Under the *order* orientation is the Caregiver, the Ruler, and the Creator / Artist. Under *freedom* is the Innocent, the Sage, and the Explorer. Under *ego* is the Outlaw / Rebel, the Magician, and the Hero. And under the *social* orientation is the Lover, the Jester, and the Everyman / Orphan.

CHARACTER SKETCHES

A character sketch is an abbreviated portrayal of a person's characteristics, and may or may not include a drawing. The term originates in *portraiture*, in which drawing characters is common, and they can be beneficial for the writer to get a sense of their characters before writing them.

Sketches tend to list physical description, personalities, attitudes, beliefs, secrets, traits, mannerisms, speech patterns, and so on. A sketch might include relationships, behaviors, habits, the characters' past, or a drawing or doodle of the physically imagined character. But characters should come out naturally, never forced upon the reader, with most left to the reader's imagination, especially physical description.

PHYSICAL DESCRIPTION

Ishmael in *Moby-Dick*, what color were his eyes? How tall was Ethan Frome? What brand of shoes does Tyler Durden wear in *Fight Club*, and what were they made of? How long, flowy, and curly was Scarlett's O'Hara's hair in *Gone with the*

Wind, and could it be described as burnt sienna, chocolate, or hazelnut? How many times does the evil villain's brow furrow, and did he hold the knife in right hand or left, and is he always laughing or chuckling or sighing or doing some mundane thing when there is nothing else for him to do? How often does whatever-her-name in *Twilight* murmur? A lot, but who cares. Physical description of character, and all that useless direction of action (nodding, shrugging, shifting, reaching), is only important if it drives the story.

Take young Harry Potter, for instance. Do his round-rimmed glasses matter? Not really, but they define him because who other than John Lennon and Gandhi wore circular-rimmed glasses? Does the lightning-shaped scar on his forehead hold significance? Most definitely. The scar tells a story, makes him memorable. Scribble a lightning scar on any young boy's forehead and slide on a pair of circular-rimmed glasses and hand him a twig and he is suddenly Harry Potter. Rowling may have physically described every detail of her hero, but what *really* matters about him?

If a character is physically described, those details better matter, otherwise it forces the reader to visualize exactly how the writer imagines a character to appear, not how the reader might imagine them. And since character is the most important part of *any* story, what better way to ruin a character than to kill the reader's imagination with forced visuals.

Ask a hundred people to list physical descriptions of an attractive person and expect a hundred entirely different lists. Ask a hundred people to list physical descriptions of an *un*attractive person and expect the same. Part of the fun of reading is letting the imagination run wild. No imagination, no fun. In other words, don't get caught up in trivial details that physically define a character; those details are boring. Think only of what should be memorable.

Writers tend to have characters made up in their minds before they write, or have already created character sketches, so it is only natural to want to describe appearance to the reader, to list every physical detail. And what is the easiest thing to write about a character? It is not their inner struggle or the complexity that drives their story arc, no, but all that meaningless stuff that pads the writing: hair color, eye color, skin tone, height, weight, etc.

When meeting someone for the first time, what leaves an impression? Is it skin tone, the color of their eyes, their hair, their exact height, and weight? Remembered most are *traits*, *mannerisms*, *dialogue*, and *emotion.*

TRAITS

A trait is a distinguishing characteristic of a person. There are positive traits and negative traits, and with any character, there is a good mix of the two. There are hundreds of good ones, hundreds of bad ones, so no sense listing them all out. Some believe there are upward of a thousand . . .

Every character is a special blend of ethics, morals, and personality, which is why traits are the most important components that make or break a character. They help the reader understand why they act / react, how they speak both to themselves and to other people, and how they present themselves to the world.

A character's ideals matter most: *core values* (personal values, theoretical ideals of thought), both the *internal* and *external.* A character trait, for example, is a person's internal—*private*—compass, whereas a personality trait could describe an external—*public*—behavior. To break it down even further, character traits are the building blocks of who a character *is*, whereas personality traits are the building blocks of what a character *does*.

MANNERISMS

Does a character consistently laugh, chuckle, nod, or turn their head and do other mundane things between dialogue or action? Those are not mannerisms; those are annoyingly unnecessary subtle actions that become less subtle the more they are used. Novice writers include them often to get more words on the page. They kill pacing and prose, and most insignificant actions are assumed or implied anyway.

A mannerism, however, is a type of conduct, a way of speaking, or a habitual gesture. They are micro-behaviors that help define, and so they must make sense and fit the personality of the character within their environment. Does a character crack his knuckles when nervous? Good. Does he do it every page? Does he snarl every time he speaks? Only include the most important of gesticulations and *only* if important. Do not move the character, move the reader.

EMOTIONS

Never hold back. Never flinch. Emotion is one of the most difficult things to write in terms of character, but crucial. For readers to connect, they need to be emotionally moved, and this is done not by being told a story *about* a character, but by experiencing a story *through* a character. Emotion is triggered through show vs. tell and point of view. Reveal emotion through action / reaction, and unveil how those responses affect the character, and thus the reader. Unmask sympathy and indifference so the reader identifies and connects through empathy and compassion. Let characters speak more so than with their words.

DIALOGUE

The way one talks (or thinks) also defines a character, but what is spoken (or thought) needs to be believable and maintained with that character throughout. A cowboy cannot start with a drawl in the first part of a story only to have it disappear over time, and likewise a cowgirl cannot develop a drawl as a story develops. Every character needs unique dialogue, a unique voice, and it needs to be consistent. Word choice matters. Inflection matters.

That is a lot of information to absorb, but what makes a character? What is the secret? *The writer.* To write a character, the writer needs to *be* the character before ever putting them on the page, before ever speaking on their behalf.

DIALOGUE

Writing believable dialogue and giving characters voice.

"The most important thing in communication is to hear what isn't being said." - Peter F. Drucker

Dialogue gives characters voice, bringing them alive on the page, whether their words are spoken or internal. What a character says or thinks can be incredibly useful for development (their own or another's), can subtly reveal backstory, and can advance the plot.

Why is dialogue so important? It can be used to define and develop characters and allow them to evolve, to breathe life, provide realism, and increase pace. If done right, it can bring information unconsciously to the reader by way of relationships, personalities, moods and—if not forced upon the reader—data crucial to the story.

If a character comes off as sounding fake, it has something to do with the words coming out of their figurative mouths. If read aloud, does the dialogue sound real, not simply there to explain what is happening to the reader? If alone, is the character saying thoughts aloud? Are characters stating the obvious?

Dialogue does not need to be grammatically correct. In the real world, people use slang. Sentence fragments. And at times they—well, they tend to interrupt one another—do not commonly use unnecessary words, such as the parts of conversation that could be assumed or implied, including names. And rarely do they use words like anfractuous, logomachy, or floccinaucinihilipilification.

Write how people talk, not how they *ought* to, and not how they never would.

Dialogue is always show and never tell, unless written unbelievably, and so it is best to get characters talking as often as they can, but only if the story warrants them speaking or thinking. Take the following example:

> "Hey, Susan Reynolds, it's good to see you, Thursday the 13th of all days, so close to noon," Jonathan Simon said absentmindedly, looking at his watch. "I never thought I'd see you at Parking Lot Espresso."
>
> "It's good to see you too, Jonathan Simon," Susan beamed, smiling. "Say, Jonathan, after that firestorm we had last week--where over half the homes in the county were destroyed, most leveled to the ground with only chimneys left behind--did you happen to lose your house in the wildfires too? I heard over 5,340 homes were leveled in the county, most in residential areas, so I was wondering." Her smile turned to a frown. "Such a sad thing to happen," she breathed.
>
> Jonathan looked at her solemnly, sighed, then vocalized matter-of-factly, "Yeah, ours was one of those 5,340 homes, Susan. As you know, we lived in the neighborhood down on Bean Street where nearly all homes were lost."
>
> Susan gasped, then took a sip of her coffee and gulped. "Wow," she managed, "I

was hoping that wasn't the case."

You and me both, he thought to himself.

What is wrong with the dialogue above? Everything. It is obvious by their conversation that Jonathan and Susan know each other. Real people would not so formally address one another. There may be a casual "Hey, Susan" or "Hey Suse," but unless they had a strange relationship and joked about calling each other by their full names, full names would not realistically be used. They would just talk.

There is a lot of unnecessary information only there for the sake of the reader, such as the day, the time, the place, and all that "data dump" information about the fires and the exact amount of homes lost, which would most likely be known by both parties, and the "as you know" and the fact that he lives on Bean Street and divulges that information to her anyhow. With his thought at the end, it is known that Jonathan is thinking this line, so "to himself" is not needed, nor is "he thought." And lastly, all that attribution . . .

ATTRIBUTES

Often called *speech tags*, or *dialogue tags*, attributions link the character's actions to their spoken words (or thoughts). In the example above, there are attributes that should never be used as attributes. A person cannot *beam* words. They might be able to *vocalize* or *manage* or *breathe* words, but wouldn't it be much easier to just *say* those words?

Think of other attributions commonly used in dialogue that should not be there.

"How many of you hate dialogue tags!" he hissed. How

many of those words in that example *can* be hissed? Zero. What about *laughed*, *coughed*, or *chuckled*, as in "I can't believe there are so many alternative forms of 'said,' he chuckled." Try to *chuckle* or *laugh* or *cough* all those words and the person on the other end of the conversation will think you are mad, or sick.

Novice writers typically start with 'said' and grow bored, thinking they should be using other words, or that they should be branching out with other creative variations of the verb 'said,' or use words that have no place in dialogue. They find a need to use dialogue attribution for everything. Consider a tasting of alternatives to 'said,' some of which appear under multiple categories:

Responding: *acknowledged, added, answered, articulated, clarified, commented, conceded, concurred, corrected, counseled, deflected, disagreed, disputed, explained, interjected, reassured, remarked, replied, responded, stated*

Debating: *concluded, considered, countered, debated, hypothesized, noted, objected, pointed out, pondered, proposed, reasoned, reiterated, rejoined, reported, restated, speculated, surmised, testified, theorized, verified*

Incoherent: *babbled, chatted, chattered, effused, jabbered, prattled, rambled, yakked, yapped*

Happy / positive: *approved, beamed, bubbled, burst, cackled, cheered, chirped, chorused, complimented, congratulated, crowed, exulted, grinned, gurgled, gushed, hummed, praised, resounded, sang, simpered, smiled, squealed, thanked, whooped*

Sad / negative: *bawled, bewailed, blubbered, comforted, consoled, cried, lamented, sniffled, sniveled, sobbed, wailed, wept*

Humorous: *bantered, chortled, chuckled, giggled, guffawed, jested, joked, joshed, laughed*

Affectionate: *breathed, confessed, cooed, expressed, flattered, flirted, proclaimed, professed, promised, purred, swooned*

Persuading: *advised, asserted, assured, avowed, begged, beseeched, cajoled, claimed, convinced, directed, encouraged, entreated, implored, needled, pleaded, prodded, prompted, stressed, suggested, urged*

Provoking: *bragged, dared, gibed, goaded, insulted, jeered, lied, mimicked, nagged, provoked, quipped, ribbed, ridiculed, sassed, smirked, snickered, tempted*

Purposeful: *affirmed, attested, blustered, decided, declared, defended, insisted, maintained, vowed*

Curious: *asked, challenged, coaxed, hinted, inquired, pleaded, puzzled, queried, questioned, quizzed, wondered*

Uncertain: *cautioned, doubted, faltered, guessed, hesitated, vacillated*

Surprised: *bleated, blurted, ejaculated, exclaimed, gasped, marveled, sputtered, yelped*

Angry: *accused, argued, badgered, bickered, caterwauled, chastised, chided, commanded, complained, condemned, cursed, demanded, denounced, exploded, fumed, growled, interrupted, ordered, raged,* *ranted, retaliated, retorted, scoffed, scolded, scowled, seethed, shot, shot back, shouted, snapped, snarled, sneered, stormed, swore, threatened, taunted, warned*

Frustrated: *exasperated, grumbled, huffed, protested*

Disgusted: *cringed, gagged, groused, griped, grunted, mocked, rasped, refused, sniffed, snorted*

Regretful: *apologized, forgave, gulped, mumbled, murmured, muttered, sighed, wished*

Embarrassed: *admitted, confessed, spilled, spluttered*

Afraid: *denied, fretted, moaned, panted, prayed, quavered, shambled, shivered, shrieked, shuddered, squeaked, squealed, whimpered, whined, worried*

Neutral or not otherwise attached emotionally: *acquiesced, added, addressed, agreed, alliterated, announced, began, bemoaned, bet, boasted, called, chimed in, coached, confided, confirmed, continued, contributed, conversed, demurred, described, dictated, disclosed, divulged, echoed, emphasized, ended, finished, gloated, greeted, imitated, imparted, implied, informed, insinuated, insisted, instructed, lectured, mentioned, motioned, mouthed, mused, nodded, notified, observed, offered, opined, peeped, peppered, pestered, pontificated, pressed, prompted, put in, quoted, read, recalled, reckoned, recited, recounted, related, remembered, reminded, repeated, requested, revealed, rhymed, spoke, started, startled, stumbled, sympathized, teased, tested, thought aloud / out loud, told, tried, uttered, ventured, volunteered, welcomed, went on*

Using speech mannerisms: *barked, bellowed, boomed, croaked, deadpanned, drawled, enunciated, groaned, heaved, hissed, hollered, howled, intoned, lisped, monotoned, mumbled, piped, pronounced, rattled on, roared, screamed, screeched, shouted, shrilled, sibilated, slurred, sneezed, stammered, stuttered, thundered, trilled, wheezed, whispered, yelled*

Skim those words or simply flip through it to the next page? So will the reader. The absurdity of that extensive list of horrible attribution substitutes proves a point: there are way too many alternatives to 'said,' and there is no reason to include them around dialogue. Do not use that list as a go-to when searching for something to use other than 'said.'

Have faith in 'said.' And since faith is having a belief in the unseen, the word never needs to be seen.

Branch out with an occasional 'asked' or 'whispered,' but consider if the attribution is needed. Is 'asked' needed if the question ends with a question mark? If dialogue ends with an exclamation point, is 'shouted' or 'yelled' needed?

Some argue that writers should never write attribution, while others argue the opposite. And some writers use them all too often. According to Jonathan Ball, PhD, in his article "Don't Attribute Dialogue," he states, "Writers write attribution all the time, but why? Why would anyone ever write dialogue attribution?" [10] He goes on to argue that the very presence of dialogue attribution weakens the dialogue itself, and that there should only ever be two instances where dialogue attribution might be needed.

If a scene is intense enough, dialogue tags are unnecessary because it is assumed the dialogue around the action belongs to the character. But what if a scene does not include much action? In such cases, attributions are needed.

Dialogue should be written in a way that distinguishes voice, but there are times when the distinction is unclear. If it is unclear who is talking, an attribution might be needed, or rewriting in a way that offers clarity.

"Less is more" is always true, especially when dialogue tags are concerned. Added words take power away from words already there, always, so cutting dialogue attribution (or never tacking in on to begin with) should be considered when writing dialogue, and later when self-editing.

Another general rule is to let each character have their own paragraph for dialogue and action.

If John Doe is moving and talking, group that into one paragraph. If Jane Doe takes over, give her a new paragraph of her own, and then give John Doe a new paragraph when he starts up again. Separating characters by paragraph will not only clarify character dialogue and action for the reader but help create white space to keep the reader flipping pages.

The placement of dialogue tags is meaningful. Rhythm and repetition matter, but too much of either can become distracting. There are three options for placement:

Beginning - when the tag precedes the dialogue:

> John Doe said, "This is one way to format dialogue."

Middle - when the tag interrupts the dialogue:

> "This is another way," John Doe said, "to format dialogue."

End - when the tag follows the dialogue:

> "This is yet another way to format dialogue," John Doe said.

How that earlier example of dialogue might look with a first round of editing:

> "Hey, Suse, good seeing you," Jonathan said. Noon, according to his watch. "Never thought I'd find you here."
>
> "It's good to see you too." She beamed. "Wait, you didn't happen to lose your home in the recent wildfires, did you?" Her smile turned into a frown. "Such a sad thing that happened."
>
> "Yeah, ours was one of those 5,340 homes." (might be well-known, no tag needed)
>
> "Wow. I was hoping that wasn't the case." (no tag needed, her reaction sad)
>
> *You and me both.*
>
> (obviously Jonathan's thought, italicized or not)

The above could also work without the "Jonathan said" if written in a way that shows the reader that Jonathan is the one starting the conversation. He could check the time on his watch earlier. And why does she need to beam?

The fewer attributions the better. A good rule is to only use speech tags when it is unclear who is talking (or thinking, depending on point of view), or when important to include crucial action around dialogue.

It could get confusing when three or more characters are in the same scene conversing, especially if the same sex, but if there are only two characters speaking, the simple back-and-forth can just be lines of dialogue, one after the other. Once it is clear who is talking, the need for clarification disappears.

Always look for ways to remove dialogue attribution. Are they needed? Would omitting them make the writing stronger? Start cutting. And always clarify who is talking as early as possible so as not to confuse the reader.

> "I told you a hundred times you'd be sorry if I ever caught you editing my work without first asking my permission," Jane Doe whispered.

Based on tone and word choice, a reader might assume the character is yelling, so the 'whispered' at the end might come as a surprise. And why not lead into the dialogue first with action, thus removing the need for the use of 'whispered'? And lastly, the phrase might be so long before Jane Doe is revealed as the speaker that the reader might have started reading the line as another character, so both the whispering and the character might come as a surprise.

Another option:

> "I told you a hundred times," Jane Doe whispered, "if I ever caught you..."

A better option:

> Jane Doe leaned in close, breath hot against his ear. "I told you a hundred times..."

Readers gloss over attribution, so the best choice is to avoid them unless needed for clarity. Readers create character voices in their heads or when reading aloud, so adverbs and over-attributing dialogue gets in the way.

If the attribution is longer than the dialogue, what is the point of having it?

Take the following example of overwriting:

> "Hey, can I borrow your pen?" Jane Doe asked nonchalantly with a certain sharpness in her voice, while motioning with her fingers for John to hand it over.

What is crucial (not a question): borrowing the pen, Jane Doe as the speaker, and the hand motion. Instead of all those unnecessary filler words, consider the following:

> Jane Doe motioned for John's pen. "Hey, let me borrow that."

The first is twenty-eight words; the second is eleven. They say the same thing, or at least create the same visual. Seventeen useless words in that first example. The writing is padded, the writer sitting at the keyboard filling time typing extra words while waiting for characters to speak. Changing the question to a demand instead, and with the implied physical motion of her hand, brings out the sharpness in her voice without specifically stating the "certain sharpness in her voice." And why "nonchalantly" (does not fit), and why mention "she motions with her fingers" for John "to hand it over"? What else would she motion with? Also, it is obvious she wants the pen.

Less is *definitely* more.

Have an intense scene? Improve the pacing with fast-paced dialogue.

```
"Cut those words," Michael said.
The novice writer sighed.
"What words?"
"All those useless words?"
"These words?"
"Yes."
"And these words?"
"Yes, those too."
"All of them?"
"Most, yeah."
"Why?"
"They're in the way."
"Whose way?"
"The reader's way."
"Who cares about the reader?"
"Writers."
```

Now imagine how *un*intense that conversation would be if it included "in-the-way" attributions that slowed down the conversation. And instead of "Michael said," what if the scene started with Michael shaking his head in disgust, red editing-pen-of-death in-hand and ready to slash?

INTERNAL DIALOGUE

Internal dialogue, also referred to as *internal monologue* or *internal thought*, brings the reader inside the character's mind. This is the closest link a reader can have to a character, a type of character-reader telepathy. And for the writer it is a valuable tool for perspective and voice. Inner voice unveils emotions, opinions, truths, insights on self-esteem, doubts, and personal things only accessible to that character.

Unlike spoken dialogue, internal dialogue does not typically use quotation marks, and instead is either italicized or not, depending on the type: *direct* or *indirect.*

Direct internal dialogue is the most common and written in first person present tense, no matter if the rest of the story is written in another tense or another point of view.

> *This is all in my head,* John Doe thought. *Great, now I'm talking to myself.*

> John Doe considered his internal dialogue options. *Is this all in my head?* (no dialogue tag)

> This is all in my head, John Doe thought. Great, now I'm talking to myself. (no italics, less common)

> John Doe considered his internal dialogue options. I can't believe this is all in my head... (no italics and no tag, rare)

Indirect internal dialogue is typically written in past tense and is not italicized.

> John Doe considered his internal dialogue options. Bleak. All of it. Only so many options for portraying thought in one's writing. Is it easy? No. Never is. It takes practice.

> John Doe considered his internal dialogue options. Bleak, he thought. All of it. Only so many options for portraying thought in one's writing...

No matter the type, internal dialogue can either contain dialogue tags or not, just like spoken dialogue. But just like spoken dialogue, it needs correct punctuation and structure.

PUNCTUATION

There is a trend in modern education not only to weed out the art of reading and writing cursive but teaching dialogue punctuation. There are rules to follow and places for quotes. When an attribution precedes dialogue, use a comma before the dialogue; however, a comma is not needed when the dialogue is introduced using a conjunction, such as with *that*, or *whether*, or when dialogue is quoted:

> He said, "Punctuation matters."

> He said that "punctuation matters."

When an attribution follows dialogue, use a comma before the end quote, but before the attribution; however, a question mark, exclamation, em dash, or ellipsis can also be used, depending on the dialogue:

"Punctuation matters," he said.

"Punctuation matters," he said. "It really does." (if the dialogue continues)

"Punctuation matters?" he said. (as a question)

"Punctuation matters!" he said. "It really does!" (as an exclamation)

"Punctuation matt--" he said. (if the dialogue is cut off / interrupted)

"Punctuation matters..." he said. (if the dialogue trails off)

Always use lowercase to start attribute when the attribute follows dialogue, unless a name is used:

"Is that a question mark?" she said. (or 'Jane Doe said.')

"That's an exclamation mark!" she said. (or 'Jane Doe said.')

"No, it's a comma," she said. (or 'Jane Doe said.')

"Yep, definitely a comma," Jane Doe said.

"But what if I get interrupted--" she said. (or 'Jane Doe said.')

Sometimes single quotes are necessary. Use single quotes when quoting dialogue *within* dialogue:

"When in doubt," he said, "Michael always suggests 'it is best to format dialogue properly.'"

Punctuation goes before the end quote (outside in some countries), unless using a conjunction, or when dialogue is quoted and either questioned or exclaimed:

"Punctuation matters." (without an attribute)

"Punctuation matters," Michael said. (like above)

Who said, "Punctuation matters"? (if the dialogue is quoted)

Michael said "punctuation matters"! (if the dialogue ends with a special character)

He said "punctuation matters"?

Yes, Michael indeed said, "Punctuation matters." (if the dialogue ends with a period)

"Yes, Michael indeed said, 'Punctuation matters.'" (if the dialogue contains quoted dialogue)

He said, "Punctuation matters"--and screamed.(with an interjection)

Michael said, "Punctuation matters"--and cleared his throat--"so it's best to format properly." (with an interjection in the middle of the dialogue)

Whenever conversations occur between one or more characters, use paragraph breaks if changing speakers:

"What's that?" the writer said.

"He said, 'Use paragraph breaks.'"

"Oh, right. Structure is also important."

STRUCTURE

If a single character's dialogue fills the page or goes long, span the dialogue over multiple paragraphs by omitting end quotes. Basically, use a double quote to start the dialogue at the beginning of each paragraph, and forego the end quote until the end of the last paragraph:

"First paragraph. (no end quotes)
"Second paragraph. (no end quotes)
"Continuation of paragraphs for as long as needed. (no end quotes)
"Final paragraph." (*with* end quotes)

If a character quotes another, use single quotes within double quotes, as mentioned above:

"Michael said, about one character quoting another, to 'use single quotes within double quotes.' "

Notice the use of the single *and* double quotes at the end, which are spaced apart in this example to stand out.

Never put "quotes" around words or phrases that do not need quotes. Was a mannerism visualized, two sets of index and middle fingers clawing air-quotes around the word "quote"?

MANNERISMS IN CONJUNCTION WITH DIALOGUE

These are the unconscious gestures characters make, not only around action, but while talking or thinking, or expressions made, or odd verbal traits within one's dialogue. Depending on mannerisms expressed in the writing, dialogue can be conveyed in a multitude of ways. For example:

Jane Doe ate the bagel and said, "This is great."

Bland, right? Nothing happens, other than Jane eating the bagel. The same but with mannerisms:

> Jane took the bagel from the counter and scoffed, flicked off a lone sesame seed and bit into it with no intention of ever enjoying the damn thing. "This is great."

Mannerisms can be useful to show instead of tell, allowing for character emotions and feelings, *showing* the reader exactly what's unfolding instead of *telling* the reader what's happening.

Each character needs a unique voice (no two characters are alike) and this is done through dialogue and everything around it. Characters live on the page and are defined by their traits, their mannerisms, the way they talk (whether spoken or internal), the way they *don't* talk. How characters act / react are equally important.

But what further helps define character personality, reveals motivation, and brings out their voice?

VOICE

Breathing life into a story through style, tone, and mood.

> "Words mean more than what is set down on paper. It takes the human voice to infuse them with deeper meaning."
> - Maya Angelou

The two most common voices in literature are *author* and the *character*. The author's voice is the style of the writer, a culmination of tone, mood, attitude, and the overall quality of what makes the writing unique; whereas the character's voice is a mix of speech and thought patterns within a narrative for a particular character, whether real or imaginary.

Which of the two is more important?

Depends on the book.

Voice is personality, and the function of voice is to grab the reader's attention.

Every word must count, or it is wasted. Filler. Padding. The author's voice, or the character voice within a narrative, needs to be consistent. Notice a degree of attitude within *Righting Writing?* A wanna-help but go-fix-yourself tone? A certain conciseness at times, diarrhea of the mind at others? Blunt word-slinging? That is the author's voice. What must always be considered with any voice, however, is personality, objectivity, reliability, and a level of omniscience.

With nonfiction, the voice of the narrator is from a real person, sharing authentic voices of others (their characters) portrayed in the narrative. With fiction, the voice of the narrator is just that, *fictitious* (albeit autobiographical, depending on the author), but first and foremost the voice needs to *seem* real to grab the reader's attention and hold on tight, along with the voices of its imaginary characters.

Author Voice, how an author writes, is defined by subject matter, prose, sentence / paragraph structure, word choice, and even punctuation. Author voice is so distinct at times that an author might be identifiable by their words alone. Think Kurt Vonnegut, Hunter S. Thompson, Mark Twain, David Mitchell, David Sedaris, Chuck Palahniuk. Think Mary Shelley, Virginia Woolf, Alice Walker, Barbara Kingsolver, Maya Angelou, Shirley Jackson. Take any remarkable writer, figuratively rip out a few pages from a random book of theirs and start reading. Could the author be identified, and if not the *author's* voice, could one of their *characters?*

Character Voice, like author voice, is a jigsaw puzzle. Every character should have a unique way of fitting together by means of the words and phrases used, their ideas, and everything that makes them. In so many words, combinations of character traits make up these complex personalities. In her article "An Explanation of the Term 'Voice' in Fiction Writing" for *The Balance Careers*, Ginny Wiehardt claims that character voice, "is one of the most vital elements of a story for readers of fiction." [11]

In fiction, what drives a story is a combination of narrator voice and character voice. And when a character's voice narrates a story, it's typically done from the protagonist's first-person point of view (or the antagonist's). But along with a first-person perspective, character voices can include viewpoints of both third-person limited and third-person omniscient, and can develop from other interesting sources.

Stream-of-Consciousness is a technique primarily used in fiction and poetry, as it portrays a character's point of view by offering that character's thought processes using sensory reactions (sight, sound, smell, taste, touch), or by way of an *internal monologue*, which roughly translates to "thinking in words." Stream-of-consciousness writing comes at the reader unconstrained, directly from the conscious thoughts of the writer, although filtered through the minds of their characters. In other words, the inner psyche of the character is portrayed in how they *think* rather than how they *speak*. [12]

The style of writing itself is a special form of internal monologue that tends to break rules of punctuation, grammar, syntax, and sometimes logic. The character's emotions and feelings and sensory reactions are often fragmented or jolty. This is different than *dramatic monologue*, in which case the character interacts directly with the reader, such as when characters on television or in a movie stare into the camera and address the audience; this is more of the reader having the ability to jump into a character's or narrator's head, such as with voiceovers. The television show *Scrubs* was known for this, as well as *Malcolm in the Middle*.

> "Imagination is the primary gift of human consciousness." - Ken Robinson

Unreliable narrative voice is used to purposefully confuse and/or deceive the reader, which takes both a certain amount of trust and *dis*trust. The narrator is either biased or ignorant to the happenings, or unknowledgeable, or has a damaged mind or is drug-addled and/or unable to think clearly because of their circumstances or are confused. They talk directly to the reader at times, even addressing them, *Dear Reader*, and this creates an open range of interpretation. This type of narrative voice comes off as unusual and, well, *unreliable*, hence the name.

Yann Martel's *The Life of Pi* is a modern example. In this highly imaginative story, a boy named Piscine Patel (Pi) is the only human survivor of an ocean freighter that sinks after his family sells their zoo in India to move to Canada. He takes refuge on a life raft with a hyena, a zebra, an orangutan, and a Bengal tiger named Richard Parker. Much of the novel is open to interpretation.

Epistolary narrative voice unravels a story's plot and its characters by way of letters, notes, emails, text messages, private messages, facsimiles, receipts, or any number of documents that help move the story along. Sometimes there is no narrator at all, only words shared with the reader in various forms from a multitude of viewpoints.

Frankenstein, or *The Modern Prometheus*, published in 1818 by Mary Shelley, is one of the greatest examples of the epistolary form. The narrator, a scientific explorer, travels deep into the arctic circle to reach the North Pole, where he runs into young Victor Frankenstein, who wishes nothing more than to reanimate—by way of lightning—a sapient creature formed of collected body parts. The novel is a collection of letters recording the explorer's journey and confessions.

Third-Person Subjective and **Third-Person Objective** narrative voice will be covered in further detail in the section on Point of View, but it is worth noting that third-person *subjective* is when the narrator narrates a story showing character thoughts and emotions (for one or more viewpoint characters), and third-person *objective* is when the narrator does not, relying instead on facts and everything conveyed through character dialogue and/or body language. Objective is sometimes called the "fly on the wall" approach, with a non-biased narrator only observing visible actions of characters from a distance.

There are pros and cons of using subjective or objective.

Subjective allows the writer to create a closer relationship between reader and character, despite a lack of intimacy compared to first-person narratives, risking information revealed to the reader by way of info-dumps.

Objective, on the other hand, allows the writer to create a more plot-driven or action-heavy narrative, with character flexibility, and exposition not as likely, despite the distance between reader and character.

Voice, along with tone, is a writer's style.

> "Style is knowing who you are, what you want to say, and not giving a damn." - Orson Welles

STYLE

According to *Grammarly's* article "4 Essential Types of Writing Styles" by Daniel Potter, style can be categorized into one of four types: *expository*, *descriptive*, *narrative*, and *persuasive*, although they often blend. Style is also one of the eight elements of a story, which include character, setting, plot, conflict, theme, point of view, and tone. [13]

This writing, for instance, could be considered a combination of expository and persuasive in terms of style, and at times a little (overly-)descriptive and narrative.

Expository - This is one of the most common of writing styles and is all about explaining one's knowledge of a concept to a wider audience. What is shared relies upon widely accepted facts, evidence, and statistics. Most nonfiction books (with exception to creative nonfiction) fall under this category, as well as instructional books, how-to guides, textbooks, manuals, business writing, scientific and technical articles and journals, medical research, news stories (with exception to editorials or opinion pieces), cookbooks, and others. Straightforward information is shared in a teacher-student like manner, which might include extensive data, tables, charts, quotes, links to other expository work, and cited sources.

Descriptive - This writing style is defined by its name: it is descriptive. The writing is poetic in nature, relying on simile and metaphor and other figurative language that teases the reader's senses, often filled with adverbs and adjectives and when overly done can be exhausting to the reader. This is the picture-painting part of writing, so why dump buckets of paint? An example: "The overly-fatigued editor sipped his bitter-lukewarm coffee before thumb-clicking his red pen to bleed out his rage across the overly-written prose, slicing away at the novice writer's overly-descriptive soul unfortunately trapped upon the page." This is known as purple prose.

Narrative - Novels, biographies, nonfiction and creative nonfiction, memoirs, and hybrid forms, contain the narrative style of writing, as well as plays, screenplays, graphic novels, comic book scripts, short stories, oral histories, and anecdotes. The narrative style tells a story with a clear beginning, middle, and end, as all stories must have to be considered a story, with characters, conflict, and setting. And a little 'ol thing called *plot.* Most narrative writing contains passages of descriptive writing, such as when describing characters or creating vivid imagery, and can also contain expository passages when there is a need for hard information.

Persuasive - The pushiest of the styles is persuasive writing, which seeks to win the reader over with well-argued perspective, justifying an opinion with supportive information and reasoning. Persuasive writing always has a purpose: to *persuade.* Consider courts, and how the arguments are crafted (much like expository writing, albeit using facts on a selective basis) to present information to build one side's case. It is commonly found in editorial and opinion pieces, introduction letters, reviews, advertising, and academia. Persuasive writing can wear multiple hats, sometimes presenting itself in the form of expository, descriptive, and/or narrative writing styles. *Go on*, write persuasively, but be sure to understand tone.

"Tone has the living soul."
- Shinichi Suzuki

TONE

Tone is attitude. Achieved through *diction* (the writer's word choice) and *syntax* (the writer's structure choice in terms of sentences and paragraphs), and the overall focus of the viewpoint character, tone is either the narrator's or the character's attitude toward events or other characters. Tone is also one of the eight elements of a story.

How do characters act or react, how do they perceive other characters and what is happening, and how do other characters perceive the viewpoint character? How do they carry themselves or speak? Or how do they *not* carry themselves or *not* speak, as tone can be created by those voids.

The purpose of tone is to build the connection between plot and *character*, and likewise plot and *reader*, all that conflict thrown at characters to help define them, which in turn builds the relationship between character and reader. Tone reveals character personality. Tone reveals motivation. Tone creates a certain *feel* the reader experiences.

Editor Beth Hill, in her article "Tone, Mood, & Style — The Feel of Fiction" for *The Editor's Blog*, explains that a "scene's or story's tone, expressed through the narrator's attitude, could as easily be one of fear*less*ness or fear*ful*ness, disbelief or detachment, or maybe unconcern or snarkiness or arrogance. Whatever attitude the narrator can take on, the scene or story can take on." And it can also change throughout a narrative. [14]

Examples of tone (or attitude): *absurd, accusatory, admiring, aggressive, ambivalent, amused, all-knowing, angry, animated, anxious, apathetic, apologetic, arrogant, assertive, belligerent, bitter, bold, bossy, calculating, callous, cautionary, chatty, close-minded, clueless, compassionate, complex, concerned, condescending, confident, confrontational, confused, crude, cruel, curious, cynical, defensive, defiant, demeaning, desperate, direct, discouraging, dismissive, earnest, egotistical, empathetic, encouraging, enthusiastic, evasive, flippant, flirtatious, foolish, formal, frank, gentle, grim, gullible, helpful, hopeful, humble, humorous, hypocritical, indifferent, impartial, impressionable, informative, insistent, inspirational, intense, jaded, joyful, judgmental, light-hearted, loving, macabre, malicious, mean-spirited, mocking, moody*, and hundreds more.

> "They may forget what you said, but they will never forget how you made them feel." - Charles W. Buechener

MOOD

Mood is what a reader *feels* while reading. These are not the emotions leaking out of readers during a particular passage or scene or even after finishing an entire book, but the *vibe* created by a writer's work, the overall *atmosphere*. Mood is crucial to engage with readers. Mood can be light, dark, reflective, heavy, chaotic, melancholy, ominous, hopeful, tense. It can help convey a central theme.

A writer can create mood by way of style, tone, tense, pacing, diction (word choice, sentence length), point of view, setting, imagery, genre (category of the book), and plot.

PLOT

The story: beginning, middle, and end.

> "Plot comes first. The plot is the architecture of your novel. You wouldn't build a house without a plan. If I wrote without a plot, it would just be a pile of bricks. Characters are your servants. They must serve your plot." - Barbara Kingsolver

All stories must contain a beginning, a middle, and an end, but to get there, what kind of voice or writing style should be used? How should a writer take a reader through the story? Who are the characters, and what happens? A sequence of events is needed to tie everything together.

Plot *is* the story. Plot is what drives a narrative forward. A certain order of events must take place with characters overcoming conflict, forced to make tougher and tougher decisions along their journey, which must lead to a climactic moment that is eventually resolved.

One of the main roles of a writer is to fulfill a promise to readers that their narrative serves a purpose and keeps them flipping pages in anticipation of a satisfying ending. Plot requires cause and effect, and requires characters to express free will, to have the ability to think, choose, and act voluntarily—and sometimes involuntarily—as they develop.

Timothy O'Connor and Christopher Franklin dissect the history of free will in their article "Free Will" for *Stanford Encyclopedia of Philosophy*, stating that the term "has emerged over the past two millennia as the canonical designator for a significant kind of control over one's actions" and that "free will has two aspects: the freedom to do otherwise and the power of self-determination." They go on to discuss intuitive moral responsibility for one's actions.[15]

Characters in nonfiction *have* or *had* free will, and their true stories reveal the control those real characters have or once had over their actions; whereas characters in fiction are only *portrayed* as having free will, for the writer is the god of those imaginary characters who are incapable of having control over their predetermined destinies. Real or not, since plot is about character choice, it needs to include expression of free will.

Although plot *is* story, story by itself is *not* plot. Story is an event, something that happened. "I wrote a book" is a story. "I didn't write a book" is another story. Those two examples are a relaying of fact. What matters is everything that led up to those stories and what made them, all those building blocks: plot.

For longer works, a narrative combines individual events to compose a solid story, connected by concept or plot. And in terms of narrative writing style, there are five common types, which have been around for as long as storytellers.

Linear: the events in a story are presented in the order they chronologically occur to the protagonist and/or other characters, from beginning to middle to end. There is no jumping around in time, no flashbacks. The timeline only moves forward. The linearity immerses the reader in the protagonist's journey as it occurs.

Nonlinear: the events in a story are presented out of order, and can include flashbacks or flashforwards, or any other type of literary device to alter a story's chronological order.

The fractured timeline(s) of the protagonist and/or other characters can move around however necessary to complete the narrative.

Viewpoint: the events in a story are presented in a powerful manner designed to express the protagonist's and/or other characters' values, beliefs, desires, thoughts, and feelings. Point of view is crucial to the narration to capture character perceptions, with the reader interpreting plot events the same way as the narrator.

Quest: the events in a story are presented with a protagonist and/or other characters pursuing a goal and facing insurmountable hindrances along the way. The storyline typically covers an extensive journey, with achieving the determined goal all-consuming.

Historical Narrative: the events in a story are presented through historical process, linking causation from one event to the next. Historical narrative is common in biographies and autobiographies, as well as in historical fiction, with the narration recounting real events from the past.

Where did all these rules and definitions for storytelling originate?

Aristotle (384 - 322 BC) was a Greek philosopher who believed all poetry or drama required a beginning, middle, and end, which were later developed by Aelius Donatus (mid fourth-century AD), a Roman grammarian and teacher of rhetoric who later developed these divisions as the *Protasis*, *Epitasis*, and *Catastrophe*.

The basic plot structure of the three rhetorical appeals forms an equilateral triangle, and on each side: *ethos* (the Greek term for 'ethics'), *pathos* (meaning 'emotion'), and *logos* (meaning 'logic'). This is known as the rhetorical triangle, which includes the *speaker*, the *audience*, and the *message*.

Ethos represents the credibility of the speaker, which must be established to earn trust of the audience. Pathos represents how the audience feels when presented a message, what emotions might persuade them to act based on what the speaker tells them. And logos represents the message itself, made up of research, facts, and other evidence to convince the audience of the validity of what is spoken.

The traditional three acts originate from the rhetorical triangle, but as storytelling evolved, audiences desired more complicated plot.

A three-act structure for a play, for example:

Act 1: setup of characters, setting, and an inciting-incident (*exposition*)

Act II: *rising action*, conflict, and the midpoint

Act III: crisis / *climax*, followed by *falling action*, explanation, or *resolution*

Simplified: setup, confrontation, and resolution.

A five-act structure, for comparison:

Act I: setup of characters, setting, and an inciting incident (*exposition*)

Act II: *rising action*, conflict

Act III: events leading to a *climax*

Act IV: *falling action*, loose ends tied-up, start of explanation

Act V: *resolution* or conclusion (denouement)

Simplified: an expansion of the three-act structure.

Whether three-act or five-act, both structures have what all plots must, a beginning, a middle, and an end.

In her article "What is Plot? The 5 Elements of Plot and How to Use Them," Ruthanne Reid states that for a reader to love a story, a writer needs to understand plot. Her definition is "a sequence of events in a story that force a character to make increasingly difficult decisions, driving the story toward a climactic event and resolution." She argues, rightly so, that plot requires cause and effect, but also character choice. [16]

To determine cause and effect and what it means to a narrative, plot can be broken down into five different components: *exposition*, *rising action*, *climax*, *falling action*, and *resolution*, also known as the five parts of the narrative.

Imagine a long slope of a mountain starting with exposition, then slowly climbing in elevation by way of rising action (events, one after the other) to get to the climax (the peak), and then the steep and sudden decline of falling action on the opposite side to get to the resolution at the bottom.

This is based off Freytag's Pyramid:

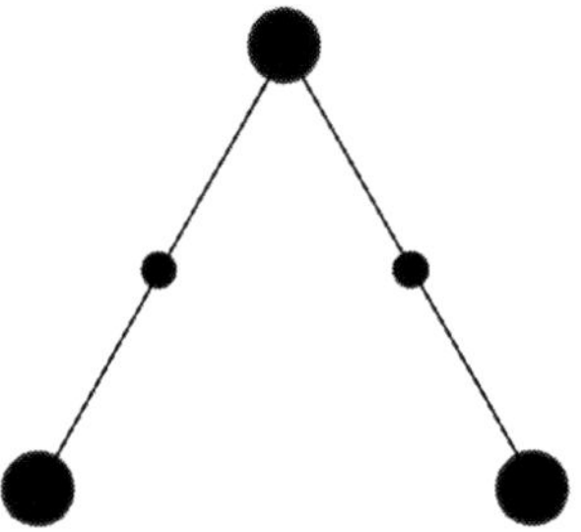

Conceived by Gustav Freytag in the mid-19th century, this is one of the oldest dramatic structures, which was diagrammed in the 1863 edition of *Freytag's Technique of the Drama*. The framework is simple in design but used (known or unbeknownst) by most writers. His theory was that effective stories had a climax split by play and counter-play, with the shape drawn out representing a triangle or pyramid shape, with the five dramatic elements going from left to right: *introduction*, *rising movement*, *climax*, *falling movement* (or return), and lastly the *catastrophe* (where all plot lines come together and all matters are resolved). [17]

A beginning, middle, and end.

Exposition is the introduction or beginning of the story, where all preparation takes place for what is about to happen. All major characters are introduced and well-established and come out and take a bow, as well as the stage dressed (the setting), upon which the acts are to transpire. This is life for characters before their world flips upside-down, and sets up the *exciting force*, what sparks the rising action (or movement) to set the plot into motion.

In Freytag's interpretation, this was called the *complication*, in which the protagonist is coerced either by the protagonist's own motives and/or complications out of their control, and/or by an outside force. But the exciting force can be summed up by a single word: *conflict.* The exciting force exposes the live wire from which the original spark ignites the fire.

Rising Action is where the main conflict is revealed, the part of the plot wherein the dry grass catches fire, then the trees, a few homes, crossing lanes of freeway, then moving into well-populated neighborhoods, and if that happens, well, there's going to be a problem. Does the character drive up the mountain to help his friends, or drive down the mountain to save his family? What about family pets, neighbors? All main characters should be introduced as conflict falls upon conflict falls upon conflict.

But rising action does not need to be a straight path. There should be twists and turns along the way, switchbacks, character decisions and flaws that help define who they are, all while creating tension and suspense. What are the characters' motivations? What are the stakes and what are the risks? What might be lost? Rising action causes complications on the way to the climax.

Climax is the moment that carries the entire body of the work (so it better count and be written well) and a reflection point for both the character(s) and the reader. In a tragedy, is the protagonist thriving? This is where their world falls apart. In a comedy, is the protagonist suffering? This is where their world comes together. According to Freytag, this is the point in the narrative where the play mirrors the counter-play, or where the counter-play mirrors the play.

While the pyramid image displays the climax as the middle, the mirror can skew the reflection from a multitude of angles. It does not have to be the middle, at times *should not* be the middle. In terms of the protagonist's fate, this is the moment the protagonist's energy is portrayed at its fullest, and once crossing that point, ambition of the protagonist is reversed. What is done in the rising action is about to be undone in the falling action.

Falling Action is a continuation of the evolution or devolution of the protagonist, all those plot points leading up to the catastrophe or *denouement* (the point in the narrative where all the plotlines cross and the main conflict is either resolved or at least explained). But before the catastrophe, falling action must include a projection of the finale and prepare the reader, whether it happens or not. According to Freytag, "It is well understood that the catastrophe must not come entirely as a surprise to the audience."

The wildfire is about to be extinguished, the rest of the community saved, but not before suspense or foreshadowing hints at a possible reverse course, a shift of wind that could spread the flames elsewhere. Freytag says it best: "Although rational consideration make the inherent necessity of his destruction very evident . . . it is an old, unpretentious poetic device, to give the audience for a few moments a prospect of relief. This is done by means of a new slight, suspense."

Resolution is a better word than either *catastrophe* or *denouement* to bookend a narrative. Freytag's focus was tragedy, hence a hard focus on the unhappy ending. The ending of a book (or any other media) is not as limiting.

A resolution for this section on plot, for instance, could have two endings. The first could be that Freytag's Pyramid is enough to explain the story arc of any narrative; the second could be that a three- or five-act story structure requires more than a simple beginning, middle, and end.

SEVEN BASIC PLOTS

Similar plots recur throughout the history of theatre, literature, and film, and are referred to as just that by literary theorist Christopher Booker in his book *The Seven Basic Plots: Why We Tell Stories*. They are otherwise known as the seven classic story archetypes. [18]

Rags to Riches - this archetype is common in fairy tales, wherein a poor or suffering character gains and then loses what they desire (fame, fortune, love, power), and by the end gets it back again. This is the typical "rags to riches" underdog climbing out of misfortune. The "American Dream" would fall under this category.

Examples: *Jane Eyre* by Charlotte Brontë, *The Princess Bride* by William Goldman, *The Wolf of Wall Street* by Jordan Belfort, *Les Misérables* by Victor Hugo. The typical five stages:

1. *Wretched conditions / call:* the physical and mental state of the protagonist is defined, revealing a dire need for change or improvement; this beginning forces the protagonist on a journey to improve.

2. *Freedom / initial success:* the protagonist seeks a better life with signs of hope, but runs into trouble, with minor successes and foreshadowing on a promising future.

3. *Central crisis:* all those minor successes are easily stripped away as the protagonist finds themselves in worse conditions than in which they started, their lowest point, and the world sees them as a fraud.

4. *Independence / ordeal:* the protagonist is back to square one, no help in sight, left with their starting qualities and traits to overcome the challenges in front of them, but eventually find their strengths.

5. *Fulfillment:* the protagonist uses what they had all along (or what they learned along the way) to overcome, revealing change and improvement; this ending shows the hero going from rags to riches.

The Quest - this archetype is found in classics, wherein the main character must go on a journey, conquering obstacles to fulfil a main goal, such as reaching a destination or attaining / returning something special, or fulfilling one's destiny.

Examples: *Watership Down* by Richard Adams, *The Illiad* by Homer, *Bird Box* by Josh Malerman. The typical five stages:

1. *Call:* the protagonist receives or decides a task must be fulfilled, the stakes incredibly high and attainable by no other means.

2. *Journey:* the task at hand will by no means be easy, everything trying to hinder the protagonist of achieving their goal.

3. *Arrival / frustration:* after many struggles, finally the protagonist makes it to their destination, but there are complications.

4. *Ordeal:* the goal is right there in front of them, but the protagonist must first jump over the biggest hurdle of them all.

5. *Goal:* the task is fulfilled, the goal met, but at a cost as something is acquired, retrieved, or destroyed.

Rebirth - this archetype is rooted in religion, wherein a character must rise from their ashes (resurrection) and change who they are, transforming after seeing the errors in their ways, or becoming a better person by the end.

Examples: *A Christmas Carol* by Charles Dickens, *Fight Club* by Chuck Palahniuk, *Pride and Prejudice* by Jane Austen. The typical five stages:

1. *Fall:* an inherently good person takes a turn for the worse, from light to dark, corrupted by evil or greed or any number of things.

2. *Status quo:* the protagonist's new status quo seems all right, everything going surprisingly well, so why worry?

3. *Threat returns / strengthens:* the protagonist realizes that everything they have done has brought upon them (and everyone around them) inescapable agony, and the thought of ever returning to their original status quo painfully impossible.

4. *Anguish:* the antagonist is unbeatable, and so the once-protagonist joins them, for there is no foreseeable other outcome.

5. *Rise:* in this final act of redemption, the protagonist makes the choice to return from dark to light, even if it means death.

Overcoming the Monster - this archetype is rooted in the ancient classics wherein a hero (or one who is not yet a hero, or even the opposite) must conquer evil or slay a beast, whether physical or metaphysical, and rise to the occasion to prove their role as hero.

Examples: *Dracula* by Bram Stoker, *Jaws* by Peter Benchley, *The Silence* by Tim Lebbon, *War of the Worlds* by H.G. Wells. The typical five stages:

1. *Anticipation / call to action:* the monster (or threat) is revealed, showing its capabilities and threat, enticing the hero to survive and/or defeat the monster.

2. *Dream:* the protagonist makes all the preparations necessary to confront the monster, shrinking the distance between them.

3. *Frustration:* the monster surfaces, revealing that it is far more powerful than originally anticipated, with the hero not yet ready for the challenge.

4. *Nightmare:* the fight between the protagonist and monster commences and the good forces seem easily overtaken, but there is a glimmer of hope.

5. *Escape / death of the monster:* the protagonist escapes and/or defeats the monster victoriously.

Comedy - this archetype is rooted in ancient Greek playwrights (such as Aristophanes), a triumph over adversity wherein a character must jump one absurd hurdle after the other to keep the laughs coming.

Examples: *Me Talk Pretty One Day* by David Sedaris, *A Midsummer Night's Dream* by William Shakespeare, *Good Omens* by Terry Pratchett and Neil Gaiman, *Bridget Jones's Diary* by Helen Fielding. The typical four stages:

1. *Establishing status quo:* life as it should be is introduced in terms of social and/or political issues, an existing situation, before any incident arises.

2. *Confusion / isolation:* misunderstandings between characters keeps everyone apart, conflicted and at odds, or alone.

3. *Raising stakes:* anything that could go wrong goes wrong as confusions amplify, no solution in sight.

4. *Resolution:* miscommunications are resolved, and life returns to how the protagonist wants it to be.

Tragedy - this archetype mirrors comedy wherein the main character is torn down by the cruelty of fate, or by their own flaws. A choice leads to the protagonist's demise.

Examples: *Carrie* by Stephen King, *The Great Gatsby* by F. Scott Fitzgerald, *The Hunger Games* by Suzanne Collins, *Anna Karenina* by Leo Tolstoy. The typical five stages:

1. *Temptation:* the status quo is established and then disrupted as the protagonist seeks what they should not.

2. *Pursuing the dream:* everything is hunky-dory, but that is about to change, the protagonist ignoring all warning signs because of their obsession.

3. *Setback / frustration:* what was once seemingly going all-too-well begins to devolve, the dream delayed and the protagonist not so happy about their predicament.

4. *Chaos / downward spiral:* anything that could go wrong does go wrong for the protagonist, and bad choices lead to ever-worsening situations.

5. *Consequence:* the protagonist, or their life as they once knew it, ends in ruin (and what / who they sought), their obsession all-destroying.

Voyage and Return - this archetype is one in which a character is sent into unfamiliar territory and must return having learned newfound wisdom from the experience.

Examples: *The Hobbit* by J.R.R. Tolkien, *The Wonderful Wizard of Oz* by L. Frank Baum, *The Lion, the Witch and the Wardrobe* by C.S. Lewis. The typical five stages:

1. *Anticipation / fall:* the protagonist is unhappy or in a lull, when something exciting or terrible (or both) transports them to some other where or when.

2. *Initial fascination / dream:* the new place or time they have entered is too good to be true, beyond all expectations, but something must be amiss, or at least foreshadowed.

3. *Frustration:* suspicions are correct, and the protagonist is faced with one conflict after another, each progressively worse.

4. *Nightmare:* the situation turns so bleak there is no return, no escape, the dull life back home not so bad.

5. *Escape / return:* the protagonist pulls off the impossible, manages to escape, damaged, and a lesson is learned before a return to "normal" life.

Some argue there is no such thing as a new story, that every story has been done to death, without any room for originality. Christopher Booker's *The Seven Basic Plots* further emphasizes that every story written is a variation of one of the seven classic story archetypes mentioned above.

But Glen C. Strathy, in his article "The Nine Basic Plots" for *How to Write a Book Now*, argues there are a few more. He outlines what he calls "The Seven . . . Actually Nine Plots According to Christopher Booker," and includes two basic plots "Booker Dislikes." [19]

The first is *Mystery*, which falls under one of the most sold fiction genres, according to Bookstr's "Book Genres That Make the Most Money." Crime / Mystery is in the no. 2 spot, according to the article, and brings in about half as much as Romance / Erotica, and a little more than Religious / Inspirational or Science Fiction / Fantasy. Those make up the top spots in terms of book revenue, followed far behind by Horror (thanks to Stephen King, primarily). [20]

The second is *Rebellion Against 'The One,'* which is the plotline of movies such as *The Matrix* or *The Hunger Games* (the series as a whole).

One argument is that these two basic plots fit under *Quest*, or one of the other highlighted seven, but they are a little different. For the sake of covering all plots possible, they are included below.

Mystery - This archetype involves a protagonist, typically either a detective, investigator, or crime scene specialist, who has no personal connection to the investigated crime. In other words, the story investigated is itself based on one of the other plots. A story buried / uncovered within a story. It is for these reasons Booker argues, "the [protagonist] has no inner conflict to resolve," only external conflict, and so it must not belong. Some argue the moral dilemma is the inner conflict, with the story based on tragedy.

Rebellion Against 'The One' - this archetype is the last of Booker's basic plots that are dismissed, which deal with a protagonist rebelling against an entity that's all-powerful, or godlike, or machine; often the protagonist submits to 'The One's' power and toward the end the protagonist is either portrayed as benevolent (well-meaning and kindly) or malevolent (having or showing a wish to do evil to others). So, the conflict is questionable.

Whether there are seven basic plots or nine, plot can be explored in wonderous forms. Rarely is that form predetermined for novice writers, unless naturally gifted with an already-polished Barbara Kingsolver-type writing ability and everything planned out in advance. For most writers, plot often identifies itself either after the first draft of a story is written, or somewhere along the way, and then tweaked during revisions and/or rewrites.

All that really matters is to write the story that wants to be written and to make sure the work has a solid beginning, middle, and end. Its uniqueness will be in its making. And together with character and setting, plot will provide context and understanding for the reader.

However, *conflict* is the soul of any story.

CONFLICT

The essential driving force of plot.

"Nothing moves forward in a story except through conflict."
- Robert McKee

Conflict is the challenge characters must overcome to reach goals, created by the doubt and uncertainty that those characters will not reach those goals. Conflict increases tension, building upon itself until the end.

According to Robert McKee, author of *Story: Substance, Structure, Style, and the Principles of Screenwriting*, every type of story requires conflict. He calls this the "Law of Conflict." He argues that inner conflict is typically best, although external conflict can become extra-personal when conflict involves an outside threat. [21]

Conflict keeps the plot moving, keeps it interesting to the reader. What good is a story without conflict, if the main character plods along, everything happening as it should, one event after the other and without opposition? Without conflict, there *is* no story, just recounted insignificance.

John Doe might wake up, use the toilet, brush his teeth, take a shower, dress, then eats granola and berries while reading a newspaper. After breakfast, he goes for a long walk, because, well, it is Saturday morning, and the weather is nice. Then, he goes home and makes a sandwich, eats it on his back porch, sits on the rocker contemplating what life was like before Jane was gone and . . . Bored yet?

What if instead John Doe is already in the shower and slips, splits his head open against the tile, and within the crack in the wall finds a golden glowing light? What if he needs to address his head wound before ever investigating and finds the first-aid kit under the sink is empty, and so he dresses haphazardly, desperately needing a hospital, the wound severe enough that he is bleeding out, only he cannot find his car keys . . .

Conflict drives plot forward and, like change, needs to be as constant as it is in one's daily life. In autobiographical work, conflict mirrors the self. Life throws challenge after challenge, and so in a narrative the writer needs to continuously put strain upon characters by creating ever-building conflict. Once one challenge is conquered, another takes its place, one stronger and more challenging.

There are two main types of conflict: *internal*, and *external*, and between those two are seven categories.

INTERNAL

Internal conflict is the psychological struggle of the mind resulting from opposing impulses or demands. Fears and/or flaws of a character are exposed and exploited to help make the reader empathetic or sympathetic because the character is more lifelike. Emotional pain therefore builds the tension.

Person vs. Self - when a character has inner moral conflict and/or wants to improve.

Person vs. Destiny - ambiguous in nature, usually when a character struggles with fate, luck, or faith / belief.

In *The Art of War for Writers: Fiction Writing Strategies, Tactics, and Exercises*, James Scott Bell says, "An inner conflict is plot-centric; it is an internal obstacle either triggered by or somehow directly connected to the story – the plot." Bell goes on to explain that while inner struggle plays against character strengths, characters bring conflict to the plot, typically from their past. [22]

EXTERNAL

External Conflict is when a character is pitted against another character, nature, society, or technology, with the conflict aggravated by an outside force, typically while the protagonist is struggling against the antagonist.

Person vs. Person - the most common conflict between two characters, protagonist vs. antagonist, good vs. evil, is richer if both sides believe they are in the right or there is no discernable wrong.

Person vs. Nature - when a character's conflict is with the forces of nature, such as the weather, natural disasters, or other living beings.

Person vs. Society - when a character is faced against law, tradition, an institution, or any other societal construct involving prejudice, sexism, racial inequality, etc.

Person vs. Technology - typically science-fiction, when characters face science or technology that surpasses control.

Person vs. Supernatural - speculative in nature when a character's conflict involves unexplained or unbelievable phenomena.

> "Conflict is drama, and how people deal with conflict shows you the kind of people they are." - Stephen Moyer

Scott Trettenero, in his article "My Way Versus Your Way: How to Handle Conflict" for *Psychreg Ltd.*, argues that "Seeking the balance between your own way of doing things and someone else's is a universal problem that nearly everyone encounters in their relationships with others." When interactions are emotionally charged at opposite ends of an argument, both sides will have viewpoints and perspectives and histories that shape their reactions. [23]

If both sides' arguments are comparable or compatible, or seen as complementary, neither side will have a reason for conflict. But if there are distinct differences, and one side wants so desperately to win over the other, then whoever is on the losing side of that battle will react emotionally and become adversarial.

Trettenero states, "It is within our conflicting differences that our inabilities to deal with others can be exposed with those who have an opposing viewpoint based upon their values. These conflicts can also show to us and others our levels of emotional maturity in dealing with conflict."

According to the American Psychological Association (APA), emotional conflict is a state of disharmony between incompatible intense emotions—such as love and hate, the desire for success and fear of failure—that causes distress.

Because of emotional conflict, one's perception is often painted into a corner, and when both sides are painted into separate corners, there is a slim chance of meeting in the middle to find resolution or compromise to get out of the paint, with each stubborn to be the first to leave the safety of their corner.

No one ever wants to be wrong—*everyone else* thought of as wrong—and so sometimes the best hope for resolution is to find an agreed-upon solution that works for both parties, which is not always easy.

Conflict opens the mind for originality, allows for the verbalization of needs, teaches behavioral patterns, flexibility, and communication skills (both speaking and listening), and allows for practicing emotional control, setting limitations, and differentiation. Conflict strengthens character.

Psychologist Sherrie Campbell authored an article for *Entrepreneur*, "The 10 Benefits of Conflict," in which she discusses the advantages of conflict. "Conflict activates our flight-or-fright self-protection mechanism, causing many of us to feel clammy and adrenalized. Some of us start shaking, voices tend to raise, and more-often-than-not things are said out of reaction which are not meant. Feelings get hurt and relationships destroyed. It is no wonder many of us want to avoid conflict at all costs." The more a person is exposed to conflict, the better they become at handling it in the future. [24]

While Campbell's benefits are aimed at entrepreneurs and not specifically for fictional or nonfictional characters in a literary work, they equally relate since overcoming conflict shapes character.

But conflict in literature is purposeful, not necessarily meant to be resolved or one side winning over the other. In narratives, the protagonist needs to win over the self, their destiny, another character (antagonist), nature, society, technology, or the supernatural.

Conflict must have a few defining characteristics. Events must be believable and relevant to the character, and not trivial or abstract. This is especially true for the protagonist or any loveable character, although even the most villainous antagonists need relevant conflict. A prime example is the movie *Joker* (Joaquin Phoenix winning the Academy Award for his role), an alternative origin story for one of the most ruthless villains created (originally as a counterpart to Batman), about a man disregarded by society struggling with a public system's inability to address mental illness.

Real or imaginary, when a character overcomes conflict, they emerge emotionally stronger and wiser, the resolution cathartic. And likewise the reader urges the character on, trying to push their own strengths to them to help overcome their struggles; the reader thus becomes connected with the fictional character, and likewise emerges emotionally stronger and wiser, the resolution-by-proxy cathartic.

Reading can be therapeutic, the reader escaping the conflict in their own lives to figuratively overcome the conflict in another's. Someone else to root for, to support; a way of experiencing resolution despite finding one's own.

And *writing* is therapeutic in that a writer has the ability of escaping the conflict in their own lives by putting it all on the page through characters, through dialogue and emotional response, through storytelling (real or imaginary). But what is a story at the basic level?

Known for the classic *Slaughterhouse-Five*, Kurt Vonnegut was an expert at simplifying conflict, which is apparent in his visual representations for stories. In his autobiography, *Palm Sunday: An Autobiographical Collage*, he wrote, "The fundamental idea is that stories have shapes which can be drawn on graph paper, and that the shape of a given society's stories is at least as interesting as the shape of its pots or spearheads." The pots or spearheads are the conflict, resembling what one might see on the graphical representation of the stock market, all those peaks and valleys. "What has been my prettiest contribution to the culture?" he once asked. His master's thesis in anthropology was his answer, "which was rejected [by the University of Chicago] because it was so simple and looked like too much fun." [25]

In his master's thesis, "The Shape of Stories," Vonnegut described eight extremely simplified graph representations on which any story can be plotted, with the main character's ups and downs revealing each story shape, the vertical axis representing the Good and Ill fortune characters experience over the course of a story, the plot—conflict points—represented by the horizontal axis, or Beginning and End.

A quick summary of each:

Man in a Hole - with conflict points beginning at the top of a single sine wave high on the horizontal axis, the character begins well, gets into trouble (down-up), then out, left better for the experience.

Boy Meets Girl - with conflict points beginning at ground zero, then creating a single sine wave above and below and up the horizontal axis (up-down-up), the main character discovers / obtains something wonderful, loses it, then obtains it again forever.

Happily Ever After (Cinderella) - with conflict points starting below the horizontal axis, continuously rising in steps only to fall lower than ever before, then finally rising off the charts into bliss.

Which Way Is Up? (Hamlet) - with conflict points mostly creating a flat line throughout, starting at the bottom like Cinderella, the character's story has realistic ambiguity that keeps the reader from knowing if resolutions are good or bad, the storyline flat.

Bad to Worse - with conflict points progressively falling from ground zero, the main character starts off in a dire situation that gets continuously worse, with no end in sight.

Creation - with conflict points creating a staircase continuously upward, a character's story progressively improves.

Old Testament - with conflict points like those of the Creation Story, a character's story progressively improves, then takes a sudden and drastic fall.

New Testament - with conflict points like those of Old Testament, a character's story progressively improves, then takes a sudden and drastic fall, only to rise off the charts into bliss.

There is a humorous YouTube video from Vonnegut's lecture at The Case College Scholars Program in which he plots out the first four of these story lines. He starts with, "Stories have very simple shapes, ones that computers can understand," and garners laughs as he describes the simplicity of the four most basic stories into which stories fall.

Worth noting is that in 2016, researchers from both the University of Vermont and the University of Adelaide tested his theory by plotting over two thousand works of fiction and found that they each fell under six unique shapes (one of which was covered in the previous section on plot):

Rise (Rags to Riches)

Fall (Riches to Rags, Tragedy)

Fall, **Rise** (Man in a Hole)

Rise, **Fall** (Icarus)

Rise, **Fall**, **Rise** (Cinderella)

Fall, **Rise**, **Fall** (Oedipus)

Conflict not only affects plot, but also setting, tone, and theme, making the central conflict one of the most important roles of the writer. And one of the other most important components of conflict is how it affects *character*.

Characters affected by conflict reveal truths about who they are, forcing them to act / react and reveal their most significant strengths and flaws (all those traits), connecting them with the reader on an intimate level.

That said, conflict should not exist for the sake of conflict. Conflict must serve a greater purpose and always feel believable to the reader, not just thrown in to create more obstacles for characters to overcome.

What are the protagonist's core values and what do they

fear most? What about the antagonist? What do both *want* or *need?* Characters need to struggle against their core values and fears, and writers need to keep them from having what they most desire, throwing everything possible at them.

> "Difficulties are meant to rouse, not discourage. The human spirit is to grow strong by conflict." - William Ellery Channing

THEME

The central topic, subject, or message.

"What we learn becomes a part of who we are." - Katy R. Jeffords.

Narrative theme is the central topic of a story and can be categorized by either *thematic concept:* what the reader thinks the work is about; and *thematic statement:* what the work offers about the subject.

Any story can have multiple themes, which are typically implied more than explicitly stated. Theme is also considered one of the main components of fiction, along with plot, character, point of view, setting, and style.

To connect with readers, theme should explore *human nature*, which are the psychological characteristics, emotions, and traits shared by everyone. The three natural aspects of humanness are self-interest, humanity-interest, and life-interest, and can be positive, neutral, or negative. Theme should also reveal the *human condition.*

According to Jeremy Griffith in his interview for the World Transformation Movement, "The human condition is essentially the riddle of why humans are competitive and aggressive when the ideals of life are to be cooperative and loving; however, it needs to be emphasized that the deeper meaning of the human condition is more allusive in that the human condition has been such an unbearable issue for humans to think about and confront that many people now have very little idea what the human condition actually is." He goes on to say that "the human condition is a much more profound and serious issue that goes to the very heart of who we are." [26]

A strong literary theme connects with a reader on a deep, emotional, human level, and when done well draws a reader back to the same story. Most readers have a handful of books they regularly return to, one they read around the holidays, or every few years, but why? Compelling characters? Witty dialogue? The plot? What makes a book 'a classic'? It is most likely *theme*, the underlying message the reader is left with long after reading a particular book.

Theme can be explored and conveyed by any combination of character, plot, or any of the fundamentals that makes a story. Every remarkable story has a moral, a message buried deep or on the surface. Take the following example:

> It was Jane's idea to bring Ally home, but the damn cat claimed John from day one, saying "You're mine" with that initial bump against his leg. The dander makes him sneeze, makes his nose run. All cats want is attention, to be let outside, inside, then out again, always wailing in the early hours of the morning and playing on the bed at night or licking themselves incessantly when the house turns silent. They want to be pet, sure, but only when *they* deem it appropriate, shoving themselves against John, transferring their hair on his slacks, always weaving in and out of his legs and tripping him and begging for food. But now that little Ally is gone, euthanized after her fight with lymphoma for more than thirteen years, John misses nothing more than those petty annoyances, if only

to feel her bump against his leg one last time...

The theme? The moral? The main takeaway? It could be that although an animal is there for a *fragment* of a person's life, a person is there for the animal's *entire* life, or that love is stronger than hate, or that all life is precious. It is whatever the reader takes away as an underlining message.

In the MasterClass article "Complete Guide to Literary Themes: Definition, Examples, and How to Create Literary Themes in Your Writing," it is offered that "there is one ingredient that stands out above the rest, catapulting works from commercial stardom to critical success and classic status: a strong literary theme." They define literary theme as a "main idea or underlying meaning a writer explores in a novel, short story, or other literary work." [27]

Below are the six most common themes exploring the human condition:

Good vs. Evil - the typical story of light vs. dark, good vs. bad, with one side pitted against another, exploring an internal struggle before an impending collision.

Love - nearly every story has love buried within it, making it one of the most universal themes, and can be sub-categorized as: *family* (love and loyalty between parents, children / siblings, relatives), *friendship* (concerning the strength of companionship through difficult times), *forbidden* (collision between star-crossed lovers or unapproved relationships), and *unrequited* (complications of loving someone without a return of affection).

Redemption - a tragic or sad tale in which the characters make amends to right wrongs, typically with an uplifting ending, or a character making a sacrifice.

Courage and Perseverance - when characters in a story endure demanding situations and survive to the end by acts of determination, survival, and will.

Coming of Age - also known as a *bildungsroman*, dealing with a character's formative years and/or spiritual education as they grow into adulthood, typically centered around an awakening moment or loss of innocence.

Revenge - the typical story involving a character facing moral dilemmas while seeking vengeance, and trials endured along the way to avenge wrongdoings.

Themes emerge naturally during the writing process or are purposefully inserted. Every writer, aware or unaware, has a message (or messages) they want to offer readers. It is one thing to write a compelling story, or poem, or screenplay, but it is another thing entirely to leave a reader pondering what they have read.

Consider the following classics: *Fahrenheit 451* by Ray Bradbury, *The Handmaid's Tale* by Margaret Atwood, *Of Mice and Men* by John Steinbeck, *The Scarlet Letter* by Nathaniel Hawthorne, *To Kill a Mockingbird* by Harper Lee, *The Catcher in the Rye* by J. D. Salinger, *1984* or *Animal Farm* by George Orwell. There is a reason these are considered classics. Not only are they incredible stories, but their themes are timeless and still relevant today.

In *To Kill a Mockingbird*, there is the coexistence of good and evil. Scout and Jem start as innocent children assuming all people are good, only to later understand that hatred exists in the world. Along with prejudice (forming judgment before understanding fact), injustice is explored through racial inequality in an unfair society. Courage is also a theme explored through Atticus' character. What is true courage? It is not holding a gun, but "when you know you're licked before you begin but you begin anyway and you see it through no matter what." Atticus reveals his own courage by accepting Tom Robinson's unwinnable case.

Fahrenheit 451 explores the conflict between censorship and freedom of thought (and speech), which also falls under good vs. evil. Although the novel never provides an explanation of why books are banned in this futuristic story, Montag, Faber, and Beatty struggle in terms of knowledge vs. ignorance, and the threat of technological innovation in an easily distractible society addicted to entertainment. Books are burned because they *need* to be, otherwise the opinions of the "minorities" who read them might freely express themselves, and so the idea of free thought (and speech) is destroyed by first eliminating that threat.

With *The Catcher in the Rye*, there is a dominating theme of the protection of innocence. In the dystopian novel *The Handmaid's Tale*, Gilead's main goal is controlling reproduction by assuming control over women's bodies by way of political domination, with language used as a tool of power in a totalitarian state. In *Of Mice and Men*, the story of George and Lenny offers an unfortunate lesson on the nature of human existence through its lonely and isolated characters. *The Scarlet Letter* explores sin and punishment around a story of adultery, individual vs. society, social norm vs. guilt, Puritan vs. non-Puritan ideals. And Orwell's *1984* and *Animal Farm* both concern the dangers of totalitarianism.

The themes in the examples above were (and still are) purposeful. The authors were pushing buttons that needed (and still need) to be pushed. Theme(s) *should* be purposeful in any literary work meant to stand the test of time.

Michael Hague describes in his book *Writing Screenplays That Sell* that theme "is the prescription for living that the writer wants to give the audience or the reader," which needs to be connected by the protagonist's journey. Lessons learned by the protagonist during their character arc illustrates the transformation for the readers so they can learn those lessons as well. [28]

Theme is the main subject revolving around the plot, the overall concept, an issue discussed often and/or repeatedly. And in both literary and non-literary terms, theme requires conflict because of its importance. Theme is the heart of the book, and its absence is detrimental for any story to be compelling and memorable.

But how exactly is theme created in a narrative?

Conflict, conflict, conflict.

Themes often need a controversial idea to work as a source of conflict, not only for the characters involved, but the reader, and society in general if really wanting to make an impact. The more conflict a character overcomes (or fails to overcome) on their journey of *good vs. evil*, *love*, *redemption*, *courage / perseverance*, *coming of age*, or *revenge*, the more opportunities will arise so they can make those difficult choices that define them.

How do the characters act / react? What do they say

/ think? And, most important, what are they going to do about it?

Symbolism (using symbolic images and indirect suggestion to present ideas) as well as motifs (recurring images and/or details used for the same purpose) are other ways to push theme through a narrative, but they can be tricky. These can be colors, words, characters, settings, or abstract ideas, if they represent things beyond their literal meanings. Recurrence of vivid images and/or details can work as reminders, although the goal is not to smash the reader figuratively over the head with them all-too-often, otherwise they become exploited, and the theme(s) overstated.

What is the lesson? What should readers take with them when they finally set the book down? What should readers return to repeatedly? What will readers be talking about ten years after the book is published, or a hundred? What is so important?

"Human life is fiction's only theme."
- Eudora Welty

SETTING

A time and a place, and sometimes a character.

"Everyone experiences different parts of themelves at different times, these different parts of themselves that come out in different settings."
- Amandla Stenberg

Along with plot, character, style, and theme, setting is one of the main components of fiction and nonfiction. This is the environment in which to immerse readers. Without setting, characters would exist in a void, their only home the page as they float around aimlessly in a world empty of all but words.

Setting is thus time *and* a place.

For fiction, this can affect the behavior and dialogue of a character, their voice, how they respond to events emotionally or even physically, and can influence the overall mood or tone of the narrative. In nonfiction, setting is the framework for the topic and/or theme. How a character reflects their own society, real or imaginary, is a crucial element of storytelling.

Imagery is where the magic happens. If a reader cannot envision a scene easily, and characters act within a two-dimensional plane of existence, a reader cannot fully be pulled into a narrative. Setting creates a necessary third dimension for the reader. Characters need to exist in a realistic environment with just enough relevant information to paint the picture for the reader by way of vivid description, otherwise, a writer is just *telling* a story, not *showing* it to the reader by way of evoking the imagination.

Details need significance, a balance of not too little /

not too much (a "Goldilocks and the Three Bears" analogy) or the story will underperform and drag on with over-description and useless fact. Sometimes this is unfortunately done by way of 'data dumps,' which is when a writer simply inserts setting between the important stuff.

An example of a data dump to establish setting:

> Jane couldn't imagine spending a weekend at John's place. Sure, it was fun going out for a night of drinks and laughs now and again, or to the theatre and disappearing not only into the dark but into a story for a while, but the thought of spending *two days* so close to him, even if hiding in the next room, sparked anxiety-fueled uncomfortableness.
>
> His house was a two-story pre-Victorian building with windows sealed in layers of cracked paint. The exterior walls were light beige with white trim, and inside every wall was stark white, like an old hospital. Nine-foot ceilings instead of ten. Crown molding everywhere. Door-less entryways separated the rooms, so there was no privacy. The floor not level. All the power outlets on the walls (and really, does the reader need to know the outlets are on the walls?) were two-prong, not three. The sink dripped a steady beat, synchronized to ticks of the plain clock on the wall, and the kitchen had

been modernized. All the appliances were stainless steel or black, including the countertops, which were made of a smooth granite. Clean, but overly sterile. Most of the flooring was porcelain tile and slippery, especially when wet, or when wearing socks. Even the ceiling fans were white, helping them blend into the blandness of the place.

John often stood too close, 'a close-talker' Jane's friends would say...

While the example paints a picture of the home (the descriptions not too bad), consider the placement. The reader is in Jane's head as she contemplates spending the weekend with him. John is the concern, not his homestead, at least not yet, and so the long paragraph between the other two makes the description of his home seem 'dumped' into place. The descriptions are fine, and might work well to immerse the reader, but they are distractions from the story.

Setting should be eased onto the reader, never forced. Why not weave in crucial details instead of dedicating an entire paragraph to them? Always consider placement.

Did the coffee shop (there is always a coffee shop in stories, it seems), or bar (also common) have bare walls (insignificant), and fans and lights hanging from the ceiling (standard)? Was the counter or bar made of wood, and the seats too (so what)? Inside, was it simply cold, or hot, or room-temperature (yawn)? Did it smell like coffee beans or alcohol (all implied details because of the mention of 'coffee shop' / 'bar')? The floor, was it tile or hardwood or linoleum (the characters intrigued by those details because they are mentioned)?

Who cares?

Details that matter most are those that define an environment as original.

Perhaps in the coffee shop there is an oversized bean sculpture upon which everyone tapes their phone numbers, and the walls are black chalkboard-painted, and customers' doodles create a warm feeling of "wow, that's pretty cool, letting everyone draw on the walls and all, the children too." Perhaps the bar itself, upon which a character drinks his woes away (there *must* be a character), is the original door from 1848, riddled with bullet holes from a shootout (because the place was a saloon back then) and still visible beneath the resin coating.

To make setting come alive on the page, in terms of time and location, avoid the "tell." Do not explain that it is cold inside (simple, boring fact). Show snow pelting patrons by a horrid wintry wind each time a customer enters. Have a random patron yell out, "Shut the door, you're bringing in the blizzard!" It could be a pub from long ago, the dialogue adding to the time and location: "Shut the door, 'long wit'cher blabberin' mouth, ya fecking gobshite, yer lettin' in a bad dose o' the arctic!"

Take the following example of bad setting description:

> John Doe entered the log cabin, which had a long porch made of old wooden planks that led to the front door. After unlocking the door, he turned the knob and pushed his way inside. He flipped on the

> light switch and the dark room brightened. There was a bookshelf straight ahead of him that was full of dusty paperbacks. On the left side of the room was a window overlooking the forest, and on the right side a fireplace with a gunrack mounted above the hearth. And in the center of the room was a round rug that...

Count the number of uses of "was" and "had," which is a telling indicator of forced setting, and be sure to look out for "were" as well and avoid *expletive construction* . . . beginning sentences with "It was" and "There were" and similar.

The when and where and the what matter. The *when* is unknown but could be estimated. The *where* is a log cabin in a forest, thanks to the description of the window. And the *what* is everything that happens in that where and when.

There is a fireplace but so what? The gun rack is important and could help inform the reader he is in a cabin used for hunting. The porch made of wooden planks, the door, the knob, the light switch, rug, the "room" in general . . . How much of that is important? The dusty paperbacks give the place an abandoned or not-visited-too-often vibe, but otherwise it is a bunch of useless information.

Now take the following version (revised):

> John Doe kicked snow off his boots and shoved his way into the log cabin, the door sticking like always. He ripped off his mittens and threw them next to the fireplace. Must have been near freezing

> with the blizzard wreaking havoc all about northern Michigan, devil winds pushing hard across the frozen lake to all who lived south of its ice. "Aye, it's wile cold out." He tossed another log on the coals, grabbed an old worn copy of *Fahrenheit 451* and tore out pages to help bring the fire back to life. He eyed the gun. Eyed it again.

The three major components to setting are *place*, *social environment*, and *time*, and with several aspects: *geographical location*, *historical time*, *immediate surroundings*, *social conditions*, *timing*, and *weather*. Consider each of those when setting up a scene. *Where* does a story take place? *When* does that story take place?

In the above example, the events in the blizzard occur after the publication of Ray Bradbury's short novel *Fahrenheit 451*, creating an estimation of time, and the weather a sense of cold, dread, and isolation. Michigan is mentioned, and a frozen lake, which could be one of the three Great Lakes surrounding the state or a smaller lake close to the cabin. More detail would narrow down the geographical location, but the details included are enough to intrigue the reader and pull them into that fabricated world. The moment takes place in a log cabin, so this could be in the past or in the present. John Doe could be on a hunting trip, or escaping city life for a while, or could have built the cabin himself. All that is to be determined as the story progresses. Even the gun has something to do with setting, and might later be used for hunting, protection, or a sinister life-ending task. Why is John Doe in the middle of a blizzard? Why is he alone? Is he alone? Why was he out in the snow? He is tearing up a wonderful book, so that must mean something, right? Why is he eying the gun, and why twice?

The paragraph dissecting the example is far longer than the example, but that says something about the efficiency of the revised version. Speculation about the story and the character and the environment takes place in the reader's mind as they read, so let as much of that happen effortlessly.

A complete history lesson is not necessary, nor is including every detail the character experiences in an environment. Leave out what is implied. Is it cold? A reader understands 'cold,' so the character's teeth do not need to chatter, nor does their skin need to redden, nor do they need to rub their hands together and blow into them, nor do they need to say "It's sure cold" or think *It's sure cold.* Such writing can help the writer—and likewise the reader—explore setting, but let the reader's imagination do the arduous work by leaving out minor details. Too many can drag down the pacing instead of moving a story forward, and a story always needs to move forward.

John Doe's passage uses long sentences, which can be effective at times, but so can short, snappy sentences. In fact, short sentences and fragments can be incredibly useful to create a sense of urgency within a setting, as well as character attitude.

That same example trimmed down for effect (rewrite):

> John Doe kicked snow off his boots. The door stuck, like always. He ripped off his mittens, threw them next to the fire.

> Near freezing out, near freezing in. The blizzard wrought havoc all about northern Michigan, devil winds pushing hard. The lake frozen. He tossed another log on the coals. Sighing, he grabbed a worn copy of *Fahrenheit 451*, tore out pages, crumpled and tossed them onto the coals. He eyed the gun. Twice.

Dialogue and voice enhance setting, and so can character traits. The way a person talks, thinks, and acts / reacts can explain—without words to describe setting—much about an environment. "Aye, it's wile cold out," for example, might not be a phrase used in modern times, and not from someone living a city life. An added thought of *What kind of hell is this place?* could imply the location is foreign to the character. Even the chosen vocabulary can help setting, such as the phrases "wrought havoc" and "devil winds."

For a less bleak scenario, the same rules apply. What kind of warmth can be brought to a scene; what kind of happier tone expressed? Pull the reader into a three-dimensional world, touching on the senses without explicitly mentioning them. If the location is a warm beach with a lot of love in the air between two characters sunning in the sand and holding hands, then bring the reader into that experience *through* the characters, not by excessive description of everything around them.

Socioeconomics and cultural conditions can also play a role. Poverty and wealth affect a story and the characters within as much as culture: language, clothing, customs, traditions, beliefs, foods, beverages.

A time and place (setting) can also represent character, although not as common. Donald Maass, literary agent and author of *The Breakout Novelist: How to Craft Novels That Stand Out and Sell*, urges that "In great fiction, the setting lives from the very first pages. Such places not only feel extremely real, but they are also dynamic. They change. They affect the characters in the story. They become metaphors, possibly even actors in the drama." [29]

One way to bring characters (and setting) alive is by immersing the reader in the senses: *sight*, *sound*, *smell*, *taste*, *touch*. Settings become real when they interact with other characters, and if they change over the course of the story. Think of novels like *A Tale of Two Cities* by Charles Dickens, *The Hunger Games* (the arenas, the districts) and the *Harry Potter* series (the castle, the landscape), Stephen King's *The Shining* (the Overlook Hotel), or his go-to fictional towns of Derry and Castle Rock, or James Ellroy's *L.A. Confidential.*

Setting must fulfill purpose. Setting creates tension and conflict. Setting establishes mood and atmosphere (how a reader *feels* while reading, controlled by the words chosen by the writer). Setting can be so important at times that it can be a plot-driver, moving all the action in a story. And setting can sometimes be the most important *character* in a book, one capable of coming alive on the page.

A second definition: a piece of metal in which a precious stone or gem is fixed to form a piece of jewelry.

Setting holds everything in a book together.

> "There are places that you long for that you might not ever see."
> - Alice Munro [30]

PART 2: THE MIDDLE

A few things to improve upon the craft.

"You will never make it to the end, if you give up in the middle."
- Joyce Meyer

Every book needs a beginning, middle, and end. The beginning of *Righting Writing*, act one of three, covered what it takes to start writing a book, dissecting and squashing impostor syndrome, emphasizing the importance of habit-writing by establishing routines and goals, and exploring each of the writing fundamentals. A quick recap:

Impostor Syndrome - Every writer is an impostor, so get over it. Not an expert? Not good enough? New to writing or have a lot of experience but feel unqualified or incapable of writing a book? Welcome to the club. Every creator experiences this phenomenon, and it is completely normal to hesitate. None of that matters, though. Brush self-doubt away and start writing. The book *needs* to be written. Write it.

Routine - Addiction and habit-forming takes time. In their book *Psycho-Cybernetics: A New Way to Get More Living out of Life*, Maxwell Maltz and Melvin Powers claim that it takes twenty-one days to form an addiction, and likewise break one. [31] As a challenge, write for twenty-one days, a thousand words each day (or more), and the first third of a book will take shape (21,000 words or more).

Character - This should be the focus. Not theme, not "the message," not even plot, although all are important. Readers enjoy reading because of relationships they develop with characters, whether fictitiously existing in fiction or actually existing in nonfiction. They need to seem real and exist enough to love and to hate. Understand who they are, then write their stories. Who are the protagonists? Who are the antagonists? Who are the supporting characters?

Dialogue - Real people talk and have thoughts. For characters to seem real to readers, their dialogue, spoken or unspoken, must be entirely believable. And if quoting real individuals in nonfiction, the dialogue needs to be verbatim, otherwise it is fiction. Write dialogue how real people talk: sentence fragments, bad grammar, long-windedness. Conversation is rarely perfect, so why make it perfect? Dialogue should be unique for each character, lest they sound the same or like the author.

Voice - What kind of *personality* will the book have, and in whose voice? There are many writing styles, which develop over time, changing as the writer changes, forever strengthening. The only way to determine one's original writing voice is to start writing and see what comes out. Like dialogue, one's voice needs to be unique, a representation of the writer, the characters, and the story. What kind of *tone* will the book have, what kind of *mood* portrayed?

Plot - The events that take place in a narrative cannot exist without character. Barbara Kingsolver argues that plot comes first, calling it "the architecture of a book." Without plot, or a *plan*, there can be no story. The basic building blocks of the narrative need to be determined by the writer. This can be as simple as the spark of an idea inside the mind, Post-It notes stuck to a wall, or a chapter-by-chapter summary. What will happen, plot point by plot point? What *is* the story?

Conflict - Plot cannot exist without character the same way plot cannot exist without conflict. All the main components of writing work together, one serving the other, and one not able to exist without the other. Internal and external conflict drive plot. No conflict, no plot; know conflict, know plot. Characters must meet challenges, whether they overcome them or not, otherwise the story is a series of insignificant *things* occurring without reason.

Theme - What kind of message will the book carry upon its shoulders, what kind of morals, lessons, or takeaways? What should the reader be left contemplating long after reading? Good vs. evil, love, redemption, courage and perseverance, coming of age, revenge . . . What kind of message might be buried between the lines or even left in plain sight? Consider the purpose of the theme(s). There must be purpose.

Setting - Lastly, but not least, a story needs to take place some*where* and some*when*. An environment must be determined. Along with creating three-dimensional characters in fiction, or utilizing real characters in nonfiction, characters must exist in a figurative three-dimensional space and within a certain period. A time *and* a place. Without setting, characters float within a void.

Everything covered in the beginning is important to consider for a book to go from concept to draft to published product, but there is much more to consider.

This is the middle, act two of three.

Anyone can have the initial thought of writing a book, and a small percentage of those who have that creative spark will finish a book-length first draft manuscript (around 1 or 2% of those who start), and a smaller percentage of those who finish the initial draft will put it through much more than a quick polish or proofread, and a smaller percentage will ever see their book in print. And if managing such a feat, how much work went into it?

A soul-crushing fact: the odds of winning the lottery (striking it rich) is 1 in almost 14 million; the odds of getting hit by lightning is about 1 in 500,000 (getting struck); and the odds of becoming a household name by publishing a book that becomes a best-seller is around 1 in 10,000 (*awe*-struck). Yet those publishing odds are somewhere between getting struck by lightning and winning the lottery because the 1:10,000 ratio only includes writers who finish and submit a highly polished manuscript to a traditional publisher, and through an agent who then sells it. In other words, it is more probable to be struck by lightning twice than for a book to be published traditionally and sell well.

This is why writing is a disease; a person must be sick to have such extraordinary ambitions. And this is why a writer *needs* to write and does not *want* to write, because the odds of "making it big" by one's writing is *want* more than *need.* And this is why writing takes more than completing a first draft, or a second, or third . . .

Book publishing has simplified over the years, so the percentage of those who go from concept to finished product has increased, thanks to streamlined publishing options, yet so much more is needed before a book goes to print.

The writing needs to be righted.

Whether vanity-published (there's a very small need for this), independent- or self-published (viable if done right), hybrid-published (a growing trend), or traditionally published (every writer's dream), a writer must spend more time in the *middle* of their book than in the *beginning*, otherwise there will not be a meaningful *end*.

What do all traditionally-published writers have in common? They put in years of dedication to writing, *decades*; they constantly improve upon their craft. The odds of making it as "an author" become less daunting with more effort. 1 in 10,000 is the ultimate goal, and a writer can chip away at those soul-crushing odds by completing a polished manuscript any traditional publisher would consider spending both their time and money on because of its potential.

A writer not only writes, but revises, and rewrites, spending more time perfecting the work than the initial writing.

Is the writing strong enough to entice potential readers, an editor, agent, or publisher? The honest answer: no, at least at first, but it can be.

Prior to publishing, manuscripts require multiple drafts, rewrites, the work self-edited and then edited by others. It needs beta readers, proofreaders, and so on. The pages will need to bleed with red ink. But before the writing can go from manuscript to published book, a writer needs to spend a lot of time with revisions.

In an interview with *The Atlantic*, Stephen King admits he spends months, even years, writing opening sentences. "There are all sorts of theories and ideas about what constitutes a good opening," King says. "It's tricky thing, and tough to talk about because I don't think conceptually while I work on a first draft — I just write. To get scientific about it is a little like trying to catch moonbeams in a jar . . . An opening line should invite the reader to begin the story. It should say: Listen. Come in here. You want to know about this." [32]

The first line of a book needs to intrigue the reader, to "hook" them, yet it does not stop there. The first paragraph needs to be equally enticing, as well as the entire first page, and all the pages that follow. Voice is crucial.

Importance of intrigue could explain the blank stare writers often have when starting a new project, always trying to write the perfect opening line, fingers paused over the keyboard, pen hovering over the page, words written then erased. In the beginning, the hook doesn't need to be perfect; it can be perfected somewhere around the middle stage of the writing process when a manuscript is steadily improved upon, or even closer to the end.

Prose is equally important to understand, which is the order and style of a writer's words and significant in keeping the reader hooked throughout by way of narration. Pace—or the speed of storytelling—and prose can change with each scene, depending on the circumstances.

The story will take place in either the past, present, or future, so what tense will be used, and from whose point(s) of view / perspective(s)? In other words, *who* is telling the story and in what timeframe?

Novice writers often rely on *tell* rather than *show*, acting as a director instead of a writer, which has a lot to do with not only point of view and prose, but imagery. How can vivid description be used to fully immerse the reader, and what unhealthy habits should be addressed to further strengthen the writing? How can the five senses be experienced by the reader *through* the characters instead of *for* them to build those crucial reader-character relationships?

The structure of a book is also important, and knowing how to frame chapters and understanding the components involved, no matter if it is fiction or nonfiction.

This is the middle. This is the hard part. This is the honing of the craft. This is what needs to be considered before ever reaching act three of three: the end.

INTRIGUE

How to entice and hold a reader.

"I'm only as good as my last work, my last hook, my last bridge."
- Kendrick Lamar

HOOK

What does it mean to "hook" a reader? The writer is the fisher, the reader is the fish, the book is the inviting water, and the hook is the lure used to attract the fish.

"Opening hook" is often used to describe that grabber first sentence / first paragraph required to snag the reader. The term is pounded into writers from an early age: "You must have a strong opening hook!" But capturing reader *intrigue* requires more than an initial flashing lure. It might be shiny, that hook, but will it hold interest long enough?

When editors and agents read manuscripts, and readers when the book is eventually published, the first line needs to impress, then the rest of that first paragraph, then the first page, and likewise the first chapter, and the entire book thereafter. Those literary "gatekeepers" might reject a story on the first sentence alone, or the first page, or they might even give the writer a chance at redemption by reading a few pages. The same goes for potential book buyers.

If a hook is not strong enough for the long haul (the *narrative hook*), the reader will at some point set the book aside, perhaps for good, and that's the last thing a writer wants after dedicating so much time to their labor of love—their book sadly tossed aside and left forgotten. Page-turners and literary works that stand the test of time require intrigue throughout, not just at the beginning or tossed about.

When requesting manuscripts, editors, agents, and sometimes publishers will typically ask for the first chapter, or first three, or first however-many pages of a completed book, depending on submission requirements. They might not even want to read the work at all but a synopsis, which always needs to be written with the same quality and care. They want to know if that sample writing can "hook" them, not only with initial story intrigue, but with the writing quality. Most have read enough pages in their lifetime to know within moments if the work is any good.

Some will even ask to see an entire manuscript, either focusing on those opening pages or flipping randomly to a page, for if page 196 cannot hold them, why should they bother with any of the others? Does the writer know what they are doing? Is the writing edited and polished and the highest of quality? Is there a distinct voice and is there conflict, plot, believable dialogue, and all the other essentials? That is what all readers are looking for in a book: a level of professionalism.

First impressions are pivotal, which is a convincing argument why one's first book (or second or third) should not be their first published. If the writing is bland, cliché, or otherwise uninteresting, why would anyone want to pursue future books by that particular writer?

One trick many unestablished and even well-established writers use (James Patterson is known for this) is to have a simple hook at the beginning of a chapter and another at the end, coaxing readers to turn the page and begin the next chapter (in Patterson's case, the one- or two-page micro-chapter could be considered part of the hook, the reader thinking, *Well, maybe just one more short chapter before closing the book*). Is the bookend or short chapter-approach enough? For some readers, sure, but these are gimmicks.

Hooks should be on every page, not inserted into one's writing to *be* a hook. Intrigue should instead naturally occur on the page. The entire written work needs pull from beginning to middle to end; every word is essential.

The book is the hook.

Consider the fundamentals: *character*, *dialogue*, *voice*, *plot*, *conflict*, *theme*, *setting*; each generate intrigue. Characters need to be likeable / hate-able / relatable, the dialogue interesting and believable, narrative voice guiding and figuratively holding the reader's hand, the plot captivating, conflict guiding readers and the characters along, theme buried but dissectible, setting vivid and engaging and memorable.

Ever not been drawn into a book, or the opposite: unable to put one down? Boring books do not have strong narrative hook, and "un-put-downable" books (a horrible term often used in reviews) do. Simply put, narrative hook is when a writer clearly knows what they are doing from years of reading and writing practice.

Knowing the target audience can help tremendously in the initial stages of writing, knowing what book categories might be used for marketing. Will it be fiction or nonfiction, or creative nonfiction or memoir? If a novel, what genre: science fiction, fantasy, horror, literary, etc., or will there be a blending of genres, often referred to as cross-genre?

Randy Ingermanson's article "Defining the Target Audience for your Novel" for Advanced Fiction Writing (which applies to most books), advises that a distinction should be made between one's *General Target Audience*: those interested in the genre as a whole; and *Specific Target Audience*:

those interested in a particular narrative, in which potential readers are determined by demographic. [35] No matter the target audience, the more a book is whittled down by category, the smaller the pool of potential readers.

Hook-writing should not intentionally be *clever*, but the writer should always consider intrigue. At Writer's Edit, the article "7 Clever Steps to Hook Your Reader Into Your Narrative" by Katherine O'Chee offers "Points to consider before writing the hook," such as the need to understand an audience, the writing having a purpose, use of strong character voice, unusual imagery, hiding information from the reader, starting in the middle of action (*in medias res*) and the use of philosophical statements. [33] These could also be considered gimmicks, but only if forced upon the reader.

What makes a book stand out within the endless libraries? The purpose for a book can be one of the greatest hooks used to snag readers. Having a catchy cover is great, and that will make a potential reader initially pick up a book ("don't judge a book by its cover" a flat-out lie), but also what is on the back cover copy, on the dust jacket flaps, or inside, especially those first pages. Determine "the message" of the book, but first determine its purpose.

Narrative voice not only hooks writers in the shor term, but keeps readers hooked from book to book. Fans of Hunter S. Thompson, author of *Fear and Loathing in Las Vegas* and *The Rum Diary*, and notable short fiction writer, return to his work because of his narrative voice. Same could be said for those who enjoy Mark Twain, Virginia Woolf, Ray Bradbury, Barbara Kingsolver, Chuck Palahniuk, and Stephen King. It could be argued that fans could blindly pick up a book by any of those writers, read an excerpt from a random page, and know the writer with a sense of familiarity, like sitting down and talking with an old friend.

Consider the classics: *1984* by George Orwell, *The Catcher In the Rye* by J.D. Salinger, *Lord of the Flies* by William Golding, *Slaughterhouse-Five* by Kurt Vonnegut, *Adventures of Huckleberry Finn* by Mark Twain, *Little Women* by Louisa May Alcott. Not only have these books survived the test of time because of narrative voice, but they also engage the reader with creative and/or unusual imagery:

> "The clocks were striking thirteen."
> - Orwell.

> "Certain things they should stay the way they are. You ought to be able to stick them in one of those big glass cases and just leave them alone."
> - Salinger

> "They looked at each other, baffled, in love and hate." - Golding

> "Everybody is supposed to be dead, to never say anything or want anything ever again. Everything is supposed to be very quiet after a massacre, and it always is, except for the birds. And what do the birds say?" - Vonnegut

> "I don't want no better book than what your face is." - Twain

"I like good strong words that mean something." - Alcott

The last quote from *Little Women* is not an example of creative and/or unusual imagery but highlights the importance of creating memorable settings that engages readers fully by way of strong words that mean something.

Holding back from the reader is also important. In the Writer's Edit article, O'Chee states, "One method of sparking curiosity within the reader is to avoid revealing all of the five W's (who, what, when, where, why) and one H (how) in one go. This applies not only for the hook, but also for the rest of your narrative. By hiding at least one piece of information from the reader at any one time, you invite them to ask questions and to keep reading onwards in anticipation (and expectation) of finding the answers they're seeking." [33] The key is not making the held information noticeable.

An example of poor holdback:

"Jane Doe knew who the killer was..."

. . . and then ending the chapter there. An intriguing revelation, but gimmicky to get the reader turning the page.

A better example:

"Jane Doe knew who the killer was. It had to be John. It just had to be."

Still on the cheesy side, but the self-doubt on Jane's part works as a ledge, not the writer smirking and teasing the reader, otherwise the writer is basically saying:

> "I know who the killer is, and so does Jane, but *you* don't, dear reader."

The latter at least reveals that it *could* be John, right? And what if the next chapter started differently:

> "Out of breath, John Doe fell to his side, the stitch under his ribs a reminder that he was too old to run so hard. He stopped at a neighbor's and stained their hose red, rinsing off what had come out of the body. So much blood. He wrung his hands, but the life buried itself under his nails, between the creases of his knuckles, his shaky hands unable to still properly, and..."

The above technique is an example of *in medias res*, a Latin phrase that translates to "into the middle of things." Quite literally, it is when a piece of writing starts in the middle of an action, which can be a powerful way to create tension and conflict without the reader—or the writer—knowing events that occurred prior. In the example, John Doe is running from the unknown, although speculated, which gets the reader involved. He has blood on his hands, but whose, and did he do it? He is nervous, but since the reader is dropped "into the middle of things" with much left to uncover, it is intriguing.

This is where a philosophical statement could be made, another hooking technique, thus pulling the reader into the mystery and becoming a part of it. Jane Doe may in fact be speculating that her husband was the murderer, but *is* he? Maybe he fought off the real killer and tried saving the life (whoever that may be), only to find himself running from that death until this point in the narrative. Instead, thoughtful prose could be useful to further intrigue the reader.

> "We are linked by blood, and blood is memory without language."
> - Joyce Carol Oates [34]

Curiosity will keep a reader engaged. Dangle the carrot, let the reader have a taste, pull it just out of reach, and then pose the question: *Why is the carrot there?* and *Is it even a carrot?* Another analogy often used for this technique is the iceberg: showing the reader what is above the water with an understanding that so much more is hidden below, then eventually bringing the rest of the ice into view. Whatever is shown to the reader, it better serve a purpose.

Red herrings are common in mysteries, when information is either intentionally or unintentionally misleading to the reader. Be wary when using such "tricks" on the reader, though. If writing a campy mystery, there might be a place for it, if done correctly, and subtly, but always consider whether they are gimmicky. Readers trust writers and have a certain level of faith in their professional abilities as storytellers, so why lie or lead them astray?

There is a concept in writing called Chekhov's gun (or Chekhov's rifle), a principle that every element in a story must serve a purpose, with all irrelevant elements removed. Nothing should ever mislead a reader (such as with those red herrings) by never coming into play. Show the gun in the first act, and it better go off by the final act.

Foreshadowing, however, is a literary device to hint to readers that something will return later in a story. When done correctly, it creates tension to keep readers engaged, wondering if speculations were right. This can be done directly or indirectly through dialogue, character actions / reactions, setting, symbolism, or by other means.

The same rules apply for the beginning of a chapter (or the beginning of any writing), but avoid using backstory, dream sequences, flashbacks, characters waking up or falling asleep, descriptions, and setting (unless used as a character) in order to attempt to hook the reader.

Backstory is just that, a *story* that happened *back*, before the events the reader cares about. What characters *did* does not matter so much as what characters *do*. With fiction, avoid backstory when at all possible; with nonfiction, stories about the past might be needed, but the narrative does not need to go in reverse. If backstory is required, weave it in subtly. No one ever watches a movie and immediately hits Rewind. With books, nothing starts before Page 1, Chapter 1, Line 1. A prologue, maybe, but is one needed?

Flashbacks are another means of revisiting the past. As the name implies, they should "flash" back and not take up much of the page, a few sentences, maybe a paragraph or two; if they go any longer, they become backstory. In general, readers do not care about backstory or flashbacks, but for some reason writers like to revisit the past (even if fictitious), which can lead to unnecessary passive voice.

Dreams are fragmented stories and images the mind conjures while asleep, so are they ever needed in a narrative? Unless the book is about dreams, the answer is a resounding no. If dream sequences are an absolute must, keep them as short as the flashbacks.

Waking up or falling asleep is a common fallback, with characters waking up at the beginning of a chapter and/or characters falling asleep by the end of a chapter. Like dream sequences, readers do not care about the waking or sleeping habits of characters. Chapters starting or ending with characters using the restroom would be equally ineffective.

Description is not how to hook a reader. Vivid description is useful to build memorable imagery, but its overuse can bore a reader with unnecessary detail. Similarly, characters looking into mirror to describe physical appearance needs to be avoided, although reflections are unfortunately common. Allow the reader to imagine what they can.

Setting, unless a character itself, does not make a great hook. Readers need to be pulled into the characters' environment, which is part of the hook, but long paragraphs of setting description are painful. The story should be the focus, and more specifically its characters, *not* the scenery.

Intrigue keeps readers engaged. Hook the reader from the first sentence, then never let go. The first paragraph and every paragraph that follows should hold on until the end.

The book is the hook.

PROSE

The order of words matter. How will they flow?

"Don't use a five-dollar word when a fifty-cent word will do." - Mark Twain

Prose is written or spoken language in its ordinary form, without metrical structure; a form or technique of writing exhibiting a natural flow of speech and grammatical structure; how words and phrases are arranged with sentences and paragraphs.

From its Latin roots, *prosa oratio*, a simpler definition is "straightforward" [36] or how a reader gets from *beginning* to *middle* to *end* as a story unfolds.

There are four types of prose:

Fictional - A literary work of fiction; novels, novellas, novelettes, and short stories fall under this category.

Nonfictional - A true story or factual account of events or information; memoirs, biographies, essays, journals, textbooks; example: Anne Frank's *Diary of a Young Girl*, composed entirely of journal entries.

Heroic - A literary work written down or preserved through oral tradition, but meant to be recited; legends, tales, fables.

Poetry - Written like narrative instead of verse but maintaining poetic qualities; can have rhythmic / rhyming patterns; examples: Oscar Wilde, Walt Whitman, Edgar Allan Poe.

Once the type of book is determined (novel, creative nonfiction, memoir, poetry collection, etc.), there are a few things to keep in mind before going too deep into a manuscript, such as the order, necessity, and value of words, or prose. There needs to be conciseness, rhythm, elegance, speed, and a nice narrative flow. The writing needs to *feel* right.

Purple prose, however, is writing so extravagantly written, ornate, or "flowery," that it breaks narrative flow and draws excessive attention to itself, often characterized by an excessive use of adjectives, adverbs, and metaphors. Too many words. Unnecessary repetition. Overwriting like this typically occurs when a writer spends too much time forcing words onto the page instead of letting them flow naturally.

This is one of the reasons many editors suggest throwing out the initial pages of first draft manuscript. Sometimes it takes a few pages—or even a few thousand words or an entire chapter or two—before a writer gets into their flow, the writing less forced. "The characters sometimes tell *me* where to go" or "The writing just took off on its own" is often experienced when this happens. Sometimes a writer will not even remember writing scenes long after finished. This is all part of the magic that is storytelling.

An example of forced purple prose:

> "Elizabeth ran her long, slender yet elegant fingers through her ever-flowing burnt-sienna hair, the luxurious wind tossing it freely about, the way orange and blood-crimson leaves might dance upon a forested floor to a silent orchestrated symphony of *blah, blah, blah.*"

Instead, write the first words that come to mind because they are typically the right ones to use. If a thesaurus is needed, it is not going to be the right word.

Write as the character / narrator, not as a want-to-be writer, and follow the wise words of not only Mark Twain, but George Orwell:

> "Never use a long word where a short one will do." - George Orwell

John Gross, in his Introduction to *The New Oxford Book of English Prose*, states that "Prose is the ordinary form of spoken or written language: it fulfills innumerable functions, and it can attain many different kinds of excellence. A well-argued legal judgment, a lucid scientific paper, a readily grasped set of technical instructions all represent triumphs of prose after their fashion. And quantity tells. Inspired prose may be as rare as great poetry—though I am inclined to doubt even that; but good prose is unquestionably far more common than good poetry. It is something you can come across every day: in a letter, in a newspaper, almost anywhere." [37]

Prose has three primary functions:

The promise of fulfillment - A writer has a story to tell, and prose is how a writer tells that story, with a basic promise to the reader that what is delivered is what is expected. Every story must have a beginning, middle, and end, otherwise what is written is only a scene or vignette of a larger story. Before getting started, consider a few questions: What happens at the beginning? What happens at the end? And what needs to happen in the middle to get the characters there? Give the reader all three.

Rapport - Familiarity helps readers connect to a story and its characters, which is why prose is often conversational. A story should be relatable to the reader. It should *sound* real. And all writing should be accessible, or "straightforward," as the Latin roots of the word 'prose' implies.

There is a reason Mark Twain is well-respected for the simplicity of his writing. Any time a writer tries to sound smart, and it comes off that way on the page, they distance themselves from their readers. And likewise, if using the *wrong* words, those who understand them better will quickly notice. "Write what you know" has multiple meanings.

Voice - When it comes to prose, everyone's writing is different, or *should* be. Each writer has their own way of handling language and has different qualities that make their writing unique. Pick up any David Sedaris book, flip to a random page and start reading, and there is David Sedaris' voice. Pick any Chuck Palahniuk book, flip to a random page and start reading, and there is Chuck Palahniuk's voice.

A writer's voice is conveyed through style, tone, and mood (attitude). Once voice flows, writing becomes easier, less forced, but it takes time to develop.

Stephen King uses long paragraphs and descriptive sentences that run pages or longer, and chapters that go on for pages. That is a combination of his "promise of fulfillment" and "rapport" and his "voice" his readers have come to respect. Constant Readers (his term) know him for deep character development, and thick door-stopper tomes.

James Patterson is quite the opposite with short, punchy sentences and paragraph structure, and chapters that might not even span a page. His books typically have a hundred chapters within a few hundred pages. Patterson's writing has his own promise of fulfillment for his readers that they have also come to expect—a different rapport, a different voice.

Prose follows natural patterns of speech and communication and the written word but does not necessarily mean one should write as one speaks (unless to convey voice) because dialogue is not always grammatically correct. But there are also times when to be grammatically incorrect.

Unless using everyday language, prose may turn purple. Long-winded sentences are great but sentence fragments are also useful. Can build tension. Help with pacing. Believable language should flow smoothly, relying on the following:

Precision - Is the writing aimed at accuracy and exactness? For nonfiction, is it true? For fiction, is it believable? Are the descriptions and details specific enough? Is the writing high quality? Does the dialogue sound right when spoken or read aloud? Is the work audience-appropriate?

Clarity - Are the messages clear? Is it distinct who is talking in dialogue? Are the voices of others clearly theirs? Is the voice clearly the writer's voice, or that of the characters? Are the characters' motives clear? Is setting clear? Is point of view clear (from the narrator's or character's perspective)? Is the language believable? Is plot clear to the reader? Does nothing seem forced?

Economy - Are the sentences, paragraphs, and chapters as short as they can be without degrading the overall story? Do any of the words exist simply to pad the writing? Has the "fat" been trimmed by editing out all unnecessary words?

Those are a lot of questions to keep in mind, and there are many factors that define a word as simple as 'prose,' but it all comes together at the end because prose is discovered and developed along the writer's journey.

A way to improve prose is to read and write poetry. Poems relay stories in as few words as possible, creating vivid imagery, often moving readers emotionally, and they can be incredibly powerful. Writing and reading poetry also has a therapeutic effect on the mind through the expression of feelings. Writing so concisely also means the writer must be disciplined in word choice and number used, hitting all three of the above: precision, clarity, and economy.

Dorothea Lasky, in her article "What Poetry Teaches Us About the Power of Persuasion" for *The Atlantic*, says that "Poetry, more than any other form of writing, trains students to take into account the style of language. This close looking and listening is crucial to writing well in any manner. It would be hard to say that any outstanding essay does not involve meticulous word choice or the ability to persuade a reader through sheer aesthetic prowess." [39]

There is no room for excess. The combination of detail and brevity connects reader to poet and poet to reader, one mind connecting to the other through the page.

> "The poet gives us his essence, but prose takes the mould of the body and mind entire." - Virginia Woolf

Writing great prose requires *reading* great prose.

Prose fiction is the most popular and widely read literary genre. They win or are nominated for the Nobel Prize in

Literature (the most prestigious of all awards), the Pulitzer, the Man Booker, and the Women's Prize for Fiction (the most prestigious of all awards for female authors). They all have incredible prose in common.

A good place to start: *The Night Watchman* by Louise Eldrich, *The Overstory* by Richard Powers, *Less* by Andrew Sean Greer, *The Underground Railroad* by Colson Whitehead, *The Sympathizer* by Viet Thanh Nguyen, *All the Light We Cannot See* by Anthony Doerr, *The Goldfinch* by Donna Tartt, *The Road* by Cormac McCarthy, *Middlesex* by Jeffrey Eugenides, *The Shipping News* by E. Annie Proulx, *Rabbit at Rest* by John Updike, *Where the Crawads Sing* by Delia Owens, and any book ever written by David Mitchell.

If a book has a gold or silver stamp on the cover for award recognition, or some other marking that it is a book club pick (Between Two Books, Book of the Month, Oprah Winfrey, Reese Witherspoon, etc.), or "Soon to Be a Major Motion Picture," there's probably a good reason for such high praise. These are the books commonly found in the storefronts and in airports, books that have sold millions of copies, not just because of author name recognition.

Why do readers love prose?

In *Literature: Reading Fiction, Poetry, Drama, and the Essay*, author Robert DiYanni says, "We read stories for pleasure; they entertain us. And we read them for profit; they enlighten us. Stories draw us into their imaginative worlds and engage us with the power of their invention. They provide us with more than the immediate interest of narrative – of something happening – and more than the pleasures of imagination: they enlarge our understanding of ourselves and deepen our appreciation of life." [38]

Determine what *type* of prose to write, and understand that it must serve three purposes: promise of fulfillment, rapport, and voice; but keep in mind that the writing should be as precise, clear, and economic for the reader as possible.

PACE

The speed of storytelling.

"If a man does not keep pace with his companions, perhaps it is because he hears a different drummer. Let him step to the music which he hears, however measured or far away."
- Henry David Thoreau

Writing has a constantly changing beat, the reader pulled in and led along. The beat can be a slow and steady pulse, can be as rapid as a heart attack, and can fluctuate and palpitate, depending on conflict. Pace is the heartbeat of storytelling, which can either keep the narrative alive or let it die.

Good prose implies good pacing. One cannot exist without the other, like many of the components of writing. There are times when words need to be slow and methodical, with long—and hopefully not run-on—sentences, the paragraphs long and powerful and not dipping into purple prose but supplying a certain weight and longevity, and there are times when the opposite is equally necessary, when the writing requires a faster pace. Something quick. Writing can explode with shocking moments. Writing can increasingly build tension. Writing can be repetitive with a chorus. Consider this paragraph (go ahead, re-read it again). How many times does the beat change to prove this very point?

"The quick brown fox jumps over the lazy dog" is not only a pangram efficiently utilizing all the letters in the English alphabet (a tool used to teach typing), but an example of speedy pace. No commas, only a string of words that creates a rhythm and serves a purpose, in this case using the entire English alphabet as efficiently as possible. It is difficult not to read that line quickly because of the word order choice and immediacy of action. The scene easily visualized.

Pace, like prose, requires efficiency. The phrases "cutting the fat" or "trimming the fat" are often used in various editing stages to instill efficiency upon the writing. The more efficient the writing, the faster the reader will be pulled into the narrative and the quicker they will turn the pages. Every word needs to matter, and words that do not should always go on the chopping block. The first line of this paragraph, prior to editing, used to read: "Pace, and likewise prose, requires a certain level of efficiency." Removing "a certain level of" (which is implied and a waste of words) made the opening line more efficient with their absence.

Sentence structure matters.

Paragraph structure matters.

Chapter structure matters.

Book structure matters.

Such fast-paced repetition instills the need to absorb such basic information.

Consider five sentence structures: *simple*, *compound*, *complex*, *compound-complex*, and *fragment*, and how each might be used to control the pacing of a story.

Simple sentences - The name is the definition. These are the simplest forms of sentences to construct and comprehend and the first learned to read and write. They follow a *subject / verb / object* pattern. The subject is a noun (person, place, or thing) supplying the action (controlled by a verb), followed by an object to describe what receives that action. For example: "The cat (subject) ate (verb) a mouse (object)."

The sentence is still considered simple with more detail:

"The calico cat finally ate the exhausted field mouse." Any number of additions could keep that sentence simple, but always keep in mind how much "fat" should be "cut" when using the *subject / verb / object* approach. If words are added to pad word count, are they needed?

Known as the "perfect structure," simple sentences can efficiently express what is otherwise complex. Despite that, repetitive use of simple sentences oversimplify and make the writing seem juvenile, especially if sticking to only the *simple* form without utilizing *compound*, *complex*, or *compound-complex*.

The cat example, using only simple sentences: "The cat was hungry. It ate a mouse. Full, the cat stretched." A reader will catch on quickly to such repeated sentence forms, a little too *See Spot Run*. Good for novice readers, bad for experienced readers.

Compound sentences - Simple sentences rely on an independent clause by use of a *subject* and a *verb*, but compound sentences combine more than one clause by use of coordinating conjunctions, which can be beneficial to bring rhythm and variety to the writing. That definition is in fact a compound sentence.

Coordinating conjunctions include: *and*, *but*, *for*, *nor*, *or*, *so*, and *yet* (in alphabetical order), which can be remembered easily by the acronym FANBOYS if putting the words in that order. The simple rule is that these conjunctions can be used to combine two or more sentences that could or would otherwise stand on their own as complete simple sentences.

With the cat example: "The cat was hungry, so it ate a mouse," and since compound sentences can combine multiple simple sentences, it might even read, "The cat was hungry, so it ate a mouse, but the field mouse put up a fight." That is an example of a compound sentence containing an example of a compound sentence, which sounds complex.

Like repeating simple sentences, repeating compound sentences can distract the reader and create awkward pacing. For example: "The cat was hungry, so it ate a mouse. The mouse put up a fight, though, and it wasn't easy. Full, the cat stretched out, for it was tired. It could either nap or it could find another mouse." Each of the compound sentences could be broken up into separate simple sentences.

Complex sentences - While compound sentences rely on the FANBOY approach with coordinating conjunctions, complex sentences use subordinating conjunctions in order to have a construction that has at least one independent and at least one dependent clause. That explanation itself is a complex sentence, with "in order to" acting as the subordinating conjunction.

A list of subordinating conjunctions: *after, although, as, as if, as long as, as though, assuming that, because, before, by the time, even if/though, how, if, in case, in order to/that, lest, now that, once, only if, provided that, rather than, since, so that, than, that, though, till, unless, until, when, whenever, whereas, wherever, whether, while, who, whoever, whom, whomever, whose* . . . There are others, and each can go in various places within a sentence.

Subordinating conjunctions bring dependent clauses (*can't* stand on their own) and independent clauses (*can* stand on their own) together "as a means of" transitioning two ideas into a complex sentence.

The cat example, using only complex sentences: "The

cat saw the field mouse that had a short tail. Since the cat was hungry, it ate the mouse. After the cat finished cleaning itself, it stretched out." All three sentences are complex, and having them often makes the writing a little too simple.

Compound-complex sentences - These are, as the name implies, sentences combining both compound and complex sentences to make them even more complicated, and are both the most challenging to write, but also the most challenging to read and comprehend, although they can be fun, despite their complexity. That explanation is an example of a compound-complex sentence.

Such phrasing articulates a certain complexity in writing, but comma and semicolon placement keeps sentences from becoming run-ons and confusing the reader.

Even though they can be complicated, compound-complex sentences can add flavor to the writing, a certain change of pace. Especially if placed in conjunction with an assortment of simple, compound, and complex sentences, and even fragments of sentences.

Sentence Fragments - The sentence prior to this one is an example of a sentence fragment. It cannot work on its own as a sentence independently because the words, in their order, are only pieces of a complete sentence.

The words might seem to form a complete sentence, depending on punctuation and length, but sentence fragments often lack a subject or a verb. They are simply words strung together. Useful though (another example).

Along with lacking a subject or verb, fragments might use the wrong verb form: "The cat eating." instead of "The cat ate." They can also have abandoned clauses: "When the cat was eating." They can also be residual phrases, which are other fats to cut: "Sounds about right." And fragments can include improper use of coordinating and subordinating conjunctions: "For instance, the cat ate the mouse."

Despite the fact that sentence fragments are not grammatically correct, there is a place for them in both fiction and nonfiction. They can increase pacing or create a sense of urgency. Immediacy. Like heartbeats.

No matter the structure (and these are just the basics), how sentences are *placed* in a paragraph matters most, and then how those paragraphs are placed one after the other, and then how the chapters are placed.

When is a paragraph complete? When it needs to be. Each paragraph can create a narrative beat, each end a pause for the reader to take a breath. For a more fast-paced narrative, rapid dialogue or short paragraphs might be needed, the whitespace on the page moving the reader along at a quicker pace. But keep in mind that long paragraphs can be just as moving for a reader if including (and excluding) the right words. So, mix it up and keep the writing original. Keep the reader captivated and know when to turn up the dial. And remember:

A writer uses simple sentences.

A writer uses compound sentences.

A writer uses complex sentences.

A writer, although they can use a blend of fragments, simple sentences, compound sentences, and complex sentences, they should also use compound-complex sentences, otherwise the writing might not set the right pace.

Control pacing by word choice and sentence choice and paragraph structure. A heartbeat can carry readers through a narrative. It can speed up. Slow down. Come to a complete stop so long as it starts up again. Whatever the pace needs to be, the writing—and the writer—needs to have control.

Writer's Digest describes pacing as "a tool that controls the speed and rhythm at which a story is told and the readers are pulled through the events." How slow or how fast each beat unfolds in the amount of time elapsed is what sets the pace, and it differs with every story, and with every scene within that story. "Pacing is part structural choices and part word choices, and uses a variety of devices to control how fast the story unfolds." And there are various devices a writer can use to hasten or slow pace. [40]

Action / Succession of Events - Novice writers tend to include unnecessary detail in high-action scenes, including direction for the characters (reaching, turning, left / right / up / down, etc.), and also implied information.

Action needs to be *shown*, never *told*, and experienced through the characters, depending on point of view. Long sentences slow pace; shorter sentences quicken pace.

Limit anything in the way with tight descriptions, avoiding clunky transitions, omitting thought and even dialogue if needed, and with as few words as possible. If a character throws a punch, the reader doesn't need to know which hand was used, nor what they were doing with their other, just that a punch was thrown and whether or not it landed.

When events happen one after the other, with no need for transitions (or minimal transitions between scenes) or heavy descriptions, pacing turns up a notch.

Scene / Chapter Length - The length of a scene or chapter can hurt or help. Short scenes and chapters take less time to read and can create a (hopefully not false) sense of urgency; longer scenes and chapters, however, take more time to digest but can be useful in character- and world-building.

To speed up pacing, cut anything in the way of conflict. To slow the pace, fill in any (necessary) details and build upon setting and characterization or any number of important components that make an engaging story.

Dialogue / Thought - Believable dialogue improves pace, no matter the speed. It needs to sound real if read aloud, and match what is happening on the page. Long monologues can be useful when characters are sitting around telling stories, but not a lot is spoken when events are intense. Dialogue, spoken or thought, needs to match the action.

Trim everything unneeded between speech or thought. Dialogue tags (he said / she said / they said) might not be necessary and can get in the way. If dialogue tags are used (minimally), characters who know each other would not use each other's names so often, would they?

For internal dialogue, consider how often real people ponder, and whether the reader needs to know a character's thoughts. Some people do not have an internal monologue.

Scene / Jump Cuts - The start of a new scene can move a reader through space and time. Not every moment needs to be on the page, so carry the reader along for the ride during crucial moments. This would be like scene changes in film.

Scene cuts, sometimes referred to "jump cuts," bring the story, its characters, and the reader to new settings in the narrative, assuming the reader is aware of that transition and the transition is smooth. This winds the clock faster, skipping the unnecessary to get to the good stuff.

Suspense / Cliffhangers - A story should always progress in a forward direction, never in reverse, and so the stopping and starting points of plot can affect pacing by pausing the clock. Prolonging the inevitable can create suspense, but if not done right can unfortunately slow a story's pace.

Since readers care about character(s) primarily, always curious about outcome(s), then delaying what happens to characters can create suspense and build tension. The reader needs to know what happens next, so consider where to leave them hanging, and for how long.

Summary - To go along with the "not everything needs to be known or relayed to the reader," summarizing events that do not need to be on the page can speed up pacing. When doing so, however, avoid pulling the reader back through time by way of flashbacks or backstory; only offer what is crucial to bring the reader to the present moment. This can be an effective way to skip through insignificant details, highlighting importance.

Word Choice / Structure - Language, or choice of words, is the easiest and subtlest way to improve pacing, so think of how each sentence will be structured, and each paragraph, and each chapter. What words will be used? What words omitted? How can word choice move the reader through the narrative and at what speed? How will the sentences be structured and in which order?

In her article for *The Pen and the Pad*, "What Is Narrative Pace," Buffy Naillon states, "The most interesting stories contain sequences that move at different speeds" to keep the reader engaged. "Through the correct use of pacing, the writer can keep the reader on the edge of his seat and then give the same reader a bit of a reprieve when the plot becomes tense." [41]

Consider what kind of heartbeat the narrative should have in each scene and in each chapter, and how the story's pulse might best be manipulated by word choice and sentence structure to build tension.

TENSE

The past, present, and future.

"As soon as you have a language that has a past tense and a future tense you're going to say, 'Where did we come from, what happens next?' The ability to remember the past helps us plan the future." - Margaret Atwood

The past, present, and future walk into a bar . . . it was *tense.*

It is an old joke, but tense can get rather, well, tense for a reader—and aggravatingly more so for an editor—if not handled correctly by the writer. Tense communicates time in relation to the plot and is identified by associated verbs. When did the events happen, or are they happening, or will they happen?

Did the writer understand tense?

Does the writer understand tense?

Will the writer understand tense?

The word 'tense' comes from the Latin *tempus*, which translates to *time.* Tense as a noun comes from *tens* (Old French) or *temps* (modern French), and in English refers to the past, present, and future.

Other languages recognize two distinct tenses: *past* and *non-past*, or *future* and *non-future*, and there are a few tenseless languages that recognize only *future* and *non-future.* But in the English language, one of the most complex languages in the world, tense expresses time relative to the words used.

There are four aspects: *simple, perfect, continuous* (also known as *progressive*), and *perfect continuous*, with the perfect aspect utilizing the verb 'to have' and the continuous aspect utilizing the verb 'to be.'

According to Prateek Agarwal in his article "Importance of Tense in English Language," the four structures of the three tenses are *simple*, *dynamic* (or ceaseless), *impeccable*, and *immaculate dynamic* (or flawless constant). "Tense is essential since we utilize it to flag what happens when. And after there's perspective to oblige Tense." Viewpoint is a "tense sharpener" in that "Tense and perspective assume an indispensable part in developing importance." [42]

There are twelve variations and so it is important to know which to use based on *what happened* in the narrative (past), *what is happening* in the narrative (present), and *what is about* to happen in the narrative (future).

The three tenses:

PAST TENSE

This is the most common, also referred to as the "reporting tense" since it is used to report on events that have already occurred. Note the changes to the verb "write" in the four examples below.

Past simple - used to describe what happened in the past: "Michael *wrote* an example of past simple."

Past perfect - used to describe what happened prior to other past events: "Michael *had written* an example of past perfect."

Past continuous - used to describe ongoing past events: "Michael *was writing* an example of past continuous when he decided to . . ."

Past perfect continuous - used to describe what started in the past and continued into the present, or to show relevance of past events compared to the present: "Michael *had been writing* an example of past perfect, and then decided to switch to present tense."

PRESENT TENSE

This is less common and the tense of this paragraph. It is becoming more common in fiction, typically with young adult and/or first person narratives, and useful when sharing one's own views. Everything in this tense occurs in the *present*, in real-time. Also note the changes to the verb "write" in the examples below.

Present simple - used to describe what is happening in the present and unaffected by the passing of time: "Michael *writes* about present simple."

Present perfect - used when events started in the past and will or are expected to continue, or to show relevance of past events compared to the present: "Michael *has written* about present perfect but will write about them no longer."

Present continuous - used to describe what is ongoing: "Michael *is writing* about present continuous."

Present perfect continuous - used to describe what started in the past and continues into the present, emphasizing relevance to the present: "Michael *has been writing* about present perfect continuous, and needs to switch to future tense."

FUTURE TENSE

This is the least used, and for a reason. The tense is awkward because it pertains to future events that have not yet happened, although it can be useful for stating hypotheses or when making predictions about what *will* happen. One last time, note the changes to the verb "write" in the examples below.

Future simple - used to describe what will happen in the future: "After writing about future simple, Michael *will write* about future perfect."

Future perfect - used when events will happen in the present for a set time in the future: "By the time future continuous is covered, Michael *will have written* about future perfect."

Future continuous - used to describe what will be ongoing and continue: "Michael *will be writing* more about future continuous later and will cover future perfect continuous next."

Future perfect continuous - used when events are expected to continue with an emphasis on an endpoint: "Michael *will have been writing* about future perfect continuous and all the others for seemingly ever when finally transitioning to the proper use of tense."

These twelve separate options might seem overwhelming, so focus on the three main tenses: *past*, *present*, and *future*. *Has* the story happened, *is* the story happening, or *will* the story happen? That is all that matters, at least at the beginning.

How does a writer know which tense to choose when starting a poem, or story, or an entire book? "Write what feels most comfortable" is the easiest advice. Try a single paragraph, or an entire page to two, and get a *feel* for the writing. Does it seem easy, or forced? Try writing in both past and present tense (and for now avoid future tense) and one or the other will feel more natural as the writing unfolds. If it seems unnatural, it is not the right choice.

The first two questions any writer should ask before working on new material: 1. *Which point of view?* and 2. *Which tense?*

Whose story is this and *when* does it take place?

Perspective plays a part in the early decision-making process for a writer—the *narration* that depicts the story—and tense is how it comes out on the page.

A future tense question: Will the all-important "I" be the main focus of the narrative with the narrator or writer as the main character, or will the narrative be more character-based, focusing on Jane or John Doe, or alternating?

A present tense question: Is it clear when the events of the narrative take place? Do they unfold chronologically, starting now, or are they in the future or from the past?

A past tense question: This story that happened (fiction or nonfiction), what was it, who were its characters, and when did it take place?

Content also matters.

With academic writing, *present simple*, *past simple*, and *present perfect* are most common. A novel, on the other hand, could bounce from one tense to another, depending on what happens from beginning to middle to end, if tenses are used correctly and the transitions are seamless.

A poem might portray a futuristic event and need a future tense, a history on the evolution of typewriters might need past tense, and a first person present tense narrative for an essay, memoir, or creative nonfiction.

Consistency is needed, otherwise switching tenses too often makes for a jolting reading experience.

ADVANTAGES / DISADVANTAGES OF PRESENT TENSE

Novice writers tend to choose first person present tense. This may have something to do with young adult fiction where it is common and trendy. It could also have something to do with movies and/or television, wherein everything is happening "in the moment," and with new writers wanting to direct characters, which in turn leads to issues with point of view and show vs. tell. A number of factors may play into the desire to write present tense, such as ease.

> "We're in an age when everything's present tense. People don't know how to be still and surrender to the music." - Pete Hamill

First person is one of the easiest points of view to write. The narrator is the main character, or the writer, everything told from their perspective. The style is less formal, intimate, warmer, everything told in *I*, *me*, *my*, *mine*, and is the most natural voice in which a person can write. And with a single viewpoint, it is more difficult to break away from that viewpoint and slip into another. From the reader's perspective, first person is much like having the narrator recounting a story firsthand, reminiscent of a story told to them orally.

The craze over book series like *Hunger Games* or *Divergent* (both written in first person present tense) has helped lead to first person present tense popularity in young adult fiction. This type of writing creates a sense of urgency and the unknown, everything happening as it happens, the main character's fate uncertain because, well, if written in present tense, they could still die; if written in past tense, on the other hand, the main character *must* have survived or they wouldn't be able to recount the story.

Helpful hint: Never write a narrative in first person past tense in which the main character (narrator) dies at the end. It is not possible, unless that narrator is a ghost, or recorded / broadcasted their lives in some manner. Do not attempt such a feat without years of practice.

A notable example of this done well is the movie *American Beauty*. The opening dialogue of the movie (script) is "My name is Lester Burnham. This is my neighbourhood; this is my street; this is my life. I am 42 years old; in less than a year, I'll be dead. Of course, I don't know that yet, and in a way, I'm dead already." It *can* be done, but keep in mind that Alan Ball won an Academy Award for Best Original Screenplay for doing it right.

Immediacy and intimacy are reasons the present tense is often used. Everything in the narrative happens in real-time, the reader becoming the main character, drawn into their head, hopefully experiencing the senses through them. The reader is as close to the action as they can be, with anything revealed by an unreliable narrator even more shocking.

Present tense is also simpler to write, typically a mix of present simple and present perfect, with occasional trips into memory lane by way of flashbacks or backstory, and the use of future simple tense when projecting aspirations or goals during those moments from the past. Present tense is a more streamlined narrative, and it is difficult to slip into more complex forms of tense.

There are disadvantages to writing in present tense, such as when dealing with time shifts. Past events are always flashbacks, which readers (editors especially) are not fond of, instead wanting the story to always travel in a forward motion and avoid jarring the timeline of events. "What happens next?" not "What happened leading up to this?"

Interruptions are created during trips down memory lane. For example, twelve years before writing this section on tense . . . No, no one cares what happened twelve years ago, only what is happening now.

Since events in present tense happen as they happen, what about all those boring moments in between the good stuff? An example of this is with crime scene investigation shows, or medical dramas, in which a single episode of television might include a synopsis-like recounting of incredibly remarkable events—that most in their fields wouldn't experience over the course of *years*—with all those boring parts of their job left on the editing room table.

When writing, it seems natural to include banal details: dreams, waking up, brushing teeth, looking in the mirror (a cliché gimmick to describe first person character), showering, changing clothes, using the restroom, walking from one place to another, taking a sip of coffee or tea, reaching for things, opening doors, sitting, standing, turning heads, smiling, laughing, nodding, furrowing eyebrows, clearing throats, going back to bed and falling asleep, etc. Bored? The reader will be too if including unnecessary details.

Readers do not care about banality, but so many unpolished manuscripts are overwritten this way, which leads to much required editing to remove the mundane.

Novice writers should stick to either *first* or *third person* points of view and using *past* or *present tense*, at least until more comfortable with tense.

To learn the most about improving one's writing, *third person past tense* is highly recommended as a starting point, but *first person past* or *present tense* might be easier, especially when still figuring out how to follow the rules of tense so as not to accidentally slip from one to another.

ADVANTAGES / DISADVANTAGES OF PAST TENSE

> "Nothing is improbable until it moves into the past tense." - George Ade

With past tense, all the events in the narrative have already occurred, with hopefully all those filler moments ignored, the writer highlighting only what is important. Past tense also allows for the timeline to be explored however suits the narrative, as long as it all makes sense to the reader by the end.

In David Chitty's essay "The Benefits and Drawbacks of Past Tense" for *Thanet Writers*, he states, "It's easier to make a non-linear story when you're writing about past events without the use of flashbacks. Doing this properly can lead to a stronger story telling experience and can feel more fluid or natural than it does in present tense." Most stories told are about events from the past, and so past tense is the most traditional of storytelling tenses, and according to Chitty, "It tends to be slightly more enjoyable for the reader." [43]

One of the biggest advantages of past tense is that the writer has more room to stretch.

With nonfiction, everything that happened already happened, so there is an entire pool of information from which the writer can pull: character (actual people), plot (real conflict), point of view (from individuals who experienced those events), setting (the actual place / time), and so on. Only the interesting ever needs to go on the page.

In comparison, with fiction, everything is made up, but hopefully the writer knows what happened or at least figures it out at some point while writing, pulling from their own pool of imagination. And again, only putting what's interesting onto the page.

With past tense, it's much easier for both writer and reader to reflect on the *why* and the *how* of the events that transpired; whereas with present tense both writer and reader are always in the moment, as everything transpires, and so the *why* and the *how* is not as clear since there's no time for reflection.

However, reflection can slow pacing, leaving the reader not "in the moment" but in the tense itself: the past. Shocking moments are not as shocking to the reader, surprising moments not as surprising.

The reader already understands the protagonist survives at the end, or overcomes the obstacle, especially if they are the narrator. First person past tense means they were alive and well to recount their tale, and third person past tense means they were most likely alive and well, as long as another character was around to finish the story. Since there's no great mystery of "the end" with present tense, past tense relies more on conflict leading up to the ending.

Another drawback to past tense is show vs. tell. Unlike present tense, with everything happening real-time, the past has already happened, and so it is much easier for the writer to slip into *telling* the reader what happened instead of *showing* them as they should, and this can lead to unnecessary passive voice.

ADVANTAGES / DISADVANTAGES OF FUTURE TENSE

With future tense, nothing has happened yet. There are no past moments, no present moments, only the uncertain future. In all accounts, future tense is far more difficult to write, and should be avoided by novice writers.

Not many *have written* in future tense. Not many *write* in future tense. Not many *will write* in future tense. It's difficult to write it right, but pulling it off allows a writer to explore uncertainty and concept, which begs the question: Does the story even have to happen?

One of the biggest drawbacks of future tense is that the reader might not care as much about characters or events because nothing has happened, at least not yet, and might not happen, everything mysterious yet uncertain.

And since future tense is so rare, a reader / writer about to immerse themselves in a future tense narrative will likely be forced to become familiar with this strange, seemingly unnatural writing style. They might not "get it" and instead fall back to writing what is more comfortable: past or present tense.

What makes writing future tense so difficult is that every sentence to be written must follow a pattern that can so easily become annoying to a reader (such as this sentence).

There are only a set number of words and phrases that can be used to express future tense: *will, will not, shall, shall not, about to, going to*, pronouns or names with the truncated *'ll* tacked to the ends of them, and awkward iterations of *'ll have been*, *'ll've*, *will not've*, *won't have*, and *won't've.*

In all its complexities, the most important thing about the use of tense is to keep it consistent.

> "Existence really is an imperfect tense that never becomes a present."
> - Friedrich Nietzsche

POINT OF VIEW

Who is telling the story and why?

"You never really understand a person until you consider things from his point of view." - Harper Lee

Point of view is one of the trickiest concepts for new writers to grasp, often referred to as POV. There cannot be smooth prose without tight point of view, and point of view cannot be tight without smooth prose.

It is all about perspective.

Who is narrating the story and how?

Point of view is the *perspective* from which the writer conveys the story to the reader. *Who* is telling the story must be consistent and always considered with *what* is told in the story.

The reader can only ever know as much as the point of view character. Any time that line is crossed, point of view slips around the page.

In nonfiction, the writer is often the narrator recounting events from their own perspective or using primary and/or secondary interviews to bring points across. In fiction, the narrator can be a single character or the story can be told from multiple perspectives.

The goal is to maintain consistent point of view throughout each chapter, or each sub-chapter, at least, with everything in that segment within the character's perspective, unless relying on an omniscient point of view.

There are rules to follow with point of view, and multiple types, so it is necessary to determine which POV should be used for a particular story. There are three main points of view:

FIRST PERSON

The singular form is the easiest for newer writers to comprehend and write and considered the most intimate of perspectives. *I*, *me*, *my*, and *mine*. In terms of the reader, first person singular is the friendliest, as if the writer is confiding in the reader on a personal level. A writer must connect with the reader, creating intimacy, sharing emotion, so many choose this option for either fiction or nonfiction narratives.

A second option of this viewpoint is *first person collective*, though not as common (we, us, our, ours), and the hardest to comprehend and the toughest to write. Stephen King and Peter Straub were able to pull it off in a lengthy collaborative novel called *Black House*, but it ain't easy!

One issue with first person in general is that it is all too easy to *tell* the reader everything instead of using smooth prose to *show* the reader. The other issue is that first person can easily lead to the overuse of *I*, *me*, *my*, and *mine* to the point where the writer or narrator is narcissistic, always talking about *me, me, me.*

Joe Bunting, in his article "The Ultimate Point of View Guide: Third Person Omniscient vs. Third Person Limited vs. First Person" for *The Writer Practice*, argues there are two big mistakes writers make with first person storytelling: "**1. The narrator isn't likable**. Your protagonist doesn't have to be a cliché hero. She doesn't even need to be good. However, she must be interesting. The audience will not stick around for 300 pages listening to a character they don't enjoy. This is one reason why anti-heroes make great first person narrators. They may not be morally perfect, but they're almost always interesting." [44]

Bunting agrees with the earlier argument that "**2. The narrator tells but doesn't show**. The danger with first person is that you could spend too much time in your character's head, explaining what he's thinking and how he feels about the situation. You're allowed to mention the character's mood, but don't forget that your readers trust and attention relies on what your character *does*, not what he thinks about doing."

Great first person writing limits the use of pronouns, and is all show, no tell. And bad writing can make characters unlikable if the prose is unlikable. For example:

> I was on my way to the grocery store and as I was driving on the freeway another driver next to me nearly clipped my car, which the family always called Betty. My hands jerked the steering wheel hard to the left and I had to quickly choose whether I wanted her to collide into me or if I should move into the next lane over to avoid her ending my life prematurely. I nearly hit the guardrail.

Count the pronouns. In all first person writing, always consider the pronouns, and then kill as many as possible. In that single paragraph above there are twelve, but how many are needed amid those seventy-eight words?

A quick revision:

> On the way to the grocery store, another driver on the freeway nearly clipped

```
Betty, the family car. Merge into the
next lane over or collide; those were the
options. Nearly took out the guardrail.
```

There are zero first person pronouns in that shorter version, although it is the same story. A pronoun could be added to add emotion at the end: "She almost killed me!" but the point is that first person narration does not even *need* pronouns, so use them sparingly. Too many and they quickly stand out.

Everything implied in the edited example above was simply removed. 43 words gone, 55%+ cut. That is the power of editing, and the power of prose. And with first person pronouns removed, the example is less narcissistic and more personal, as though the reader is driving the car and not the first person character.

SECOND PERSON

Second person is from the point of view of a word not even used (outside dialogue or context or writing examples) until the end of this sentence: *you.*

This second of viewpoints addresses the reader, the writer or narrator speaking directly to them by way of the pronouns *you*, *your*, and *yours*.

But like first person, it is a stronger viewpoint with fewer pronouns, otherwise the writer is making the reader an empath, which is the opposite of a narcissist, making it all about *you, you, you.*

In *The Writer Practice* article, Bunting states, "In this point of view, the narrator is relating the experiences of another character called 'you.' Thus, *you* become the protagonist, *you* carry the plot, and *your* fate determines the story." [44]

The second person viewpoint is not often used in fiction but appears regularly in nonfiction. If done right, this unique viewpoint puts the reader in the driver's seat, pulling them directly into the action, putting words in their mouth through the spoken dialogue, placing thoughts in their head through internal dialogue, and providing a new voice (the reader's), making the story more personal.

An example of poorly written second person (over-using pronouns to prove a point), modifying the previous example of poorly written first person:

> You were on your way to the grocery store and as you were driving on the freeway another driver next to you nearly clipped your car, which the family always called Betty. Your hands jerked the steering wheel hard to the left and you had to quickly choose whether you wanted her to collide into you or if you should move into the next lane over to avoid her ending your life prematurely. You nearly hit the guardrail.

Second person is difficult to write, and awkward, and the unexperienced writer will exhaust the reader. In the paragraph above, there are also *twelve* pronouns, but how many are needed? What is interesting is that *all* second person pronouns can once again be removed, making it *identical* to the edited first person version:

> On the way to the grocery store, another driver on the freeway nearly clipped Betty, the family car. Merge into the next lane over or collide; those were the options. Nearly took out the guardrail.

Despite using the same words and in the same order, it is still written in second person point of view. The rest of the narrative will eventually use pronouns, but the same rules apply to tighten all points of view.

While not often used, second person can be useful if kept short in fiction, or if used in nonfiction since nonfiction is often directed at the reader if the story is not about the narrator.

Whenever using second person, the writer poses the risk of sounding preachy, a know-it-all, making the reader a knows-nothing-at-all.

If new to writing, start with either first person singular or use third person.

THIRD PERSON

He, *she*, *it*, and *they* are pronouns most used in third person narratives, told from the perspective of characters outside the action. There are other gender neutral and gender inclusive pronouns to consider as well.

Third person is the POV of choice when the story is not about the writer. It is used when the story is about Jane or John Doe or any number of characters. Jane said / John said, and he said / she said / they said.

The only time first person appears within third person

is for character thought (inner voice, always in present tense and often italicized), such as in the following example:

> Jane Doe slid into bed next to John, careful not to rustle the sheets, not to make a noise lest she wake him. *What am I doing?*

Most fiction is written in first person or third, as most nonfiction is written in either first person or third. Writing instructors tend to coach new writers to first learn third person because it helps teach point of view, and because first person is often an easy out for beginning writers.

The first decision a writer needs to make is if the narrative will be in third person **limited**, or third person **omniscient**. For beginners, it is highly recommended to start in third person limited, meaning the narrator has "limited" access to a particular character's mind—knowing their thoughts, feelings, and emotions, experiencing what that particular character experiences; whereas in omniscient the narrator understands *all* characters.

Bunting in his article states that "this distinction is messy and somewhat artificial. Full omniscience in novels is rare—it's almost always limited in some way—if only because the human mind isn't comfortable handling *all* the thoughts and emotions of multiple people at once." That is not to say it cannot be done; it must be done *right*. When *all* emotions and inner thoughts and feelings of *all* characters pop into a narrative, it degrades the story, typically by telling and not showing what is happening to the characters. Bunting says it best: "Drama requires mystery. If the reader knows each character's emotions all the time, there will be no space for drama." [44]

An example of poorly written third person narration using a mix of names and pronouns:

> Jane Doe was on her way to the grocery store and as she was driving on the freeway another driver next to her nearly clipped her car, which the family always called Betty. Her hands jerked the steering wheel hard to the left and she had to quickly choose whether she wanted the other driver to collide into her or if she should move into the next lane over to avoid the other car from ending her life prematurely. Jane nearly hit the guardrail.

Along with names and pronouns, "another / other driver" was needed for clarity. How it would look if pronouns were not used often enough, and names too often:

> Jane Doe was on her way to the grocery store and as Jane was driving on the freeway another driver next to her nearly clipped Jane's car, which the family always called Betty. Jane Doe's hands jerked the steering wheel hard to the left and she had to quickly choose whether she wanted the other driver to collide into her or if Jane should move into the next

```
lane over to avoid the other car from
ending her life prematurely. Jane Doe
nearly hit the guardrail.
```

In third person narration, there must be a nice balance between name and pronoun use, and to introduce the point of view character as soon as possible. And if multiple female characters are in the same scene, or multiple male characters, too many pronouns might become confusing to the reader, so that is when names are necessary for clarity.

A quick revision:

```
On Jane Doe's way to the grocery store,
another driver on the freeway nearly
clipped Betty, the family car. Merge into
the next lane over or collide; those were
the options. Nearly took out the guard-
rail.
```

While first person and second person are limited to a single viewpoint (*I* or *you*), third person can have multiple viewpoints, and so the same rules apply to limiting use of pronouns and names to keep the writing from becoming awkward. Each chapter, or at least sub-chapter, should be from a single point of view, and the number of POV shifts kept to the main characters, typically.

Omniscient third person is another variant. This is when the narrator has complete access to the thoughts and experiences of any or all characters within a story. The key is to avoid shifting to another character's perspective within a single chapter unless designated by sub-chapter break, making it clear to the reader who they are following, otherwise the narrative will float between characters.

If using first person point of view, stick to first person. If writing in second person, stick to second person. And if writing in third person, stick to third person. Avoid swapping back and forth.

The term 'point of view' is derived from the Latin *punctum visus*, or "point sight," meaning "where you point your sight." The German word for 'point of view' is *gesichtpunkt*, which translates to "face point," or "where one's face is pointed."

Imagine not having a camera over a character's shoulder, but having one inside the character, one that not only provides visuals, but *all* the senses for the reader, allowing them to experience everything *through* the character.

Point of view is the filter through which everything pours. To go with a coffee analogy: it keeps the grounds from getting in the mug, keeps the drinker from swallowing chunks of bitter bean.

> "From the dog's point of view, his master is an elongated and abnormally cunning dog." - Mabel Robinson

The above quote includes a lesson with its humor. No matter which point of view is used by the writer, the reader can only know what the perspective character knows, experiencing everything *through* them. If the character is a dog, for instance, how might that dog see the world?

Before writing from a character's perspective, a writer must spend time inside that character. A writer needs to understand them intimately, whether or not they exist (fiction or nonfiction), *becoming* the character, seeing what they see, hearing what they hear, smelling what they smell, tasting what they taste, feeling what they feel—all the senses. Everything experienced *through* the character, not *for* them, and only when that happens should words go on the page.

With first person, it is much easier to accomplish this feat, with second person it is difficult, and with third person it takes finesse and much practice, as well as a deep understanding of show vs. tell.

SHOW VS. TELL

Fully immersing readers.

"Don't tell me the moon is shining; show me the glint of light on broken glass." - Anton Chekhov

What makes reading pleasurable? What makes a reader fall in love with a novel, a nonfiction narrative, a poetry collection, or any number of books? There are many possible answers: when the words draw the reader in from the first sentence, first paragraph, first page, then hold on until the very last; when the prose is smooth; when the pages flip by one after the other; when the reader doesn't want to ever put the book down lest their journey end; when the writing is finely-tuned, effortless; when worlds are created and destroyed; when characters are memorable, loveable, deplorable, and the reader connects to each and every one; when pacing is intense at times, delicate at others, emotions free-flowing, the language beautiful; when the reader closes the book after that final page and thinks, *Damn, that was good.*

A better question: 'What makes writing unpleasant?' The answer: bad writing. Every writer starts with bad writing, but every great writer learns the techniques required to break habits and write well.

Opposites of those more pleasurable moments of reading can easily lead a reader away from a book. If the first page is not polished, the first paragraph, the first *sentence*, it may be the end of a reader's journey from page one, paragraph one, *line* one. What every writer wants is for the reader to enjoy the entire shared journey from beginning to middle to end.

Novice writers lean toward telling instead of showing.

It is easy to fall into that habit, but the habit must be shattered like those unnecessary words that get in the way of point of view and prose. Beginning writers tend to over-explain action, or over-describe the senses, with over-written detail and description. *Over* is the common word here.

With show vs. tell, less is more.

In her article "Showing vs. Telling in Your Writing" for *Writer's Digest*, Roseann Biederman offers three tips: [45]

> **1. Be brief.** Make sure that all of your "telling" details are actually necessary to advance the plot, either by developing backstory, establishing the mood/tone, or describing the setting.
>
> **2. Avoid the dreaded "info dump."** Do not overwhelm your reader with information in your story's first few pages. Focus on capturing her attention with a compelling character and an interesting situation, then fold in the details as the plot develops.
>
> **3. Steer clear of clichés.** Never start a story with a character waking up and starting his day—unless you want to put your reader to sleep.

TELL

"Telling" is *explaining*, *informing*, and at times *understanding*. It's blandly stating facts and relaying feelings: the air was cold; the night was dark; he was tired; she ate a sour lemon; the carpet felt warm.

An example of telling vs. showing:

> ...with his left hand he held a sword while in his right he struggled with a shield and the dragon approached him angrily as he looked at the treasure chest of gold behind the beast and smiled with his mouth from ear to ear.

SHOW

"Showing" is *channeling*, *evoking*, and *presenting*. It is pulling the reader into the story, letting them become the character. Was the air cold and the night dark? Why not paint a better picture? The character's breath could puff out in chattered wisps, the night a void through which all light is devoured. And all lemons are sour. Instead, show what happens to the character when tasting that lemon. Their lips might pucker, one eye asquint, or they make a noise and cringe. There are endless ways to make the lemon not so generic. Was the carpet warm? First, *why* was the carpet warm, and how does the character know this? Are they barefoot? Are they touching the carpet with their hand? Did something spill? And for that final example of the dragon-slayer . . . what could be cut, and what might be added to make it showier?

A first attempt at a self-edit:

> ~~...with his left hand he~~ The fearless knight ~~held~~ readied his ~~a~~ sword ~~while in his right he~~ and struggled with his ~~a~~ shield ~~and~~ as the dragon approached with fiery breath. The ~~him angrily as he looked at the~~ overflowing treasure chest of gold

behind the beast made him ~~and~~ smile~~d with his mouth from ear to ear~~.

What is not important in the example with those first round of edits, and why:

with his left hand he (unless the knight's left-handedness is important to the story, there is no need to mention it; also, what else would he hold a sword with but his hand?)

held (what he does with the sword is important, and 'held' is lazy and obvious if the sword is unsheathed)

while in his right he (like his left hand, his right is not important; what he does with the shield is important)

angrily (show the reader the dragon's anger instead)

as he looked at the (having characters 'look' at things is always telling; show the reader what the knight sees)

with his mouth (what other body part would someone use to smile?)

from ear to ear (unless pruning shears were used to cut his mouth open, this is impossible).

The suggested edits are harsh, but they are necessary to improve show vs. tell. But there is still improvement to be made. How could "made him smile" be better phrased? Even "fearless knight" is telling since the phrase is cliché.

Edits also need edits, but the point is to first remove the *tell* and replace with *show*. How could the example of the dragon-slayer be revised even further to not *tell* the reader the knight is fearless, and to *show* his smile more naturally? This could be done through dialogue, through character thought, using stronger words, or by any number of things, which is why writing is never finished, only abandoned. A writer could self-edit until no words remain. And sometimes even that is needed when the writing cannot be salvaged.

A second attempt, technically a re-write because it was scrapped and begun anew:

> The knight, having struggled with his shield, threw it to the stone floor and raised his sword high. The dragon's breath, was it not merely a ball of ignited stomach gas, a fiery belch? "Prepare to die," he said as the glint of gold from the overflowing treasure chest behind the beast drew him forward.

Follow the advice of Chekov. Do not *tell* the reader the moon is shining; *show* them "the glint of light on broken glass" (or gold coins, in this case). The moon always shines, unless behind heavy clouds or on the opposite side of the earth, so instead show the reader *how* the moon shines. Stating the obvious, or the implied, is never necessary.

Showing vs. telling is by far one of the most challenging concepts to learn when writing, but the most common mistake. Even experienced writers do it often, especially during first drafts. Overuse of telling is one of the top reasons manuscripts are rejected by editors, agents, and publishers. Luckily, there are tools to learn to kill *telling* for good, or to at least limit its use. Although there are numerous ways to improve show vs. tell, here are four big ones to keep in mind:

Believable characters. Let the characters carry the heavy lifting, letting their actions / reactions and dialogue move the story. This can be done through characterization, body language, internal dialogue, etc.

Believable dialogue. Characters rarely say what they are thinking (unless in poorly written television dramas), they do not always speak grammatically correct, and they *never* explain what is happening.

Descriptive telling. Understand differences between *telling* description or detail and *showy* language.

Plot exposition. Let plot unfold naturally, never summarizing using blunt description, or having characters explain what is happening in the narrative.

Showing is like leaving a path of chocolate chips for a reader to eat along the way, prodding them to keep turning the page, pulled in by the story and what happens next, occasionally leaving a larger chunk of chocolate at the end of a chapter. *What happens then? What will become of these characters?* Eventually the reader will get to the end, having enjoyed all those tiny morsels, with a big payoff at some point.

Telling, on the other hand, or *over-telling*, is a five-pound chunk of 100% unsweetened cacao. It is raw and bitter and chaulky; no one ever spent time refining it into chocolate to make it any better.

Giving the reader vital information all at once takes enjoyment out of the reading experience, time wasted stumbling over words to figure out exactly what is supposed to be happening in the story, or who is speaking. Readers want to be challenged, but that is the wrong kind of challenge. Readers want to be entertained, not put to work.

Imagine watching a movie and the director is on the screen the entire time, or sitting in the adjacent theatre seat, telling the audience what is happening, scene by scene, line by line, and he is over-describing, relaying every unimportant detail, eye color, hair color, the exact distance to the wall across from John Doe, explaining why the character is constantly smiling and laughing and nodding and turning his head and reaching for things as his feelings are described in great detail.

> "John Doe sees the wall and walks toward it and with his left and right hands placed above him on the plaster he begins to slam his head into a bloody mess, feeling ashamed."

Jeff Gerke has great show vs. tell writing advice in his book *The First 50 Pages* in which he asks the question, "Can the camera see it?" [46] The argument could be stated *Can the writer see the telling?* He mentions how description is not *necessarily* telling because the camera *can* see it, so without description, a reader would not be able to visualize the story; in other words, do not leave it out. But he also mentions exceptions to the rule, such as the fact that cameras are unable to *see* sounds, or *see* smells, or *see* what is felt, or *see* tastes, yet all those can be *telling*.

But the senses should not be ignored. All the senses should be included whenever possible to fully immerse the reader. Reading should be an immersive experience for the reader, never boring. Show the senses instead of telling them, *through* the character, and through tight point of view and beautiful prose.

Telling is boring; telling puts up the wall against which a bored reader bangs their head.

Below are some skills all writers should try to perfect to improve show vs. tell:

Unrestrained creativity. A book is like a jigsaw puzzle. Lots of parts, all different shapes. *How* they are put together does not matter as much as how the pieces *fit* together. And they need to fit together, otherwise what is created is an unfinished puzzle. How the reader is pulled along until the very last word is likewise as important.

Language subtlety. Subtlety in the written form requires creativity with word choice. Having an idea is great (a poem, story, chapter, book, whatever), but going from concept to finished product takes effort. Character action, dialogue, plot points, setting, and all those descriptions and previously covered topics need to be subtle. Anything implied or assumed is not needed. Find a way of subtly showing.

Understanding humanness. Humanness is the quality or condition of being human. Much of showing is derived from human psychology. Characters need to first be understood by the writer (how they act / react, speak, their nuances, their ticks, all their traits) before the reader can understand them. Develop characters before writing them. Realistic characters (and their traits) should come out naturally through the narrative. Readers connect to characters when they are more human.

Reader trust. Over-telling results from a writer's fear of the reader not understanding what is on the page. Clarity is always important, but solid writing walks the razor's edge, over-explaining on one side of the blade and "just enough" on the other. A writer should trust the reader will understand the writing. If the writing is forced, it is more difficult to understand.

Self-editing. A writer not only writes, a writer edits, revises, rewrites, and constantly works on improving their craft. Working through show vs. tell is one of the most difficult parts of self-editing. It is easy to edit another's writing but editing oneself is more challenging.

Practice, practice, practice. Every writer starts at the beginning. Every writer, good or bad, has issues with show vs. tell. If they say they do not, they are lying. It takes practice but, like any skill, the more one practices, the better one gets. No writer is perfect. No writer ever can be, or ever will be. So, keep working toward perfection.

What can a writer look out for early on? What are the signs? Besides heavy description and detail, one early indicator of telling vs. showing is the use of *sensory words* and *directional / positioning* words.

SENSORY WORDS

Just as the phrase implies, sensory words are related to the five senses: *sight*, *sound*, *smell*, *taste*, and *touch*. Be on the lookout for verbs that deal with the senses.

Sight - Characters *looking, seeing, gazing, noticing, spotting, glimpsing, spying,* or using similar or other versions of those verbs: *look / looked, see / saw, gaze / gazed, notice / noticed* . . .

Sound - Characters *hearing, listening,* or using other versions of those verbs: *hear / heard, listen / listened* . . .

Smell - Characters *smelling* . . .

Taste - Characters *tasting, relishing, savoring* . . .

Touch - Characters *feeling, reaching, touching, holding, moving, walking, picking things up, putting things down, grasping, pushing, pulling* . . . *Feel* and *felt* are the worst offenders.

Let the reader experience the senses *through* character. Instead of "`Jane Doe looked at the hummingbird as` `it fed from the daylily,"` go with `"The hummingbird fed from the daylily."` The reader should already be in Jane Doe's point of view, so there is no need for Jane Doe to look at anything; the hummingbird can simply do what the hummingbird does, and Jane's ability to see things is assumed.

Likewise, instead of `"Jane Doe heard the hummingbird as it fed from the daylily,"` go with `"The hummingbird buzzed as it sipped from the daylily"` or something similar, choosing another way to describe the sound.

DIRECTIONAL / POSITIONING WORDS

Directional or positioning words are the other easy *tell*, which can be useful in screenwriting but not prose writing. Direction does not matter to the reader, only the writer, the same way direction does not matter to the person watching the movie, only the director.

Leave direction to directors. Show, don't tell.

Words to avoid: *up, down, left, right* (the worst offenders), *in front of, behind, between, above, below, toward, forward, backward,* etc. Direction / positioning words are assumed anyway by the action, such as with "standing up" or "sitting down." *Left* and *right* and *up* and *down* and similar words do not mean anything to the reader if point of view is tight, since the reader should be within the character already and not looking over their shoulder; there's no reason for the character to turn right or left, or pick up things with their left hand or otherwise.

DIALOGUE

Dialogue is real-time action, speech happening at that exact moment in time. This means dialogue is always *show*. Action and speech tags in front of and between and at the end of dialogue can be telling, however, which is why dialogue is so important and why it is important to get it right.

According to the American Time Use Survey for 2019, by the U.S. Department of Labor's Bureau of Labor Statistics, men in the United States spent an average of 3.00 hours (180 minutes) per day watching television, and women spent 2.64 hours (158.4 minutes). In comparison, the average time reading for pleasure was 0.23 hours (13.8 minutes) and 0.31 hours (18.6 minutes), respectively; 13x the amount of time watching vs. reading for men, and 8.5x for women. [47]

Why is this important? Besides the fact that people spend way too much time watching screens and not enough time reading, most new writers copy dialogue from poorly written television. Do not copy television dialogue. Ever.

Most film is over-written, the dialogue terrible, characters revealing inner thoughts, or explaining plot, the writer "dumbing it down" for the audience. Next time a crime show is playing (or any kind of drama), listen for repetition in the dialogue:

> "I understand your concern, Officer Obvious. I'm listening . . . I'm listening."

How many real people talk like that, and with repetition at the end for emphasis? Not many. No, *not many*.

Trust the reader. Readers read. Watchers watch.

Character perception should also be considered in terms of show vs. tell. If there is an overabundance of *perceiving, distinguishing, recognizing, realizing, ascertaining, discerning, catching, learning, gathering, discovering, finding out, making out, taking in*, etc., other versions / similar verbs and phrases, be wary.

Search for sensory and directional words, then weed them out. And strengthen the dialogue, taking out all those unimportant or implied actions. There is always a better way to arrange a sentence. Less is always more.

Writing will never be perfect but can be beautiful.

> "Show the readers everything, tell them nothing." - Ernest Hemingway

IMAGERY

Creating vivid description and detail.

"Words are tools of imagery in motion."
- Sam Shepard

One way to overwrite is using excessive detail in descriptions, but if handled with the appropriate balance, *description* by way of *detail* can create vivid *imagery*. And doing so helps create those much-needed visuals for the reader, even helping to flesh out characters and improve dialogue. But what is the difference between the two, and what is imagery?

DESCRIPTION

According to Merriam-Webster, description is a) an act of *describing*; specifically, discourse intended to give a mental image of something experienced; or b) a statement or account giving the characteristics of someone or something; a descriptive statement or account.

DETAIL

On the other hand, detail is defined as a) extended treatment of or attention to particular items; or b) a part of a whole, such as "a small and subordinate part," "a part considered or requiring to be considered separately from the whole," "the small elements that collectively constitute a work," and (in terms of photography) "the small elements of an image corresponding to those of the subject." [48]

The difference between the two is that details are countable somethings within description that are (or should be) small enough to escape casual notice, whereas description is a more in-depth layout of the essential qualities (details) or "portrait" of what is being described with language. Description is an explanation of what happened or what something is, and details are the petty things that bring it to life.

"The air is cold" would be a bland description of the air, and the only detail included is "cold." That *telling* statement can change to *showing* by including better detail with a better description of the air. "Constant frigid wind ached every bone, her bottom lip about to split, her throat raw." The air did not ache "every" bone, of course, but it paints a picture. Also, the air is no longer the concern with good description, but the *character*, and how the air affects the character in terms of the senses. The word "air" is not used in the second example, nor "cold," although both are implied.

In terms of dialogue, or the "stuff" around it, assumed or implied description should be left out.

```
"This is wonderful!" Jane Doe exclaimed
loudly, smiling, and nodding to herself,
her eyes wide with excitement.
```

Instead, let the dialogue do the heavy lifting.

```
"This is wonderful!" Jane Doe said.
```

Those six words are enough to create the visual. Even "Jane Doe said" might not be needed, so perhaps three words will do. Everything else is overwriting. *Telling.*

```
"This is wonderful!"
```

Unnecessary detail around dialogue can quickly become noticeable, words added that do not need to ever be there. They get in the way of conversation and hold up a Stop sign and say, "Wait, but check out all this nodding, smiling, laughing, grunting, and shrugging this character is doing."

In terms of character, only description crucial to the story is needed. Does John Doe have a limp because he is missing a leg and relies on his prosthetic? Those are vital details to include in his description because they matter.

If a character is described as "beautiful," every single person on the planet has their own concept of beautiful. If a character is described as "thin and curvy and platinum blonde with luxurious scarlet lips" and . . . well, that may have just described what might not be considered beautiful for a particular reader, or could have just described a much-hated ex-wife, or a nemesis.

Think of character description in terms of W.G.A.S., coined by Thomas F. Monteleone, F. Paul Wilson, and Douglas E. Winter for attendees of the Borderlands Press Writers Boot Camp. "Who Gives a Shit?"

Does Jane Doe have long and flowy brownish-blonde hair, cinnamon eyes that sparkle, legs that never end? Is John Doe tall and gangly and six-foot-three, or a short and stalky five-foot-two and walks with a long or short stride, always smiling, chuckling, or laughing like a maniac, nodding like a bobblehead? Who cares about any of those details? Show the reader he is tall by having him tower over other characters or show the reader he is short by others towering over *him*. All those other details are unnecessary.

Show the reader John and Jane Doe, do not describe (tell) them.

Vivid description should bring to life what would otherwise seem lifeless to the reader. The goal as a writer is to be the brush that paints a picture in a wonderful display of color across a canvas (in this case, the page). Without vivid detail, a writer is simply dipping a paint-less brush into an empty can and slapping nothing across a canvas.

IMMERSION

Imagery is the magic that happens when details transform description into visuals in the mind. Imagery is language used by poets, by novelists, and by all great writers to invoke imagination using figurative and metaphorical language to improve the reading experience through the senses.

Merriam-Webster lists three definitions for imagery, but the last two are most important: 2) figurative language, and 3) mental images; especially, the products of imagination. Always strive for more arresting or unusual details. Make description stronger, more vivid, hitting all the senses.

To enjoy a book requires envoking imagination, which means the writer needs to make sure the writing creates life-like imagery, pulling the reader directly onto the page and putting them inside the character(s) by full immersion.

A writer can pull a reader deep into their book through unique, original detail, and by way of simile and metaphor, and by other means of figurative language.

Is a character wearing "pants," or are they wearing "holey cargo pants stained with a rainbow of paint splatter"? Is a character's hair "messy," or "a rat's nest of filth"? Are a character's eyes "surrounded by wrinkled skin and deep-set," or "as dark and ancient as a pair of puckered assholes far too close together" (something like that was used in a national bestseller). The key is to make description specific, and *figurative.*

> "Figurative language can give shape to the difficult and the painful. It can make visible and 'felt' that which is invisible and 'unfeelable.'"
> - Mary Oliver

FIGURATIVE LANGUAGE

Figurative language is described well by Neil Gaiman in his MasterClass video where he shares, "It's tempting to think that direct language is the easiest for us to understand, but sometimes we respond better to more creative wording. Writers and poets use figurative language to build imagery and give words more power. Simile, metaphor and a host of other non-literal methods of expression help make foreign concepts familiar and graspable." [49]

The word *figurative* is derived from Old French *figuratif*, meaning "metaphorical," and from Latin *figurativus* ("figurative") in terms of speech, as well as *figurare*, meaning "to form, shape" from *figura*, meaning "a shape, form, figure." [50] According to Gaiman, figurative language can be expressed four different ways:

Simile - A comparison of one thing to another to make description more vivid or empathic, using "like" or "as." For example: "description as tasteless as water," or "description like unflavored water."

Metaphor - A transformative comparison by calling one thing another and regarded as symbolic, representative, or abstract. For example: "The writer's page is a canvas" or "the writer bled his ink onto the page."

Personification - An attribution of a human characteristic or something of a personal nature to something that is not human. For example: "The stars danced in slow rotation across the night sky." Stars cannot dance, but the description creates a figurative visual.

Literary devices that heighten imagery - *alliteration*, *assonance*, *onomatopoeia*, and *hyperbole*.

ALLITERATION

Alliteration happens when similar sounds are used in close proximity. Alliteration entails an entirely challenging choice of "wonderful whimsical words" that dance off the tongue, such as "sheep should sleep in a shed." There is rhyming in the latter, but also much alliteration. And there are numerous types of alliteration, depending on the alphabet: *plosive* (repetition of *p* and *b* letters or sounds), *sibilance* (repetition of *s*), *dental* (repetition of *d* an *t*), *guttural* (repetition of *g*, *r*, and *c*), *fricative* (repetition of *f*, *ph*, and *v*), and *assonance.*

ASSONANCE

Assonance is the repetition of a sound with nonrhyming syllables near enough to each other that it creates an echo, or when there's a *diphthong*, a sound that begins as one vowel and moves toward another, or are combined, such as with the character *æ*. It is confusing to describe, so best left to example, such as: "The beam of light shone green in her eyes." While "beam" and "green" do not rhyme, they are alike enough to create alliteration. For the diphthong, think of the word "coin" and how the "oi" quickly changes the annunciation mid-word. For the echo effect, consider the first line in this snippet from Edgar Allan Poe's poem "The Bells" (published in 1849), wherein "mellow" and "bells" create the effect before the rhyming:

Hear the <u>mellow</u> wedding <u>bells</u>
Golden bells!
What a world of happiness their harmony
 foretells

ONOMATOPOEIA

Onomatopoeia, on the other hand, could easily be compared to the colorful and fancy-font words found on the pages of a comic book or graphic novel: *crash, boom, bang, splash, mumble*. In the Poe example, if the bells *clang*, that would be the imagery. It is a way to poetically create sound because the words appear the way they sound, as though heard by the reader when read. For example: "The pans fall and clang and crash across the floor." This works much better than stating that the pans fall to the floor. It not only creates a visual, but sound, hitting *two* senses in that single sentence (although "the pans fall" is bland). A few more lines from "The Bells" to show how onomatopoeia works in poetry (with "air" and "ear" and "danger" working as assonance):

> How they clang, and crash, and roar!
> What a horror they outpour
> On the bosom of the palpitating air!
> Yet the ear, it fully knows,
> By the twanging,
> And the clanging,
> How the danger ebbs and flows

Dialogue should never utilize onomatopoeia in place of dialogue or speech tags. Characters never need to "boom" words across the page when an exclamation point could be used, nor do they (or can they) "beam," which is impossible for all but Care Bears. When flipping through the pages of *Twilight*, an international bestselling series with hundreds of millions of copies sold, circle each time "murmur" is used as a dialogue tag. The definition of the word itself means those who murmur can barely understand each other, and in that novel, there are thousands upon thousands!

HYPERBOLE

Hyperbole is overexaggerating for dramatic effect: phrases like "hungry as a horse" (simile), or "starving to death" (metaphor), or the all-too-familiar story of having to walk uphill both ways "when I was your age" through two feet of snow and hurricane winds and other unrealistic descriptions of how the past happened. Hyperbole is when details are blown out of proportion, opposite of an understatement.

Unlike simile and metaphor, hyperbole is extravagant and ridiculous overstatement. They are never meant to be taken seriously. When used right, they can add a flare of humor to a scene, or add to one's character, especially by way of dialogue. For instance: "Susie, I asked you to clean your room forever ago!" With inner dialogue (thought), it can be just as useful. An editor might be thinking a particular writer's work "uses more telling words than craters on the moon." Hyperbole is less common in nonfiction but can be useful to stress a point or catch a reader's attention.

All forms of imagery help with prose, with point of view, and with show vs. tell. And everything mentioned creates that imagery, but too much detail in description and too much use of figurative language can be *too much*, resulting in purple prose, or simply bad writing.

The perfect amount of figurative language by use of simile and metaphor and personification, and a limited use of alliteration, assonance, onomatopoeia, and hyperbole, can create poetic writing a reader will always remember. With vivid description, it is a matter of finding balance.

> "Literature, like memory, selects only the vivid patches." - T.E. Hulme

John Doe doesn't need to huff and crouch down in front of the library shelf and reach out with his left hand to retrieve a book, his amber eyes gazing over the titles of each spine, his light-brown hair atop his head well-combed and described in detail with his eyebrows furrowing, and he doesn't have to be angry that he has to choose a book from the millions on display, murmuring to himself and *blah, blah, blah*. John Doe can simply storm across the library and take a book off the shelf.

Only enough imagery to cover what the reader absolutely *must* experience by way of vivid description is ever needed. Paint the picture and let readers enjoy the art. Do not point out every detail or throw on so much paint that what is intended is unrecognizable. Leave visuals up to the reader's imagination, which can be one of the most powerful tools for creating memorable imagery.

A little paint goes a long way.

FRAMEWORK

What needs to go in each chapter.

"Writing doesn't mean necessarily putting words on a sheet of paper. You can write a chapter while walking or eating." - Umberto Eco

While that is true, words eventually go on the page. To be considered a book, there needs to be a whole lot of words strung together within a digestible framework. Large chunks of text need to be organized in an order that makes sense and allows the reader to pause and reflect, to slide in a bookmark if distracted or desired.

Depending on scope, a printed book could be 25,000 or 125,000 words (or more), but how those tens of thousands of words are arranged are incredibly important. It is rare for a reader to start and finish a book in a single sitting. Considering the average printed page is 250 words, within the hundreds upon hundreds of pages of a book there needs to be a certain amount of whitespace.

According to data published by Statista, Amy Watson suggests, "The average daily time spent reading by individuals in the United States in 2020 amounted to 0.34 hours, or 20.4 minutes. Adults over the age of 65 were the most avid readers, and those aged 75 or above spent almost an hour reading each day [0.95 hours, or 57 minutes]. Meanwhile, those between the ages of 15 and 19 years read for just 8.4 minutes per day on average." [51]

That is a small reading window for most age demographics. Twenty minutes per day. And that is an average for *all* age ranges, and only considering avid readers, those with a keen interest or enthusiasm for reading. Individuals in the 65 to 74 age bracket were next highest at 0.72 hours (43.2

minutes), so a vast majority of those who spend a decent amount of time reading each day are over the age of 65.

Teenagers spend the least amount of time reading, but that number only *slightly* increases for the span of ages 20 to 64, going from 0.20 hours (12 minutes) to 0.29 hours (17.4 minutes). Around 15 minutes for anyone under 65.

Also worth noting is a little math. Paul Nowak, founder of Iris Reading, the largest provider of speed-reading and memory courses, suggests that "the average reading speed of most adults is around 200 to 250 words per minute." College students are around 300, or a page per minute. [52]

When comparing reading speeds to reading windows, this reveals how many pages the avid reader digests per day, which could also be referred to as one's *reading attention span*. For teenagers this is about 8 minutes, for those 20 to 64 it is between 12 and 17 minutes, and for those 65 and older between 43 and 95 minutes.

These numbers are slightly higher than the two years prior, so either COVID-19 played a role in getting more people to read for additional seconds (not a big jump), or reading is slowly gaining in popularity as a pastime.

In a hilarious but frightening article called "You Now Have a Shorter Attention Span Than a Goldfish," Kevin McSpadden shares that, "The average attention span for the notoriously ill-focused goldfish is nine seconds, but according to Microsoft Corp., people now generally lose concentration after eight seconds, highlighting the effects of an increasingly digitalized lifestyle on the brain." The study shows that since the start of the mobile revolution (2000), this number has dropped from twelve seconds, and the data correlates with the study on average read time published by Statista. "77% of people aged 18 to 24 responded 'yes' when asked, 'When nothing is occupying my attention, the first thing I do is reach for my phone,' compared with only 10% of those over the age of 65." [53]

What do these statistics of a distracted world have to do with chapters? Attention span and word count.

CHAPTERS

Chapters are main divisions or sections of a book, organized by topic or story beats. The space between one and the next works like a Pause button, a chance for the reader to become distracted by something else for a while, despite the fact that the book is intended to be a distraction *from* that busy world.

A cellphone chimes, a child calls, or someone says, "Hey, I see you're reading, but got a moment?" Once pulled into that alternate time and space (fiction or nonfiction), the magic is severed by the interruption. "Yeah, let me just finish this chapter (or section)" and soon after the book is set aside. The book could be revisited later that night, the following day, weeks or months, or never again depending on the distracted reader. Maybe they flip through the pages and realize they don't have the dedication for X-number of pages, or eventually re-shelf the book entirely because they "just couldn't get into it," which typically means not enough time was dedicated to reading.

If the average *avid* reader is only going to spend 20 minutes reading at a time, books benefit from digestible segments. A chapter on the shorter side might make a reader think, *Okay*, one *more before* [fill in the blank].

8 minutes of reading for adults is about 2,000 words. 20 minutes of reading is about 5,000. An hour of reading is about 15,000. This should all be taken into consideration for chapters and/or subchapters. The speed at which younger readers read should also be considered.

From the same Iris Reading study: "By the middle of the year in first grade, a student should read around 23 words per minute. In second grade this should have increased to 72 wpm, by grade three to 92 wpm, grade four 112 wpm, and 140 by grade five. Speed increases continue steadily through middle school, and by grade 8, they should be reading around 151 words per minute. For most students, speed increases will continue more slowly through high school as youngsters pursue other interests, but they should continue to progress steadily toward the average adult reading rate of 200-250, or better."

This is why books intended for younger audiences have shorter chapters with fewer words, and why children are fascinated by number of pages and number of books read. It may take little Jane fifteen minutes or longer to read *Where the Wild Things Are* by Maurice Sendak, but the average adult Joe could read it in under two because the entire book is only 338 words.

Ideally, chapters for mainstream books for adults run between 1,500 words and 3,500 words on average, toying with the reader distractibility mindset. There is a sweet spot somewhere around 2,500 words, but every book is different. Beach reads might be 300 pages and have 50 to 100 chapters, letting readers commit to only one or two pages at a time. Books of more literary merit might have chapters spanning 20 pages or more.

The average number of chapters in mainstream books is between 12 and 20, depending on genre and intended audience, and anywhere from 10 to 20 pages per chapter.

Most books are segmented in this fashion. A new chapter could mean time has passed in the story, a continuation from another plot point, or a switch in point of view. For nonfiction, there could be sub-chapters within those chapters, and for fiction, chapters could be arranged linearly or nonlinearly. It all depends on what kind of arrangement the story warrants.

The book could be structured like a three-act play (beginning / middle / end), or five parts, or two halves, or no parts at all. There might not even be chapters, only breaks either designated by blank space or with a *dinkus*, a symbol placed between sections of text. This is a way for the writer to cue the reader that it is okay to take a pause because the story has transitioned.

SCENE / CHAPTER BREAKS

In an article for *The Paris Review* called "Ode to the Dinkus," Daisy Alioto defines this strange term as "a line of three asterisks (* * *) used as a section break in a text. It's the flatlining of an asterism (⁂), which in literature is a pyramid of three asterisks and in astronomy is a cluster of stars." [54] Depending on the publisher, different symbols can be used in its place.

Common in manuscripts is the use of hashtags centered on the page between section breaks: #. This allows for a quick find and replace to change the symbol into something else later or helps designate breaks when the manuscript is printed out. They are incredibly useful when a section ends at the ending of a page or begins at the beginning of a page, or to help a typesetter designing the interior of the book, since sometimes a blank line without such a marking can cause confusion when text runs from one page to another.

Without places for the reader to pause in the narrative, the entire book can seem daunting, the reader forced to not only use a bookmark but to figure out exactly which *line* on the page to return to the next time they crack open that spine, resulting in unnecessary re-reading.

Long chapters, such as this one, can benefit from chapter breaks as well.

* * *

Technically, a novel does not need chapters or chapter breaks, but perhaps *should.* And technically, chapters and sub-chapters do not need titles, but maybe they *could.*

Chapter title options:

1

One

Chapter 1

Chapter One

I, II, III, IV ...

The Title of This Chapter

Chapter 1: The Title of This Chapter

(or any combination)

Parts of a book could be named similarly:

```
Part 1
Part One
I, II, III, IV . . .
The Title of This Part
Part 1: The Title of This Part
(or any combination)
```

Both chapter and part titles follow the standard naming convention of *title case*, in which major words are capitalized and most minor words are in lowercase. When using title case, also known as *headline case*, refer to style guides such as the *AP Stylebook* or *Chicago Manual of Style* since there are differences in what words are considered "major."

* * *

Another dinkus, another designation that this section will have a different focus than the previous, although fitting within the same theme of the chapter framework, otherwise the writing would perhaps better fit in another chapter.

Every manuscript is formatted a little differently, but all should follow general guidelines so they do not sorely stand out from other manuscripts. What should make a manuscript stand out is the writing, never the "cleverness" of the writer, and this applies to query letters, synopses, and all correspondence related to submission and follow-up. Cleverness gets tossed aside as inexperienced and amateur.

Knowing how to write and knowing how to put together an industry standard manuscript are both required of professional writers. Chapters cannot be thrown together and blocked off by word count; they need to each stand on their own, as though separate publishable short stories or essays. They can be open-ended, of course, but only if there is a smooth transition to the subsequent section of the book.

Chapters thus require certain components. The main ones: beginning, middle, and end. Just as a short story or essay needs a *beginning*, *middle*, and *end*, each chapter does as well, and this framework is established by the following sub-components, covered in length earlier but recapped below:

Intrigue draws the reader's attention; the "opening hook" needs to serve a purpose other than simply snag the reader, and needs to add to the scene and/or create or resolve conflict. The intrigue, or pull of the narrative, needs to continue throughout the chapter and not be gimmicky. A strong voice helps.

Character development needs to take place for the *protagonist* (the main character at the center of the story); the *antagonist* (a character presented as the nemesis of the protagonist); or *secondary characters* (anyone who plays smaller roles to advance the plot positively or negatively). Character is the most important part of the chapter, and likewise the entire book.

Plot / Conflict is what happens in the story; *plot* is the action sequence and relevance of character action / reaction, and in terms of the overall story is the beginning, middle, and end of a sequence of events. Conflict is the source of internal or external tension that moves the plot, and so characters need to struggle and/or face obstacles, otherwise there is no story and events are happening without reason.

Dialogue / Voice brings characters alive on the page; characters need to talk, whether realistically or imaginarily portrayed (nonfiction vs. fiction), and their dialogue needs to sound real to the reader if read aloud; *dialogue* is internal or external words spoken or conveyed through thought between one or more characters, whereas voice is a writer's / narrator's / character's style.

Point of View is the narrator's position in relation to the story, most often experienced through a single character's perspective; this can be in first person (I), second person (you), or third person (they/John Doe), and must stay consistent since POV contains what is experienced by characters through the senses. Show vs. tell is crucial for tight point of view

Setting is the time and place within a narrative that initiates the main backdrop for a story and can be referred to as the world or milieu in which to include or build context; the *where* and the *when*. Setting can also be a character and should be equally as developed. A reader needs to be fully immersed in the characters' environment whether real or imaginary.

Style / Tone / Mood likewise help immerse the reader into the story; a writer's *style* needs to engage the reader by way of everything mentioned above, while *tone* creates an overall feeling for the reader, and *mood* needs to build upon the sensory atmosphere / environment created to enhance the reading experience.

Theme is a central topic, subject, or overarching message within a narrative, divided into: *thematic concept* of what the reader thinks the work is about and *thematic statement* of what the work conveys about the subject.

Intrigue is needed again at the end to provide a reason for the reader to continue reading (if not the final chapter, in which case the conclusion needs to be further developed). For nonfiction, a chapter might include a solid yet concise wrap-up of what was covered, touching on main takeaways or lessons; and no matter the book the ending of a chapter can be a cliffhanger, resolution of a problem, or create a new problem. A chapter needs to *feel* right upon completion.

> "Who can't relate to the idea of leaving one chapter behind and moving on to the next." - Mike Shinoda

Nonfiction requires additional chapter components:

Personal Stories can offer vulnerability to the reader while also exploring theme. These should be genuine, compelling stories that add to the believability of the text and support any arguments or claims. This is a section of writing based on the author's personal and/or professional experience(s), usually anecdotes in which the writer is the primary character or assisting alongside the primary character.

Primary Interviews are directly performed by the writer, resulting in the inclusion of useful quotes, background information on the interviewee, and directly addresses the chapter topic. Primary interviews are conducted by the writer and should flow naturally within the narrative by way of seamless transitions.

Secondary Interviews are direct or sometimes indirect interviews or case studies used to support the chapter topic. These can include elements the writer read second-hand or gathered from information available to the public but are not interviews conducted by the writer.

Teaching Moments / Lessons are clear arguments in support of the writing, drawing information from either primary or secondary interviews, as well as direct and indirect research (see below). This is also known as commentary, what the writer learned from a particular experience.

Thematic Narrative is a central topic, subject, or overarching message within a narrative. Themes can be divided into two categories: a work's thematic concept of what the reader *thinks* the work is about, and its thematic statement of what the work *reveals* about the subject.

Direct Research / Data is information supporting the topic in the form of stats or quotes from relevant and properly cited sources. This is information the writer has sought out personally; direct support from sources, statistics, theories from respected public collected data, interviews, trends, surveys, etc. that add credibility. Such research and data do not require inference or writer commentary to be understood by the reader in direct support of the argument.

Indirect Research / Data is information not related to the main topic that help support the topic. This is indirect support from psychology, sociology, academia, historians, etc., which requires the author to provide additional commentary for the reader to understand how the disparate information supports the argument.

Quotes support a nonfiction writer's research, which can be directly spoken or written work, or dialogue taken from an interviewee, or material available to the public. Quotes should be short, and verbatim (without modification), and always sourced properly to avoid plagiarism.

Each component builds framework for a chapter, and despite word counts and time spent or not spent reading, a chapter needs to be as long as it needs to be, the way a book needs to be as long as it needs to be.

But a writer should always keep potential readers and potential *reader attention spans* in mind. 20 minutes / 20 pages is the average for *all* avid readers, so that is a good place to start for each section of text, or maybe half of that since on the low end it is more like 8 minutes / 8 pages (19 years old and younger), as it slowly creeps up to around 15 minutes / 15 pages (20 to 65 years old) on its way to the extreme end at 60 minutes / 60 pages (75 years and older).

A good length for an average chapter is 2,500 words +/- 500. With the reader in mind, consider how often breaks might be needed in the narrative, whether represented by white space, symbols, dinkuses, hashtags, or new chapters entirely, and keep in mind the power of each section of text and how the words flow from one to the next.

Is each segment engaging, not just the opening or closing? Are each equally engaging, and do they fit neatly together to tell a story? If all those pieces are in place, the entire book will be engaging.

> In that book which is
> My memory...
> On the first page
> That is the chapter when
> I first met you
> Appear the words...
> Here begins a new life.
> - Dante Alighieri

STRUCTURE

Order of operations.

"In limits, there is freedom. Creativity thrives within structure."
- Julia Cameron

A book can be any culmination of gathered words: a chapbook (small pamphlet or paperback booklet), a fiction collection (collected work from a single author), anthology (collected work from multiple authors), novel, memoir, creative nonfiction, bibliography, essay collection, poetry collection, or whatever it may be.

Righting Writing focuses on what is required to start, follow through, and finally finish a book to help writers prefect their craft, but the offered advice applies for any type of writing, despite how the words are bound or what word-length boundaries are observed. And word count defines what is written, so it is okay to ask, "What have I written?" or "What am I writing?" or "What will I write?"

Word count guidelines for fiction:

Micro-Fiction - 100 or fewer
Flash Fiction - 100 to 1,000
Short Fiction - 1,000 to 7,500
Novelette - 7,500 to 17,500
Novella - 17,500 to 40,000
Short Novel - 40,000 to 60,000
Novel - 60,000 to 110,000
Epic Novel - 110,000 or more

Those all have loose boundaries. Anytime word-length is defined, there are subtle differences in word counts and plenty of arguments, depending on the source, which is why they are labeled as "guidelines." The ranges are flexible, to an extent.

In an article by Blake Atwood for The Write Life, the question is asked, "What's the ideal book word count?" to which he answers laxly, "If you're writing your first novel or any book, you're probably asking these questions. The short answer: long enough to tell the story but short enough to consistently hold the reader's interest. The long answer is, well, longer." [55]

25,000 words of manuscript will translate to roughly 100 pages of printed book. Most printers require 100 pages to have a spine with printable text, otherwise what is created is more of a spineless chapbook, and anything over 400 pages (100,000 words) will have a significant spine.

Higher word counts result in higher price points and potentially lower profit margins, which is why publishers are interested in the number of words a writer has written. Anything shorter than novel-length is a tough sell, although there has been a reemergence of short novels and novellas. Anything shorter than novella-length will end up published within either a collection or anthology or other venue.

All books are different, depending on category and genre, so the ranges of commonly published books vary. But anytime a writer (especially novice) pushes boundaries of industry specifics, manuscripts will be more difficult to sell to traditional markets, or may be tossed aside because of a number.

Time must be spent researching the market, and if the word count is on the higher end of the spectrum, consider what Chuck Sambuchino wrote in his article "Word Count for Novels and Children's Books: The Definitive Post | How Long Should a Book Be?" for *Writer's Digest:* "Almost always, high word count means that the writer simply did not edit their work down enough. Or—it means they have two or more books combined into one." [56]

Typical word counts for younger readers:

Picture Book (Fiction) - Fewer than 1,000
Picture Book (Nonfiction) - Up to 2,000
Early Reader - Up to 3,500
Young Middle Grade / Chapter Book
 - 4,000 to 10,000 or higher
Middle Grade (General) - 20,000 to 55,000
Middle Grade (Fantasy) - 65,000 to 85,000
Upper Middle Grade (General) - 40,000 to 65,000
Upper Middle Grade (Fantasy) - 65,000 and higher
Young Adult - 50,000 to 80,000

Word counts seem to be on the rise for younger readers, thanks to authors like Rick Riordan (Percy Jackson series), Veronica Roth (Divergent series), and J.K. Rowling (Harry Potter series), who keep pushing boundaries and creating larger books, but the adult reader has a more solid word count structure for fiction.

Typical word counts for adult fiction:

Crime / Mystery / Thriller / Horror - 70,000 to 90,000
Fantasy / Science Fiction - 90,000 to 120,000 or higher
Historical - 80,000 to 100,000
Romance - 70,000 to 100,000
Western - 50,000 to 80,000

There are exceptions. Stephen King tends to write in the range of 150,000 to 200,000 words, hence the term "doorstop" for some of his books. The uncut version of *The Stand* is around 500,000 words, or 1,153 pages (eventually published that way), which he originally cut by 150,000 to bring it closer to 350,000 for its initial release. His novel *It* was published at 1,138 pages, so probably close to the half-million-word mark (or between six and seven normal-sized novels). Unless widely popular with a backlog of titles, agents and publishers are not interested in such hefty tomes.

Generally, published nonfiction tends to be around 75,000 words and fiction around 85,000, on average, sometimes venturing closer to or slightly above 100,000.

Word counts are malleable, but for first books, aim for the averages.

Typical word counts of adult nonfiction:

Short Essay - 1,500 or fewer
Essay - 1,500 to 5,000
Dissertation - 25,000 to 50,000
Nonfiction (General) - 50,000 to 100,000
Nonfiction (Creative) / Memoir - 60,000 to 90,000
Self-Help / How-To - 20,000 to 50,000
Biography - 80,000 to 150,000
Travel / Nature - 40,000 to 70,000

Nonfiction is all over the place, and there are endless genres and sub-genres, so be sure to research the market and understand expected word counts. Along with obtaining a desired word count, though, those words need structure.

Creating a book is not merely authoring a story and

all the editing and suffering involved (organizing chapters, providing headings or titles, creating a Table of Contents, numbering pages, slapping on a cover, and placing the book on sale). Numerous components make a book. The interior layout is crucial and there are professional standards to follow when putting together a manuscript.

Similar to the three-part story structure of *beginning*, *middle*, and *end*, there is a three-part order of operations for interior layout: *front matter* (beginning), *body* (middle) and *back matter* (end), and various sub-components within each of those.

To understand the placement of each sub-component, there should be a basic understanding of pagination, which is the number sequence of pages within a book. Every physical page technically consists of two: an odd-numbered page on one side and an even-numbered on the other. When opening a book, odd-numbered pages are on the *recto* side (right) and even-numbered pages on the *verso* side (left). Along with page number, *headers* and *footers* should include valuable information for the reader.

HEADERS / FOOTERS

An early definition of "header" is "one that removes heads" to per chance be lopped off and placed into a wagon (wheat or noggins or otherwise), but in document layout terms, the header is the top-most area of a page above the bulk of the text. With nonfiction, headers typically include the book title on the verso, and the chapter title on the recto, and with fiction, the author's name is usually on the verso and the book title on the recto.

A "footer," on the other hand, is a line or block of text at the "foot" of the page, below the bulk of the text. With both nonfiction and fiction, footers tend to include the page number if not already included in the header. Footers can also include footnotes [1], which work as interruptions to the text, which forces the reader to temporarily shift focus to the bottom of the page to the footnote included there, then back to the main body of text to resume reading. [2]

Other things to consider with page numbers: they should not be placed on inside margins; they are not needed for blank pages, either those intentionally left blank, illustrated pages, or blank pages that fall on even numbers.

For the sake of simplicity, left or right will be used for page side reference going forward, and it can be assumed content typically appears on the right-hand page if not mentioned specifically.

The front matter is also not part of the book's pagination, and the page numbering before the main body of work should either use lowercase roman numerals (i, ii, iii, iv, v, etc.) or not be numbered at all.

---

[1] Sequentially numbered explanations, comments, or references that coincide with superscript numbers placed within the text on that same page such as in the example above. If this were the end of the printed page, for example, a line would appear before the footnote, like this.

[2] The use of footnotes is considered an outdated practice, with publishers moving toward the use of endnotes instead (listed at the end of the book, definition coming soon).

FRONT MATTER

Front Matter is everything that comes *before* the story. Some elements are more common than others, and not all are required (having them all would result in a painful reading experience), so consider a balance of what's included, depending on the book. This is not necessarily the specific order of components, as order sometimes changes depending on the publisher and the book layout.

Half Title - Most often the first page of a book, containing only the book title.

Series Title - Also referred to as the "Other Works" page, listing previous titles by the author. It can be organized by release date, alphabetically by title, and/or grouped by subject matter.

Frontispiece - In terms of architecture, the frontispiece is the façade of a building, and in terms of books, the term refers to a page opposite the main title page, with an illustration on the left and the title page on the right.

Title - Similar in appearance to the *half title* page (and on the right, depending on book design), this main title page not only includes the title of the book but any subtitles, and most importantly the author's name or pseudonym.

Copyright - Sometimes referred to as the *colophon*, this left-facing page includes the book's copyright notice, including the year of publication (not of creation), copyrights, dates of print editions, ISBN (International Standard Book Number), translation notes, and may include notes on used typefaces / fonts, etc. Notes on typefaces are optionally found at the ends of books.

Dedication - A right-facing page that is usually simple in design and consisting of a dedication message, such as *For Jane Doe*, or a short personal note to someone (or multiple individuals) directly from the author.

Epigraph - A right-facing page that includes a common phrase, poem, quotation, or lyrics related to the overall theme of the book; epigraphs are typically from works in the public domain, otherwise the author will have needed to request permission for inclusion.

Contents - A Table of Contents is typically found in nonfiction books, but sometimes appears in fiction if warranted, such as with a fiction collection or anthology. The "ToC" often lists parts or section titles, chapter titles, subheadings, along with corresponding page numbers where each begins.

List of Illustrations / Figures / Tables / Maps - If a book includes illustrations (partial-page, full-page, multi-page spreads), or any type of figures, graphs, tables, maps, or other visual content, a separate page might be used listing page number locations for those items.

Foreword - Not to be confused with the Introduction or Preface, this is an introduction written by someone other than the author. They are most often found in nonfiction.

Preface - Although the preface precedes the main body of work and is written by the author (or also the co-author if the book is a collaborative effort), it is part of the *front matter.* A preface offers additional context, such as inspirations and/or notes on the book's creation.

Acknowledgments - This is a list of individuals and/or organizations (and sometimes short notes of thanks about each) found helpful or inspiring by the author. Spelled "Acknowledgements" in certain countries, this can sometimes appear within the preface itself, or be included as part of the *back matter.*

Prologue - Depending on style guides, such as *The Chicago Manual of Style*, a prologue is considered either part of the book's *front matter* or part of the *body*, but always precedes the chapters / narrative. Prologues are used (most often in fiction) to provide readers important or helpful information prior to the story, sometimes to set a mood or present past events, thus setting up the story.

Including all those components, if only a single page apiece, would result in thirteen pages leading into the heart of the book: *the body*. Many are single-page, but consider the Foreword, Preface, and Prologue could each run ten pages or more and create padding. Should the core of a book start on page forty or later? Always consider the reader.

Other items that appear in the *front matter* list of abbreviations, blurbs (comments about the book or the writer's work in general from other professionals), a chronology (order of events by date), a conversion table, or a genealogy.

BODY

The Body is the main text of the book, the *story* (or stories). All the other stuff is formality and appreciation and lead-in. How much is included for the writer or for those involved in the book's creation, and how much is there for the reader's benefit? Many readers flip through those first potential elements, only reading the prologue, yet some readers might read every single page. But how much is *needed* to get them to this largest middle section?

Second Half Title - Identical to the *half title* page, the second half title page is used when the front matter of the book runs long, there mostly to remind the reader that they have finally made it after so many pages. Flip the page, and the book officially starts.

Introduction / Author's Note - Just one more interruption before a book begins. Considered the beginning of the main body of a book, the Introduction is not to be confused with the Foreword or Preface, which both appear in the *front matter*. Introductions are not meant to "introduce" the author, necessarily—handled in the Preface—but to introduce the book's purpose. Same goes for an Author's Note, which is similar. Often Introductions are found in nonfiction (and longer), whereas Author's Notes are found in fiction (and shorter).

Narrative / Chapters - What readers are after, the main body of text. *Finally*, readers are thinking after fifteen or more steppingstones, *the story*. The narrative can be broken into chapters, or parts, and/or with chapter titles, depending on the author's intention, broken up into scenes by use of breaks in the text, or can be one continuous narrative. Again, consider the reader and their journey.

Illustrations - Throughout the narrative, illustrations may be included either at the beginnings of each section / chapter or placed wherever needed. Illustrations are seldom created by the author and are not part of the main *body* of work, although they may appear somewhere within.

Epilogue - Found immediately after the narrative or closing chapter, an Epilogue provides closure or comments or a hinting that the story continues. They are mostly found in fiction and on the shorter side.

Afterword - Written by the author (and sometimes by other professionals in the same field, or the co-author if the book is a collaborative effort). The Afterword is like a Preface in that it offers additional context, such as inspirations and/or notes on the book's creation.

Postscript - The last component of the *body*, usually short. A postscript supplies further information after a narrative has ended, can wrap up anything outstanding, or can pose questions to the reader.

BACK MATTER

Back Matter is everything else that goes at the end of a book to support the writing or to further acknowledge the writer. Like the *front matter*, readers are typically done with a book by this point and ready to set it aside. Some readers like to dig deeper, depending on the content. Some readers want to read to the very end, which may entail any of the *back matter* components below.

Addendum / Appendix - A listing of supplemental material that can be useful for a reader to help clarify the main body of work. This can include background research, a chronology, data, figures, maps, photographs, references, (re)sources, tables, etc.

Endnotes - Like footnotes, endnotes can be included in the back of a book for additional information that is not essential but might enhance the reader experience. Source citations can also allow the reader to reference specific pages based on content, or by use of superscript numbers throughout the main body of work.

Glossary - When commonly unrecognized foreign terms are used in nonfiction, an author can include an alphabetized list of words or phrases and their definitions to help educate. With fiction, this could be a list of character names and locales or can act as a dictionary for original words created in the narrative.

Bibliography / References - A listing of *all* sources used in the creation of the book, no matter if they are ever referenced. Format styles include APA (American Psychological Association), which is used in education, psychology, and the sciences, CMOS (Chicago Manual of Style), used in business, history, and the fine arts, and MLA (Modern Language Association), used by the humanities.

Index - The last relating to the main *body* of work, usually only found in nonfiction. In alphabetical order, an Index includes terms and topics covered in the text. As the name implies, indexes include corresponding page numbers matching such references.

Contributors - When certain parts of a book are written by other authors, the main author should include a listing of these contributors in the final pages to give credit where due.

Author Biography - Typically found at the very end of the book, the "author bio" is a quick biography of the author, as the name of the page implies. A short resume highlighting major accomplishments, awards, previous books, future projects, and personal details about the writer that the reader might find fascinating.

There are more than twenty-five components that can be included within a book's structure, but this covers most. Each book is different, and so each book must be structured differently, appropriately, with everything in proper place in terms of *front matter*, *body*, and *back matter*; otherwise, a book may come off as amateurish and not professional.

The reader is interested in the story, not so much all the fluff that might appear before and after. Story structure is as equally important as book structure: the framework within the framework. The narrative itself must have a *begin-*

ning, *middle*, and *end*—as much as the overall layout structure does—and likewise each chapter or segment that makes up the narrative must have its own structure. Everything that makes a book needs to hold together within its framework.

Structure defines purpose, so everything purposeful must have structure. Never distract the reader. Only include what is crucial. Let the arrangement of words illustrate to the reader the writer's intent.

PART 3: THE END

A few things before / during / after publishing.

"A book is never finished; it's abandoned." - Gene Fowler

Creatives can go through endless revisions: a painter using paint (the artwork thickening), a writer adding or cutting words (revising *ad infinitum*), a sculptor chipping away at a statue (turning stone into dust). A perfectionist might not *ever* finish a project, and so creative types must learn to abandon their work. When does that moment happen? A better question: *How many* of these moments happen?

WRITER'S BLOCK

Writer's block is another type of abandonment, hopefully temporary. Everyone has heard the phrase, and all writers have experienced this strange phenomenon at one point or another, whether or not it exists.

According to Royal Literary Fund, "Writer's block is a temporary or lasting failure to put words on paper. It can hit every writer, if only for a few minutes or a day or two, but it becomes a real problem when the writer is not reaching targets and when they feel incapable of completing a piece of work." [57]

"Lasting Failure" seems a bit harsh, so 'postponement' might seem more appropriate. Like impostor syndrome (not a real thing, only a mindset), writers need to find ways to get over this blockage. And they need to do so as quickly as possible, otherwise writer's block (not a real thing and a mind-*un*set) might become the ultimate end.

Take the following advice from fellow writers:

"I don't believe in 'writer's block.' I try and deal with getting stuck by having more than one thing to work on at a time. And by knowing that even a hundred bad words that didn't exist before is forward progress." - Neil Gaiman

"I don't believe in writer's block. Think about it – when you were blocked in college and had to write a paper, didn't it always manage to fix itself the night before the paper was due? Writer's block is having too much time on your hands."
- Jodi Picoult

"Writing about a writer's block is better than not writing at all."
- Charles Bukowski

Writer's block must exist, to some extent, but there could just be a distraction acting as the block, the creative mind too busy, life getting in the way, a chemical imbalance, physical or mental fatigue, or the writer not writing the right thing at the right moment, or a temporary lack of passion. An absolute favorite:

"Do you ever go into the bathroom and sit on the toilet when you don't need to take a shit? Do you ever just sit there completely empty and sit there and push? No, you don't. You go eat something and then you live your life and what happens, happens. It's the same thing with writing. If I don't have an idea that I'm not absolutely terrified of losing, then I don't bother to write." – Chuck Palahniuk

Does writer's block exist? Does impostor syndrome? Or are these made-up *things* to warrant why the writing isn't written? As Palahniuk says, do not force what is not there. If experiencing writer's block, get over it and move on to writing something else; if experiencing impostor syndrome, get over it and move on to writing something else.

To abandon or not to abandon one's words is the conundrum, but once the last of them end up on the page and the writer says or thinks, *I'm done. It's finished*, it is really a new beginning. Now comes the hard part.

FIRST DRAFT

The first "end" is the completion of the initial manuscript, the *first draft.* However many words were written, whether a short story, essay, screenplay, poem, novelette, novella, novel, or a multi-hundred-thousand-word epic, a writer must decide to stop and either write or not write "The End" on that final page. And it is the end, for now. The first end.

Like boxing, writing is a fight. There can be any number of rounds, but at some point, a white towel is thrown in the ring or a fighter falls; without a cap set on rounds, a battle would last until death. Rarely is there a knockout in the first round. It usually takes three or more rounds to finish (sometimes double-digit territory) to "end."

One recommendation for first draft manuscripts is to put them aside, letting the words "marinate on the page," some say, in a desk drawer or in a virtual folder. Backing up the manuscript both online and offline should be done regularly, and/or a physical copy printed out, but then the work needs to be left alone for a long while.

Finishing the first draft of a manuscript is a prideful moment. Take time to celebrate with a favorite meal or drink, or by doing anything rewarding and memorable. Write the date on the last page and/or location where it was finished so the moment can be later remembered. Some print out manuscripts as keepsakes. Whatever is chosen, there is still a lot of work to be done.

REVISIONS / REWRITES

Round two—of *many*—is about to commence: *self-edits*, a crucial talent all writers must learn; and then round three: *revisions*; and maybe four: *rewrites*, and so on, until the fight is over. A book may take two or three drafts or significantly more. A dozen? Perhaps. A writer's first book needs multiple drafts. They may even need to "trunk it," meaning either to set the manuscript aside for an extended period or indefinitely. Some writers keep many manuscripts in the trunk.

Having the writer disease means possessing the *need* to write, not just the *want*. To have passion means "to suffer" and there will be lots of suffering involved, especially if ever wanting to get the book published. After literally or figuratively writing "The End" on a manuscript, move on. Starting something new with the understanding that past work can be revisited or forever forgotten. But also understand that revisiting older pages will hurt.

Self-editing is an art that evolves with a writer. Newer writers tend to have an impression that their writing is good enough after a quick check for spelling, grammar, and punctuation errors. They look for those red-squiggly underlines in their word processor, or run a computer-aided diagnosis, or send the text through a program like Grammarly. Those options fix trivial things, but an elementary school child about to turn in a book report for *Where the Red Fern Grows* is capable of such feats.

It is difficult to see flaws in the self, which is why waiting to revisit first drafts is vital. Letting a manuscript sit untouched will allow a creator to experience the work with a fresh set of eyes, like a first reader. *I wrote that?* Yes. Now it is time to un-write that and start reconsidering whether or not writing is still "fun" and if the writer disease is worth having or should be left untreated.

ADDITIONAL DRAFTS

The second "end" occurs after exhausting self-editing on the initial draft, then creating a "second draft" by going chapter-by-chapter, line-by-line, eyes and mind tired. For first-time writers, that might mean cutting 20% to 25% of the first draft, or more. It also might mean *adding* words in those same ranges, or more. This second round of revisions is when a writer puts the complete manuscript through hell once again. This process can take as long as writing the first draft or significantly longer.

A third "end" (or fourth, fifth, sixth, or however-many it takes) happens when a manuscript has gone through a decent number of revisions to bring the writing as close to professional standards as possible. This could mean numerous rounds of self-edits, further revisions, or a complete rewrite. Plot holes may need to be filled, paragraphs restructured, chapters reordered, or other significant changes.

FINAL DRAFT

There's no such thing as a final draft. Writing can be revised until there's nothing left. Eventually, though, a writer needs to be happy enough to abandon their work, lest they find themselves in an endless loop of self-edits and revisions and rewrites. The work should not be sent out for consideration yet. Others besides the creator need to do their magic. But where can a new writer find such help?

Writers slip into the industry by attending conventions, participating in writing workshops with other writers, taking online courses, publishing shorter works, finding mentors, joining professional writer organizations, seeking craft-improving / craft-propelling programs, and forming strong bonds with fellow writers, editors, and other professionals.

Every novice writer starts at the bottom, yet the bottom is simply a community of fellow creators going through the same struggles. Being new at something is never shameful but highly regarded, especially writing a book. Most professionals in the industry are willing to help lead new writers in the right direction because without recognizing emerging talent, the written word would die off, or at least diminish in quality. All are welcome at this invisible library.

How can a writer better their craft? When can a draft of a manuscript be considered "final" by the author? When is it time to abandon the work and move on to something else? When is it *really* time to publish? Remember that *anyone* can become an "author" and that not all people who write have the writerly disease and are *writers*. It is simple enough with technology to string a bunch of words together and tell a story, then grammar- and spell-check and proofread those words and ultimately "publish" a book by whatever means are available at the time.

A writer, if they have a *need* to create and not merely a *want*, must continuously invest in their writing if they ever want to be great. A writer needs to learn bad habits and then how to break them; they need to have an understanding of manuscript formatting, book layout and design, as well as etiquette; and they need to know it is completely fine to reach out for help and to create a support system of other writers, editors, and industry professionals.

Turning a first draft manuscript (and all the drafts that follow) into a "final draft" that will eventually turn it into a book first requires learning the art of self-editing.

"Everything has to come to an end, sometime." - L. Frank Baum

SELF-EDITING

Forever-improving upon the craft.

"I have rewritten - often several times - every word I have ever published. My pencils outlast their erasers."
- Vladimir Nabokov

Rough drafts are called "rough" for a reason. Once the initial draft is out of the way, and the document formatted to industry standards, the writing is not finished. It has only just begun. Now comes the hard part: *revisions*, an essential part of the writing process. Every manuscript must go through multiple drafts, and this should take as long as or longer than it took to write the original.

Revision is where real writing takes place. Revision is how writing gets better, and there are multiple stages—different for each writer. As Roald Dahl is noted as saying, "Good writing is essentially rewriting."

Along with establishing a *writing* routine, writers must establish a healthy *editing* routine: words per day, or chapters per day. The editing should be broken up into manageable chunks so as not to exhaust the writer while wearing their editing hat, with the same dedication and accountability used to create the original manuscript.

Finding and fixing typos, grammar mistakes, and other errors is not editing; it is proofreading. Editing is thorough and repetitive and requires revisiting paragraph structure, organization, and content. It requires the dissection of character, dialogue, voice, plot, conflict, theme, setting, as well as the style, tone, and mood. And it requires reexamination of the writing essentials: intrigue, prose, pace, tense, point of view, show vs. tell, imagery, framework, and structure.

This self-editing chapter has gone through more than seven revisions, with sections added, paragraphs rewritten, and long stretches of text removed entirely. This chapter, in fact, was one of the first written, yet appears in the last third where it belongs. The "Self-Editing" chapter was itself self-edited multiple times throughout this book's journey, and then edited multiple times by others, and then revised, rewritten, etc.

Self-editing is more important than the initial writing, and is another type of art every writer needs to learn if they are to ever be any good. A writer needs to become an editor to become a writer.

The more time spent editing one's own work, or another's, the less time it will take editing future work. A writer's abilities progressively strengthen with experience, requiring less self-editing and less editing or critique from others. The initial writing becomes stronger as the number of drafts required for a work to feel "finished" reduces. And there is nothing an agent, editor, or publisher loves more than working with a writer with polished writing.

Slush reading also improves a writer's abilities. Publishers sometimes seek help from "slush readers," also called "first readers," to go through the bulk of their manuscripts to filter out good from the bad. One definition for "slush" is *excessive sentiment*, and so it is a slush reader's job to sift out excess by way of quickly judging another's work. It is typically an unpaid position, but a healthy practice for an up-and-coming writer to understand the hell that is reading unpublished manuscripts.

The first lines of a manuscript suddenly become all-important, and likewise the first page, and all the pages that follow. After reading hundreds if not thousands of manuscripts, "hook" is understood, and bad writing habits quickly surface as well as high-quality writing. All the fundamentals pop out on the page.

Would the agent / editor / publisher want this? Would they want my own work?

A similar harsh judgment will someday be made on a writer's own manuscript, which is why it is crucial to put their work through multiple rounds of self-editing, cutting every word that is not essential and leaving behind only those that shine. Why use more words than necessary?

> "So the writer who breeds more words than he needs, is making a chore for the reader who reads." - Dr. Seuss

THE ESSENTIALS

Use generally known words, not words that are generally unknown. Is the character a *biblioklept?* No, they are simply a "book thief." Which of those two made more sense, without explanation? If a thesaurus is needed, it is not the right word. The first word that comes to mind is best. Was the night air *glacial?* The night air was just *cold*, depending on the character's vocabulary.

Avoid clichés. These are phrases or opinions overused and lacking original thought: blood boiling or freezing or curdling, hairs rising on the napes of necks or arms or other places, objects as dark as the night or the night as dark as pitch; instead, create future clichés other people might steal.

Diversify sentence structure. Do sentences often start with action? *While he was walking, he . . .* or *As she smiled . . .* In most cases, be more direct and do not repeat patterns. Make it simple: *He walked to the car. She smiled. They ran down the street.* But do not be formulaic. Change up sentence structure regularly to avoid readers noticing patterns.

Consider paragraph length. White space plays a significant role in keeping the reader flipping pages. Long paragraphs can seem intimidating to the reader. If a page is 250 words, break up anything that might seem longwinded, always with pacing in mind. Sometimes a narrative calls for short and punchy paragraphs; other times the writing needs to be long and flowy. Long sentences and paragraphs can slow pacing. Short sentences and paragraphs can intensify pacing. Sentence fragments too.

Clean up dialogue. Avoid adjectives and adverbs around dialogue and primarily stick to "said" for speech tags, or do not use them at all if clear who is talking.

"Shut up, Michael!" ~~she yelled loudly with her mouth.~~

The yelling is implied because of the exclamation point; "loudly" is implied by the exclamation point; and she did so "with her mouth" because what else would she use?

A better option:

"Shut up, Michael!"

Unnecessary words cluttered around conversation can be distracting, taking away from what is most important: the dialogue. Readers gloss over speech tags anyway, so use them only when necessary, and do not give the voices direction unless warranted. Let the dialogue speak for itself.

Each character should have their own paragraphs dedicated to action and dialogue, each with their own breathing room on the page, which will help keep things clear.

Read dialogue aloud. Does it seem a little disjointed? Make it *sound* right. If the dialogue is unbelievable, readers will notice. Does the dialogue sound like something from a television show, or do characters say their thoughts aloud?

Word choice. There are four major classes of words: *nouns*, *verbs*, *adjectives*, and *adverbs*. Less common are adjectives and then adverbs. The uses of each can either help or hurt a piece of writing, so it will be beneficial to understand when and where to use them.

Nouns - The persons, the places, the things.

Verbs - Words used to describe actions, states, or occurrences.

Adjectives - Words or phrases that modify nouns, adding to or modifying their descriptions, such as *small, cold, blue*, etc. Use them sparingly.

Adverbs - Words or phrases that modify verbs or qualify adjectives, such as *gently, strongly, only, quite*, and most *-ly* words. Also use them sparingly.

Character names / pronouns appear more often in the narrative than most other words, especially around dialogue and action-heavy scenes, and so they must not become over- or under-used. Look for places to clarify action and dialogue, and make sure the pronouns are not confusing.

Directional / positioning words. These are words relevant to pointing out unnecessary direction for the character, similar to how a director might provide instruction for an actor: *left, right, up, down, turned*, etc.

```
He turned his head and she was holding a
knife in her left hand, a spatula in her
right, and he wondered which she'd throw
at him first.
```

A better option, and without passive voice:

```
She held a knife and spatula, and he
wondered which she'd throw first.
```

Direction does not matter to the reader, and neither does pointing out the senses by way of sensory words. All that matters is the knife and the spatula, and what she is doing with it.

Sensory words. These are words related to the five senses, commonly found alongside directional / positioning words: *felt, noticed, looked, heard, smelled*, etc. When removed, this allows the reader to instead experience the senses *through* the character instead of *for* them.

```
He noticed the train smelled like smoke
as he heard the engine choke to life, and
felt the seat beneath him vibrate and...
```

A better option, which is sometimes as simple as removing the sensory word(s) and modifying the verb that follows:

```
The engine choked to life with a stank of
coalsmoke, his seat vibrating.
```

The implied. If something is implied, why state it? This is everything suggested but not directly expressed. In the example of the self-edit above, everything implied was removed: the *noticing*, the *smelling*, the *hearing* (sensory words) and "beneath him" (useless words).

```
John Doe walked to the door and turned
the knob, opening it outward, and...
```

A better option:

```
John Doe walked out the door.
```

Lazy verbs. *Get, got, is, was, were* are boring and overused. In the manuscript, search for *was*. There will be a surprisingly high number, and in terms of tense, search for *is* or *were*.

```
He was staring at the page.
He got cold from the wind.
```

These could be made stronger:

He stared at the page.
The wind chilled him.

Search for and destroy *it was* and *there was / there were* as well, which are often found at the beginnings of sentences.

Show vs. tell. "Show" is using description and action to help the reader experience the story through the character, whereas telling is when the writer summarizes or uses exposition to "tell" the reader what is happening.

He saw the red car as it sped down the road.

The seeing is implied, so a better option:

The red car sped down the road.

Instead of telling the reader something like *It was cold*, show the reader how cold it was through the character:

Jane shivered.
Jane wore a blanket of snow.

Passive voice. Let verbs do what they are designed to do and avoid having the subject of a sentence acted on by the verb, which can result in passive writing.

He was running. The knife was thrown by the woman.

Better options:

`He ran. The woman threw the knife.`

Both revisions are more immediate, less in-the-past.

"Began to" and "started to" and similar phrases can also interrupt action and slow pace, so avoid when possible.

`They began to run` could be `They ran.`

Unless characters are in the act of "beginning" or "starting" to do something, they can simply do those things.

Filler words / phrases. These are short, meaningless pauses that occur when a writer, or speaker, is stuck deciding what words should be used. While they can be useful in dialogue to make characters sound believable, they never belong on the page: *I mean, like, okay, so, and stuff, uh, um, you know . . .*

Useless words / phrases. Stronger words are always better than those that do not add value, or create redundancy, or *are* redundant. A word that adds nothing extra to a sentence is called a *pleonasm*; a word that repeats the meaning of another word is called a *tautology*. Both are useless and easily forgettable, and a reminder of why complicated words are not always the best choice. Useless words to avoid:

> *actually, basically, highly, essentially, for what it's worth, in essence, in my opinion, in reality, just, needless to say, of the, really, some, that* (unless it serves a purpose), *truly, very*, etc.

Everyone uses these words. *This book* uses these words. But how many are unhealthy habits and how many have purpose? They have their moments of usefulness but could be replaced with something stronger. Instead of *really cold* or *very cold*, it can be frigid.

Mark Twain once said, "Substitute 'damn' every time you're inclined to write 'very.' Your editor will delete it and the writing will be just as it should be."

Other words are made useless when combined with synonymous words. 'Ask,' for example, means 'to pose a question,' so to ask a question would add redundancy. Other examples: *standing up*, *sitting / knelt down*, *smiled with his mouth*, *squinted his eyes, hunched his shoulders*. If a verb is strong enough, it never needs help.

Search for the following words / phrases while self-editing and determine which can be removed to improve the writing. Culling tightens prose, improves point of view, and keeps writing lean. Not a full list, but a starting point:

> *up, down, left, right* (if used for direction), *turned, rather, quite, realize, very, truly, really, actually, completely, absolutely, totally, virtually, literally, only* (adverbs in general / most -ly words), *just, that, then, sudden / suddenly, all of the, most of the* ('all the' or 'most the' is cleaner), *some* (in all forms: *somebody, somehow, someone, something, sometimes, somewhat, somewhere*), variations of the lazy verb 'to be' (*are, is, was, were*), leading words or phrases (*in order to, often / oftentimes, mostly, most times, so), start to, begin to / began to, begun* (unless an interruption to the action soon occurs), dialogue tags other than 'said,' the overuse of verbs around

dialogue (*shrug, nod, reach, laugh, smile*, etc.), sensory words (*feel / felt, see / saw, look / looked, gaze / gazed, notice / noticed, hear / heard, smell / smelled*, etc.)

Keep in mind that words are not always trimmable. If used in dialogue, for example, they might be useful to express how a character speaks, for the spoken word is often not grammatically correct. This is not a list of words to simply seek and destroy, but words to be cautious of over-using. If a word can be cut and it changes nothing, weed it out. Pluck them before they take root.

Stating the obvious. What is implied and what is assumed are also filler and useless. If someone "crouched down from a standing position to the floor with his knees bent" and so on, the sentence is thirteen words too long to describe the act of crouching. A character can simply crouch.

Repetition. This goes without stating (a useless phrase to prove the point), but many writers stop and start writing at various points, and it is easy to fall into repetition. Be on the lookout for jarring moments caused by writing pauses and smooth out as needed.

In terms of repetition, though, two things make a better writer:

READING

The more quality writing devoured, the more personal writing flaws (or unhealthy habits) will stand out in one's own work. Read to know what the writing should look like and listen to audio books to know what books should sound like when read aloud.

Nonfiction readers should read fiction. Fiction readers should read nonfiction. All should read poetry to master skills on prose, for poems are as concise and efficient as it gets. Read magazine and newspaper articles, books on writing, books on editing. Read as diversely as possible.

WRITING

The more a writer writes, the stronger they will write. And as diversely as a reader should be reading, a writer should be writing as diversely. Reading takes years of dedication and practice, as should solid writing.

Sometimes it is best to write out all the ugly until the pretty emerges. Wait until the words start flowing, until the word count at the bottom of the page no longer seems important, until the clock no longer seems important.

When word count and time are both lost, that is when the magic happens and a writer falls into "the zone," which is where they should stay for as long as possible. Everything written before that moment can always be thrown out or revised to bring the quality up to speed; it was not wasted time if what came out next was better.

Scott Summers, in his article "8 Tools and Tips to Use When Self-Editing Your Work" for *Business 2 Community*, includes a section on the importance of stepping away from the screen. "Using pen and paper makes self-editing a tactile and active experience. You're not just moving a mouse around or pushing the typing cursor along the page one letter at a time. You can feel the weight of the pen when you strike out typos. You actively flip between pages as you edit. It's a physical indication of progress and achievement."[58]

Editing from a different medium—holding something physical, a red pen, for example—helps give the eyes and brain a break from what they are accustomed to digitally, making it easier to find flaws. Let the eyes refresh. Let the hand hold something other than a mouse or touchpad, touching paper instead of keys.

Summers goes on to state, "Your eyes are off a screen—and we all know that we spend too much time looking at our screens, anyway. Sometimes, switching up the format and the visuals can help you catch mistakes that you wouldn't otherwise see."

There are many tricks to self-editing. The key is becoming aware of bad writing habits and working through them. Let others point out the flaws but take criticism as constructive. Squash one flaw, then work on the next, then the next, always improving. Keep slashing with the editing pen and making the pages bleed until it feels *finished*, or "final."

Self-edit until it hurts, and then do it again, and again.

And lastly, as the King says below, kill all those darlings. Cut every single word that is not absolutely necessary. Make the writing look effortless. Make it "straightforward" as the word 'prose' implies.

> "Kill your darlings, kill your darlings, even when it breaks your egocentric little scribbler's heart, kill your darlings." - Stephen King[59]

PRESENTATION

Manuscript formatting.

"A great magician is not more magical than other magicians; he is just more magical in his presentation."
- Amit Kalantri

Storytelling is magical and every storyteller's magic unique, yet there is a skill all writers need to learn to highlight their talent: formatting manuscripts. Industry standards are not difficult to understand and follow, but many writers ignore formatting and submission guidelines.

Words go on the page, but there is more to it than that. Rules need to be followed to properly present a writer's work and convey professionalism. Putting together a manuscript properly, along with correspondence etiquette, prevents unnecessary headache and embarrassment.

A movie called *Wonder Boys* came out in 2000 based on the novel by Michael Chabon. It is a movie for writers, a movie about a writer. The title is in fact the book the main character is writing throughout the film. In one of the opening scenes, Grady Tripp types a number on the top of a sheet of paper in his typewriter: 261. He hesitates, then adds another 1. He is starting page 2,611 of his unfinished masterpiece, and the look on his face says it all.

Keeping in mind that the average printed page is about 250 words, this means he is a little over the 650,000-word mark, and *yet* to be finished. In fact, he does not know how much more of the book remains. One of the story arcs is Tripp's character (played by Michael Douglas) finishing that novel and his agent Terry Crabtree (played by Robert Downy Jr.) pressuring him heavily for it. Tripp has old writing habits, composes his pages on a typewriter, and after nearly two hours of movie (years upon years of writing in this fictional world), he has finished his magnum opus and excited to let it go.

In one of the final scenes, perfectly bookending that original shot of him in the painful act of writing, everything he's created falls apart around him as he loses hold of that mammoth, loose stack of papers, his only copy. Winds quickly scurry them around the city, the manuscript lost forever. This single moment of humor and horror reveals a few things a writer should put into practice when putting words on paper, digital or otherwise.

STORAGE / BACKUP

Save copies of the work, always, in multiple places. Digital copies can be saved on computers, laptops, tablets, or on portable flash drives, memory cards, or by using online storage in the "cloud," or can be emailed to oneself.

Many writers like to print a physical copy of the manuscript (for later editing or as a prideful relic), which also works as a backup. Hardware crashes. Websites fail. Imagine the worst-case scenario and prepare ahead of time.

Most online word processors save in real-time, or close to it, some every few moments, others every typed character. For word processor programs, there is usually a default auto-save feature, which varies by product; some save every fifteen minutes, others every hour, although this can be (and should be) modified. A writer who types 75 words per minute might compose 4,500 words in an hour, so how much of that might be lost if there is a "glitch" in the system, or any type of outage? None of that has anything to do with presentation, but preservation of presentations.

THE MANUSCRIPT

A manuscript is simply an author's text that has not yet been published. Merriam-Webster defines it as: 1) a written or typewritten composition or document as distinguished from a printed copy; also: a document submitted for publication, or 2) writing as opposed to print. [60]

The word manuscript evolved from the Latin *manu scriptus*, which translates to "written by hand," referring to works created prior to bound books. Manuscripts *can* still be written by hand, and some writers find the practice therapeutic for first drafts, but eventually the manuscript needs to become digital, and there is an order of operations.

Create a new document, organize the page formatting, headers, line spacing, font style / size, and all the small details that make it stand out as professional. Have a template ready, and plan for its storage and salvation ahead of time.

What follows are formatting guidelines intended for traditional publishing and healthy practice. Everything can be setup ahead of time to create a traditional, old-school manuscript: a beautiful stack of pages when printed out.

FILE TYPES

The preferred text file format is mainly .docx, an updated version of the previous preferred format .doc. The format is preferred because of its "Track Changes" feature, which allows multiple participants to leave comments and track changes within the document and allows for the accepting and rejecting of such changes. While .docx is native to Microsoft Word, it has become the industry standard across multiple platforms.

Originally, either an "m" or an "x" was added to the end of the .doc file extension, meaning it was either a document *with* macros (.docm), or *without* macros (.docx). The .docx extension is an XML format, or "extensive markup language," so it is popular. This type of file includes tags or codes that describe the text in the document, like hypertext markup language (HTML) used often for websites to beautify text.

History of the digital file format aside, manuscripts should only contain text and minor formatting.

Manuscript guidelines are typically posted on calls for submissions, whether for an agent, editor, or publisher. Spending time researching file types desired is better than assuming they are able or willing to open a file in the writer's preferred format. If a potential reader cannot open a manuscript, they will move on and send a rejection, or if nice, politely request an acceptable format.

Every publisher (traditional, independent, hybrid, etc.) has different manuscript requirements, so always research beforehand. Never send a manuscript blindly, and never assume an intended recipient accepts file attachments. Most will only accept attachments if requested specifically.

Avoid sending a portable document file (.pdf), which requires a program like Adobe Reader to read and expensive software to edit. While this is a great format to protect a piece of writing, it is a middle finger to agents, editors, and publishers, saying, "You *can* read my work, but you ain't gonna touch it." And they will not; they will move on to files they can open. Agents and editors and publishers want to work with a writer willing to work *with* them, not a writer already pushing back with the initial manuscript submission.

Refrain from sending text only files (without formatting), such as .txt, or pasting the text within an email, unless requested. As a last resort, format as .rtf, which can be opened using most text programs. This format was also created by Microsoft for cross-platform document exchange, with limited formatting capabilities, although most are veering away from accepting such antiquated formats; while a few, on the other hand, request .rtf because it strips out markup language.

When in doubt, research what is required of the writer.

IDENTIFYING INFORMATION

Whether using a word processor or typewriter, the page number often goes on the top right of the page, and sometimes appears on the bottom of the page within a footer. If the winds were calmer and the circumstances better, Grady Tripp could have saved his book if all the pages were found, reorganizing them in their proper order. And if he had his name and title of the book on every page, maybe it could have been salvaged.

Word processors keep track of page numbers automatically, but they do not automatically appear on the digital or printed page without the writer putting them there. A header (most common) or footer should be used for this purpose.

Also in the header (or footer), the author's name and title of the work should appear near the page number and can be truncated to save space. For the manuscript of *Righting Writing*, each header on the top-right of the page above the main body of text (besides the cover page), would have the following:

Bailey / Righting / [Page Number]

The author's full name and complete title of the work can be included, but less is better; however, all three identifying marks should appear on every page of the manuscript. This is not the time to get fancy and format such things how they might appear when bound, for the manuscript is simply the workable text of the book before it becomes a book.

There is a reason for including this information besides helping the writer stay organized. Others who read the manuscript also require the organization. The digital version might be physically printed (without the use of staples or other binding materials), so having this header information is crucial.

Pages should always be loose and never bound, at least for physical manuscript submissions.

COVER PAGE

Every manuscript starts with a cover page. Writers often only include a name and email address, and this is not enough. This is saying to the recipient, "If you want to reach me about this project,'I can only be contacted by email." Agents, editors, and publishers each have their own communication preferences, so all options need to be provided.

The top-left of the page includes the author's legal name (not pseudonym), mailing address, email address, and a phone number (including country code information if necessary). Each go on a separate line, single-spaced. This is the most important part of any manuscript, as it allows for easy contact with the writer. Long ago, it was common to include a Social Security Number for tax purposes; this is now strongly *not* recommended.

An example of how the top-left of a cover page might appear:

```
Legal Name
Address Line 1
Address Line 2 (if needed)
City, State ZipCode
email.address@domain.com
+1 555.555.5555
```

Word count is necessary and goes to the direct right of the contact information, rounded up or down (or the exact count), and optionally the genre on the following line, all single-spaced. Rounding up or down to the nearest thousand is common but this is never the place to falsify numbers.

If requesting books in the 60,000- to 80,000-word range, rounding down 100,000 to 80,000 or rounding up 40,000 to 60,000 will be quickly noticed based on the page number and formatting, and because word processors provide the entire word count anyway. A 320-page manuscript in the

80,000-word range would not pass as something significantly larger or smaller. Agents and editors and publishers know manuscript sizes and will sometimes flip through to check if everything is in order.

An example of how the top-right of a cover page might appear:

```
                                        85,000 words
                                               Genre
```

Listing the genre is optional, depending on what the recipient is seeking. "About 85,000 words" is also acceptable, or the exact word count: "85,234 words".

A manuscript cover page would thus appear like the following:

```
Legal Name                        About 85,000 words
Address Line 1                                 Genre
Address Line 2 (if needed)
City, State ZipCode
email.address@domain.com
+1 555.555.5555
```

The title of the work is placed halfway down the page, centered (sometimes in ALL-CAPS, sometimes not), and a few lines below that, also centered, is the author's by-line. A by-line contains who the work is "written by," not necessarily the author's real name but how they wish to have the work published. If using a pseudonym, this is where a fictitious name would go.

An example of how the cover page might appear:

BOOK TITLE
Subtitle: if needed

by Author Name

Also acceptable:

BOOK TITLE
by Legal Name,
writing as Fictitious Name.

This first page does not have the same header and footer information as the rest of the manuscript, which is why word processors offer the ability to have a different first page when setting up headers and footers.

The beginning of the story starts a few lines below the author's name, and this is where additional formatting is required for the pages that follow.

INDUSTRY STANDARDS

Fancy formatting is a mark of amateurism. A manuscript is not the place to "design" the book. A manuscript should be raw and formatted in a way that helps whoever is reading the work do their job easier. Simple formatting guidelines:

Page size (letter): 8.5" x 11" or A4 (non-US) - Use the most common paper size determined by country, not the book's eventual printed size (6" x 9", 5.5" x 8.5", etc.).

Margins: 1.0" all around or about 25mm (non-US) - Mirrored margins allows adequate space for editors and first readers to make notes on the printed document without having to write in the space between lines reserved for editing. 1.25" and 1.5" margins are also common, but add unnecessary pages.

Line spacing: double - The main body of the book should be double-spaced throughout. This creates white space on the page that leaves editors room to leave editing marks.

Paragraph alignment: left justified - Printed books and digital books use full justification for text, but manuscripts should be left justified. Also known as "ragged right text," left justified aligns words on the left side of the page, leaving it nonuniform (unjustified, or *ragged*) on the right.

Indents: 0.5" or equivalent - The Tab key is often used to indent, or abusing the space bar: *space-space-space-space-space*, but it is much easier to set a pre-defined margin for new paragraphs. Editors will also be grateful. Setting a tab and hitting the Tab key are not the same, and spacebar abuse is an ancient practice. No indent is required for first paragraphs, or for paragraphs that start new chapters or sub-chapters.

Font type: Times New Roman / Courier - These are the two most used fonts, with the latter like a typewriter and the former a serif font (one with feet, so to speak). It was originally commissioned for a British newspaper called *The Times* in 1931, created by Stanley Morison, who worked for the Monotype printing equipment company. According to

The New York Public Library, the font was created with two goals in mind: "efficiency—maximizing the amount of type that would fit on a line and thus on a page—and readability." [61]

Font color: black - When printed, colored fonts will switch to black, but use a black font within the file itself to make it easier on the eyes for the reader. Using anything other than a black font is amateurish.

Font size: 12-point - 250 words per printed page considers a 12-point font, 1" page margins, and double-spaced lines. While younger eyes can read smaller fonts at a faster rate, and older eyes require larger fonts to read at a normal pace, 12-point has become standard.

For first-time writers, formatting is not often considered until *after* the first draft is written, or along the way, but it is important to organize those words in an industry standard format. For more experienced writers, this takes place before the writing, or a template is used, allowing the writer to jump right into the story and not have to worry about such trivial things. No matter the case, manuscripts need to look like manuscripts.

There is no longer a purpose for using two spaces after punctuation. A quick find and replace of two spaces for one is easy enough using word processors, but save editors and typesetters the hassle.

In *The Complete Manual of Typography: A Guide to Setting Perfect Type*, James Felici and Frank J. Romano state that inconsistency with spacing after punctuation has been around for as long as print. It is still argued today whether one space should be used or two. [62]

Typewriters created part of the problem, as they rely on monospace type, meaning every character occupies equal space on the page horizontally. Skinnier letters and numbers thus take up less room with black ink and allow for more white space around them, making spacing after punctuation not so obvious, and so two spaces became the norm, mostly to help with now-extinct printing machines. Fast-forward to post-1970, with fancier typewriters and eventually computers, and this is no longer an issue, thanks to modernized fonts, but still a controversy.

CHAPTER LAYOUT

With every new chapter, a new page is warranted. Centered on this new page is the chapter number and/or title, and a few lines below that the start of the text. For Chapter 1, this might mean the title page is blank except for the contact information, word count, and the title / author, and that is completely normal. The start of Chapter 1 can go on the following page, and contain any of the following:

```
1
Chapter Title
Subtitle
```

The chapter number might be spelled out, or might be in Roman numerals, or that part of the page might only include the chapter title, or "Chapter 1: Title." Each book is different, so include whatever is necessary.

It is also common for chapter title pages to start at the top of the new page, a quarter of the page down, or even halfway down the page. All that really matters is that there is clear delineation between chapters. This also includes prologues, epilogues, and other additional content. New sections of a book start on a fresh page.

If beginning a new *part* of the book, the information can go at the top of the page much like the chapter title page, or can be centered on the middle of the page, such as:

Part 2
The Middle

"The middle path is the way to wisdom"
- Rumi

SUB-CHAPTER BREAKS

If one scene ends or another begins, such as with a new character vantage point, or a break in the story to let the reader know time has passed, there are a few ways of expressing this on the page. Avoid using multiple line breaks. As words shift around on the page with editing and reformatting, the starting / stopping points can be confusing or become lost entirely if they start at the top of a new page or stop at the end of one.

To work around this, center a hashtag (#) on a new line when one section ends, or a dinkus (three spaced asterisks in a row: * * *), then start the new text below. Then, no matter how the text shifts, the breaks are noticeable wherever they fall.

PROFESSIONALISM

A polished manuscript reflects a professional writer. When first starting out, words matter most, so it is easy to overlook formatting and focus on the story at hand, which is important. But at some point, a writer's manuscript needs to be arranged accordingly, so why not create a template with all the formatting already handled?

The first priority should be to write. Get it all out, every word. Hopefully, a routine is in place with daily or weekly goals in mind to continuously build word count. But with any editing or revisions, a rough draft should be formatted properly so that it can be edited.

LAYOUT

Order of operations and potential additional content.

"Content is anything that adds value
to the reader's life."
- Avinash Kaushik

A writer may wish to include additional content before or after the main body of work but should keep in mind overall book length. Additional components add to word count, which add to page count, which add to the cost of the book by way of more pages and likewise diminishes profit margin. Some of these components include:

DEDICATION

This first text from the author goes after the Half Title, Series Title, Frontispiece, Title, and Copyright pages. The dedication allows for a quick shout-out to a specific person or group of people meaningful to the author. Most are centered on the page and simply read, *For FirstName*, with the identity a mystery to all but few.

Some books are dedicated to the living, and some to the memory of those no longer living, and some are to inspiring causes or ideas. In Alice Walker's *The Color Purple*, for example, are the poetic lines:

TO THE SPIRIT:
Without whose assistance
Neither this book
Nor I
Would have been
Written.

EPIGRAPH

In literary terms, one of the purposes of the epigraph is to suggest *theme*, such as with the quote by Avinash Kaushik from his years working at Google. They can also establish *mood* or *tone*, which is why they appear at the very beginning of a book, typically only after a dedication page if one is included.

In non-literary terms, epigraphs are also symbolic, appearing on buildings, coins, or etched / printed elsewhere. On the Statue of Liberty is the sonnet "The New Colossus" by Emma Lazarus with the famous "Give me your tired, your poor, your huddled masses yearning to breathe free," which became a symbol for immigration.

The statue itself was originally a symbol of freedom—a gift from France to the United States following the Civil War—serving as a reminder of friendship between the two countries. And the poem's title, etched onto the statue's pedestal, was itself inspired by "The Colossus of Rhodes," an ancient statue in Greece depicting the sun god Helios. Inspiration begetting inspiration is the point of the epigraph.

"To write on" is the rough translation from the Greek origin *epigraphein*, which adapted over the years into what it is today. Sometime in the mid-1800s, epigraphs were used as prefaces in literature, either placed at the beginnings of books or before chapters.

They can be short quotations, common phrases, stanzas from poems (or entire poems), or a segment of prose. The epigraph from Ray Bradbury's *Fahrenheit 451* is a single line from Juan Ramón Jiménez: "If they give you ruled paper, write the other way," which sets the theme of conformity in the novel. *To Kill a Mockingbird* by Harper Lee starts with a quote from Charles Lamb: "Lawyers, I suppose, were children once," pre-exploring the moral nature of human beings.

Along with establishing *theme*, *mood*, and *tone*, an epigraph can also foreshadow, help with characterization, and reveal expositional details or context otherwise difficult to portray in the narrative.

One thing to consider, however, is whether permission might be required to use quoted material.

FOREWORD

The foreword and preface often get mistaken one for the other, and for some reason novice writers want or think they should write the foreword to their own book, even going so far as to actually write a "forward," which is both a misspelling and a level of ignorance. Forewords are short essays preceding the main body of text.

This first section is typically written by someone other than the author to provide critical reception of the work, touching on why the book is necessary and what it aims to accomplish, and/or a personal history of the author or other details readers might find interesting. They are usually written by public figures, field experts, or other writers.

Always with an "e" and never a "ward," forewords are placed near the beginning of the book, hence the combination of "fore" (*before* or *first*) and "word." Before the word, or first word. 'Foreword' may have derived from the German *Vorwort*, meaning *preface*, a similar but different beast.

PREFACE

A calque (loan translation) of the Latin *praefatio: prae* and *fatia* ("spoken before") or *prae* and *factum* ("made before"), the preface is another type of introduction written before the main body of work.

The preface is often mistaken for the prologue, which is the story before the story, whereas the preface is more of what a writer needs "to say beforehand."

Before you jump right into this thing, you need to know a few things . . .

While a foreword is written by someone other than the author, a preface is written solely from that writer's point of view. They are never written from the perspective of the narrator or one of the characters, whether the book is fiction or nonfiction.

Prefaces are rarely used in fiction and serve nonfiction to give a brief history of the story's development, legacy, origin, or purpose. In some cases, they serve as a place to acknowledge those who assisted in the book's creation, similar to the purpose of an acknowledgments page.

PROLOGUE

A prologue, on the other hand, which goes before the first chapter in a book, derives from a mix of *prologe / prologus / prologos*, which roughly translates through its Latin, Old French, and Greek evolution to an "introduction to a narrative or discourse." In Ancient Greece, prologues were used in dramatic theatre as the first act of a play. A prologue for a book can serve many purposes:

- Introduce key information
- Supply backstory or background detail
- Foreshadow future events
- Establish point of view or provide counter perspective
- Set the tone
- Set the mood
- Identify theme(s)

They often do not fit the same timeline as the narrative and are primarily backstory, a place to put things from the past that should not go in the main body of text to unfortunately "rewind" the reader instead of propelling them forward. Prologues help get the reader excited about the journey they are about to take or bring them up-to-speed to the present moment.

Prologues exist to allow a book to have two beginnings and can run as short as a single paragraph or multiple pages, sometimes as long as subsequent chapters. Consider "The Prologue" to William Shakespeare's *Romeo and Juliet*, which sets the stage of the tragedy, so to speak:

```
Enter Chorus.

Two households, both alike in dignity
(In fair Verona, where we lay our scene),
From ancient grudge break to new mutiny,
Where civil blood makes civil hands unclean.
From forth the fatal loins of these two foes
A pair of star-crossed lovers take their life;
Whose misadventured piteous overthrows
Doth with their death bury their parents' strife.
```

The fearful passage of their death-marked love
And the continuance of their parents' rage,
Which, but their children's end, naught could remove,
Is now the two hours' traffic of our stage;
The which, if you with patient ears attend,
What here shall miss, our toil shall strive to mend

Chorus exits.

Everything aforementioned is considered part of the *front matter.* Additional components that might be included in the main *body* of a book include:

INTRODUCTION / AUTHOR'S NOTE

This is not necessarily the place to introduce the author but to introduce the book. *What is this book I am holding? Why read it? What is the purpose?*

For nonfiction, an introduction can be in the form of a foreword or preface as the first piece of *front matter* or can stand on its own after those individual components as the first piece of the *body* leading into the main narrative. Either way, these words are likely the first read after flipping past all the other front matter, and so there's a small period of time to snag a reader before they close the book.

A book introduction can be written by the author or by someone else, and works much like a movie trailer, a quick preview designed to engage the reader. How succinctly can a potential reader be intrigued or turned away?

There are times when an introduction might be necessary; otherwise, consider *if* one is needed and if the rest of the book is "hook" enough. Examples when an introduction could be useful:

- If the book is a writer's debut
- If the book is a new edition, previously published
- If the book is fiction and that world needs a lead-in
- If the book is nonfiction and needs credibility
- If the book is a collection (single author)
- If the book is an anthology (multiple authors)
- If the book is co-written or co-edited

With collaborations, introductions are a good place to describe the writing process and share how two distinct voices created a third; for new editions, an intro might include important information about revisions or additions; collections and anthologies might include details about the gathering of individual works and/or address theme; and if the book is a debut, an introduction could help sell the writer, especially if written by a more established writer.

Seven elements of an introduction:

1. Hook the reader
2. Address the subject matter(s) / topic(s)
3. Address issue(s) to which the book relates
4. Create credibility / trust for the author
5. Present a hypothesis / theory
6. Address the intended audience
7. Provide a reason the book is worth a reader's time.

A typical introduction is shorter than most chapters, 1,000 words +/- 500, and if included needs to be as strong and not take away or distract from the rest of the book.

While introductions appear at the beginnings of books, an "Author's Note" or "From the Author" section might appear in the front (less common) or back (more common). An author's note is meta-writing, a story behind the story, addressing the reader directly from the author's perspective.

EPILOGUE

Immediately following the closing chapter of a book, a writer may choose to include an epilogue as a supplement. This part of the story, typically only seen in fiction and narrative nonfiction, can take place long after the events of the book.

An epilogue is from the perspective of the fictional or narrative nonfictional world, not the writer's real world. They work as extensions of the main story, not from something separate. They can be opportunities to tie up loose ends not covered in the main story, reveal fates of characters, or offer a taste of what is next and/or hint at future books.

In *Animal Farm* by Orson Wells, readers are offered a glimpse into the future lives of the animals:

> "Years passed. The seasons came and went, the short animal lives fled by. A time came when there was no one who remembered the old days before the Rebellion, except Clover, Benjamin, Moses the raven, and a number of the pigs."

AFTERWORD

Opposite the foreword, the afterword (never "afterward," although in terms of the narrative placed *afterward*), is a concluding section of a book. Like the foreword, its purpose is to offer additional context.

An afterword works like an epilogue in that it adds further commentary, which can add additional closure for the reader, and can include some of the following:

- Inspiration / influence for the book
- Information / research about the writing process
- Significance of the book in relation to subject matter / theme
- Concluding thoughts on subject matter / theme
- Publication history
- If written by someone other than the author, the writer's relationship to the author

While an epilogue takes place in the same world as the narrative, an afterword is a concluding note outside that world, written by either the author or another contributor from *their* perspective, never that of a character or narrator.

An afterword, along with a postscript, are the final two additional components that appear as part of the main *body* of work; everything that follows is part of the *back matter*.

ACKNOWLEDGMENTS

Acknowledgments should be brief, since they only pertain to the author of the book and those named. While some span multiple pages, it is best to keep them short. Not many will recognize the listed names, as the honors tend to go to editors, beta readers, and others close to the author. Basically, this is a "thank you for helping" section of the book.

ENDNOTES

Footnotes and endnotes are essentially the same, the difference being that cited material in footnotes (considered an outdated method) can interrupt the reader and appear at the bottom of the same page, whereas endnotes appear at the end of the book, all gathered in one convenient place.

The Endnotes of this book would include the three sources cited for this particular chapter, formatted to Chicago Manual of Style standards:

[63] Betts, Jennifer. "Using Endnotes and a Bibliography." Bibliography.com, October 7, 2020. https://www.bibliography.com/chicago/using-endnotes-and-a-bibliography.

[64] Goldman, William. *Marathon Man.* New York: Ballantine Books, 2001.

[65] Max, Tucker. "How to Write an Author Bio & Why (with Examples)." Scribe Media, February 9, 2021. https://scribemedia.com/write-author-bio.

The use of endnotes has become the preferred method. Instead of the reader putting a finger on the page to mark their place and scrolling down to read the footnotes, they can instead keep reading, or if so desired mark their place on the page and flip to the back of the book. Endnotes give the reader the option of not being distracted.

A downfall is that dedicated readers who want more information readily—or who are used to antiquated ways of doing things—can be put-off by having to flip to the back of the book instead of temporarily shifting their focus. Other disadvantages: unless organized conveniently, such as by chapter, readers might have trouble linking citations; or the cited information might be taken as proverbial fine print while reading the narrative, as in *What is this writer trying to hide?*

Three main purposes for endnotes: citing source material; supplying copyright information for cited material; providing additional information about the content of the narrative.

BIBLIOGRAPHY / REFERENCES

The bibliography, on the other hand, also known as the "references" section of a book, appears after the endnotes section. While citations in endnotes are listed as they occur in the main body of work, the sources cited in a bibliography are listed alphabetically.

Bibliographies offer further information about a writer's list of sources and where to find them, whereas endnotes offer further information on where the writer's arguments or claims connect to such sources.

In Jennifer Bett's' article "Using Endnotes and a Bibliography" for Bibliography.com, she states, "Endnotes will provide a short citation of all the different sources that you used in the paper, article, or essay. A bibliography is an entirely different creation that provides all the sources that went into the inception of the paper. That doesn't mean that all citation pages are bibliographies, however."[63]

AUTHOR BIOGRAPHY

Biographies change over time and should be updated when and where possible so as not to appear outdated, especially online. They should summarize merit using a limited number of words, and sell the writer, which in turn might sell the book. Potential readers need to think, *This person seems interesting, so why not give 'em a shot?* The author biography is a constantly changing writer's resume.

Having a working biography is always handy. Publishers want to know who they will be working with, along with editors, agents, other writers, or anyone who may eventually want to work with the writer. Like an "elevator pitch" quickly explaining the synopsis, a biography quickly explains the writer. Take the following example:

> Michael Bailey is a recipient of the Bram Stoker Award (and eight-time nominee), the Benjamin Franklin Award, and a four-time Shirley Jackson Award nominee. He has written several novels, fiction & poetry collections, and has edited numerous anthologies. Recent publications include *The Impossible Weight of Life*, a memoir about surviving the California wildfires called *Seven Minutes*, as well as *Righting Writing*, a nonfiction explo-

> ration into the madness of writing. He lives in Costa Rica where he is rising from the ashes and rebuilding his life.

That biography would work for a book published soon after *Righting Writing*, but would become outdated, which is why an author biography needs to constantly adapt with time and profession. Perhaps "eight-time nominee" becomes "nine-time" or "ten-" or he ends up winning a Shirley Jackson Award, or the memoir turns into a major motion picture or changes titles, or years from now maybe the author wants to highlight another previously published title. The tough middle-ground is fitting in accolades yet not sounding boastful.

This is one of the reasons why author biographies are so difficult to write. Once printed, the words are cemented, but, like an author photo, it is okay for the words to age like the book will eventually age.

It is also strange to note that with professional merit and quantity of books published, author biographies shrink over time, first starting long to sell the writer, then with fewer words once the writer is more well-established. In William Goldman's novel *Marathon Man*, for example, it reads:

> William Goldman has been writing books and movies for more than forty years. He has won two Academy Awards (for *Butch Cassidy and the Sundance Kid* and *All the President's Men*), and three Lifetime Achievement awards in

> screenwriting. His novels include *The Temple of Gold* and *The Princess Bride*. [64]

Goldman's biography could run dozens of pages, but all that is needed are the essentials, those bigger moments in life that will forever sell him now that he is gone.

Sadly, more people will read an author's bio than that author's work, often flipping to those last pages of the book or dust jacket flap or read about them somewhere online. According to *New York Times* bestselling author Tucker Max, writing for Scribe Media, "It takes a long time to read a book, but it's very easy to make a snap judgment based on a short paragraph, and most people do that." [65]

What else might be included / considered when a writer is new or less established?

Everything should be written with a third person viewpoint (never first person, which is seen as amateurish). It feels odd writing about the self in third person, but proper names and pronouns should be used, as though the biography was written by someone else.

Keep everything under a page. An author biography could appear halfway down the page, or the page designed similarly to chapter title pages. 150 words or fewer is a good starting point. 100 might be better. 50 might be best.

Include publishing credits, such as previously published books (if any), or shorter works sold to reputable, recognizable markets. This is a resume, so only include the best.

Without much credential, feel free to include books not yet published, although publishers can request title changes from writers, so "currently finishing a psychological thriller" works better than name-dropping a title that could change. This is a statement that the writer is serious about writing.

Awards, prizes, or other accolades (that will mean something to potential readers) should be included. A generic label of "Award-winning" does not cut it. "Amazon bestselling" does not cut it. Awards and prizes need names. Include achievements, accomplishments, or anything that adds credibility for the book's subject matter or is interesting.

Blurbs from recognized writers can be useful. "National Book Award winner Established Name calls Author Name a 'fresh voice.'" Keep them short and know that name-dropping is terrible when done incorrectly or without permission.

If writing about forensics, or any other work around studies or professions, why not include degrees or certifications that lend merit and expertise?

A website. This is suggested for secured domain names that will stick around for a while, such as authorname.com or booktitle.com, not blogs. The author's name can seldom change, but a writer will potentially write more than one book. Unless they want everybooktitletheyeverwrite.com, a website to cover multiple books is preferred.

Social media handles, if relevant, as long as they will not turn readers away based on content.

Do not include fabricated information . . . *ever*.

A book reflects a writer, so presentation is essential. Any content included other than the main narrative needs to add value for the reader, not for the writer. It is tempting for novice writers to include anything and everything that might go in a book, but any book, especially a debut, should have the most professional layout possible.

ASSISTANCE

Never write alone.

> "Dare to reach out your hand into the darkness, to pull another hand into the light." - Norm Rice

A writer becomes an editor becomes a reader. This may seem mirrored of the natural order it took to first become a writer, pivoting around the editor role, but the order flips. Writer. Editor. Reader. A writer cannot simply stay a writer. A writer must become their own editor and, after editing, their own reader. "Write what you'd want to read" is a common expression. Is that the origin of the writerly disease?

Time passes and pages are revisited, the creator removing their "writer" hat for a while and applying their "editor" hat, putting the work through revisions and rewrites. The book goes through a few rounds of self-edits, makes it to a third or fourth draft, or a tenth. Once satisfied, the "editor" hat is removed and on goes the "reader" hat.

The creator reads their work as others would for the first time, and so they sit back and take in this still-not-so-final version. They may have printed out a physical copy, red pen in hand. Writing is lonely, editing even lonelier, but reading one's own work is sometimes misleadingly divine if the pages have not had much time to settle. "Everyone's going to *love* it, right?"

So much time has been spent in their world of creation—months, years, decades—that flaws are overlooked by the creator, the writing close to perfect. Maybe small tweaks are made along the way during this not-quite-last "final polish" (what an inexperienced writer might consider the proofreading stage), a handful of typos addressed, and once again the work is considered as finished as it needs to be.

The writer, god to their own world, having created something from nothing and turning that something into a book they ultimately want others to read, and are proud of (a book they *themselves* would want to read), at some point is happy. But first their work needs outside help from either paid or unpaid services.

"Never pay for your writing" is a misconception when taken out of context. While it may not be best to pay a vanity publisher for outside assistance with editing, or pay for reading fees or writing contests or award consideration, a writer will have to pay to become a writer through much pain and suffering, and unfortunately money.

A writer should continuously develop their craft, spending years practicing and perfecting like they would any other talent. Olympic swimmers do not jump in the pool that first time and become gold medalists, and writers likewise should not jump into the murky waters of publishing without training to become professionals.

The credit line conundrum of youth: establishing credit without having credit. The hen / egg. The writer / book. How can a want-to-be "author" publish (obtain writing credit) without having published (having writing credit)?

No matter the developing talent, there must be investment in the self. Much of this is time and effort, but also a substantial amount of money when considering how much work needs to go into that investment. Writing is pay-to-play and so "never pay for your writing" is bad advice as a flat statement. Reasonable advice: "Pay for the *writer*, not for the *writing*."

No amount of money is a loss with self-improvement.

Writing seems free, since it can be done freely, but it can be costly when done right.

Attending writer workshops is one of the quickest means of turning professional. And they cost money (sometimes in the thousands) unless receiving grants or scholarships, but they are well worth the investment. Some are in-person, some online, although networking and establishing long-lasting relationships with writers and editors is much easier in-person. There, future professional writers join current professionals in the publishing world and a sampling of the novice writer's work is put through hell over the course of a weekend or weeks or months.

Some will not survive and will quit having not grasped "constructive criticism," which is the point. These programs are designed not around high praise but self-dissection and *construction*: "the building of something" or "style or method used in building of something," in this case the writer's talent. The goal is to improve the writer, always.

According to BusinessTerms.org, "Constructive criticism is providing feedback in a manner that acknowledges both the positives and where there is room for improvement instead of solely focusing on the negatives." [66] Negatives need to be pointed out, but writers occasionally take negatives to heart as personal failures, not as potential positives. Their work was near-perfect before so horribly disassembled in front of future peers and professionals.

A writer may be wonderful at editing, but all writers need to distance themselves from their work and seek outside help because self-editing is significantly more difficult than editing the work of others.

Even the best editors need editors.

Turn to any acknowledgments page and there will be a list of names. These are not just friends but those the writer entrusted to read early drafts prior to getting manuscripts as close to perfection as possible.

> "Only a blank page needs no editing."
> - Marty Rubin

DEVELOPMENTAL EDITORS

In Scott Norton's introduction to *Developmental Editing: A Handbook for Freelancers, Authors, and Publishers*, "The DE's role can manifest in a number of ways. Some 'big picture' editors provide direction by helping the author form a vision for the book, then coaching the author chapter by chapter to ensure that the vision is successfully executed. Others get their hands dirty with the prose itself, suggesting rewrites at the chapter, section, paragraph, and sentence levels." [68]

The job of the developmental editor is often referred to as *substantive editing*, with a goal of improving the writer's potential by taking a deeper dive into the work and helping them improve with early constructive feedback and constructive criticism; helping to further *develop* not only the writing but the writer.

A developmental editor offers advice on basic writing fundamentals but does not necessarily correct spelling or grammar mistakes, although often points out such things. They can either be brought in during the book's development—even prior to any writing whatsoever—or after the first draft of a manuscript is already complete.

In Norton's article on developmental editing for The

University of Chicago Press, he states that "[editing] requires analytical flair and creative panache, the patience of a saint and the vision of a writer. Transforming a manuscript into a book that edifies, inspires, and sells? That's the job of the developmental editor, whose desk is the first stop for many manuscripts on the road to bookdom." [69]

Questions for developmental editors prior to utilizing their services:

- What is your experience / training?
- What are your editing styles or how do you edit?
- What are your specialties / strengths?
- What are your expectations?

And while utilizing their services:

- What goals / routines should we establish?
- What can I expect and what is expected of me?
- What are my strengths and weaknesses?
- What can I do to improve my writing?

Developmental editors offer general feedback on what works well, what does not, and point out recurring issues.

STRUCTURAL EDITORS

Much like developmental editing, structural editing, either paid for or provided by a publisher, requires a look at the overall structure and content of the writing but also makes changes for the writer. Such help is sometimes labeled *developmental editing* or *substantive editing* as it is the first stage of the editing process following a writer's self-editing endeavors.

The entire manuscript is reviewed with target audience in mind. For fiction, this requires addressing issues with the components covered in the middle section of *Righting Writing* (character, plot, point of view, dialogue, etc.), and for nonfiction addressing problems with overall organization (consistency, clarity of arguments, etc.).

Changes are not typically made without the author's involvement, unless relatively minor; however, significant changes require consultation with the creator to cover why such changes are necessary. Depending on the relationship created, the writer may also allow a structural editor to make changes without involvement. The ability for word processing programs to track changes has made it easier to suggest and then either approve or deny changes to the text.

Along with structure, this type of editor will correct spelling, grammar, and punctuation mistakes, or not depending on how many other editors are eventually involved. In fact, if a manuscript needs little help, a structural editor may advise that the work goes directly to a copy editor.

LINE EDITORS

Before copy editing is line editing. Sometimes referred to as *stylistic editors*, line editors take special care to protect the writer's style and approach the manuscript as an incredibly careful reader, going line-by-line (hence the name) to insure the work is clean, but also observing word choice and syntax, overall tone, as well as pace and narrative flow.

Line editors look for extra words, kill digressions (temporary departures from the main point of the writing), compare every sentence and examine how one flows to the next, and slight or abrupt shifts in point of view. They make sure the language is as precise as it needs to be.

COPY EDITORS

Going hand-in-hand with line editing, copy editing (*copyediting* as a single word is also observed) covers the mechanics of writing, making sure the words follow style guides and basic rules of sentence structure, spelling, grammar, punctuation, terminology, continuity, diction (choice of words and phrases), formatting, and factual errors, which is especially crucial with nonfiction.

Such specialized editors have a keen attention to detail at both the sentence and word-use level, working their fine-tooth comb through the entire manuscript looking for mistakes but also consistency. The "copy" is thus reviewed and "edited" to improve readability.

Copy editing is considered the final stage of the editing process, although proofreaders may be brought in to check for anything missed by all editors involved before the book goes to print.

PROOFREADERS

This is the last step required before publication. Proofreaders review a completely edited manuscript or *proof copy* of the work searching for anything missed by prior editors, for sometimes the editing process itself can produce mistakes, such as omitted or repeated words, formatting issues, etc. This is the final set (or sets) of eyes.

Along with professional help, writers—even before seeking or introduced to such services—might reach out for help in other ways, paid for or not.

CRITIQUE PARTNERS

The name says it all, but this is a free, one-on-one, *quid pro quo* approach to receiving and providing feedback, someone with whom to share the suffering that is writing and editing. Compared to a beta reader, this type of support is reciprocal and the scope of the work malleable. Feedback can be much like that from a freelance editor.

Whether page by page, chapter by chapter, the entire manuscript, or even multiple drafts of the manuscript, time spent on the work can be bartered. "You do this for me, and I'll do this for you." It needs to be an equal trade, since 'partner' in this case could become long-term, much like the relationship created with beta readers.

Once finding someone comfortable to work with who provides constructional feedback, and likewise offering the same in return, those relationships tend to stick around for future projects. Expectations from both parties must be clear from the start, and the work performed in parallel with respect to response time.

ALPHA READERS

What is working? What is not working? These are typical questions for the alfa reader, those first entrusted to read early drafts and provide feedback. They might even look at the work before a first draft is finished, such as individual chapters or outlines, or to offer peer feedback during writers' workshops. They should be *casual readers*, or those considered average readers. Do not pay for alpha readers, unless provided through a professional workshop.

According to IngramSpark, "Alphas should approach your work as a writer-reader—someone to help you find the holes and disjointed edges," not necessarily pointing out spelling or grammar issues, but looking at the work as a whole. "Alphas help you find the major points to strengthen, and the weak points that may not need to be there." [67]

Questions for alpha readers:

- What is working / not working?
- What did you think of it?
- Any questions?

BETA READERS

Another unpaid gig, beta readers are the next to read and provide feedback, typically for more complete manuscripts that have gone through a few rounds of self-edits or professional edits. Beta readers are important prior to sending the work to agents, editors, or publishers, as the critiques are more in-depth and provided by those who know what they are doing.

Such critiques dive deeper into the writing, pointing out typos, grammar issues, sentence and paragraph structure for the entire manuscript. They cover character, dialogue, voice, plot, conflict, theme, setting, as well as prose, pace, tense, point of view, show vs. tell, imagery, etc. They help bring the manuscript up to professional standards.

Questions for beta readers:

- What kind of feelings / emotions did the writing evoke, what kind of tone?
- Did the writing hold interest throughout?
- Does it feel right?
- Any questions?

GHOSTWRITERS

Never publicized, ghostwriting is when one writer writes for another writer (or a non-writer), with all work credited to the "author" who hired the ghostwriter. They are typically hired by those who either don't have enough time or experience to do the writing.

Freelance Writing, a website source for freelancing work, provides a breakdown of the two parties involved in that professional relationship: "The 'author,' who hires the freelance writer to produce content for an agreed upon fee, takes the credit for all the original work produced" and "The 'ghost,' the freelance writer who is generally paid in advance of completing the job, gets the money as a 'work for hire' job and assumes none of the credit for their ghostwriting work." [70]

The ghost is simply the pen, or *should* be, whereas the author is the storyteller whose story and literary voice are carried out through the writing. NDAs, or non-disclosure agreements, are often signed to protect the creator, and so ghostwriters are unable to divulge names of authors they have worked with in the past.

> "Ask for help. Not because you are weak. But because you want to remain strong." - Les Brown

There are many other types of outside help for writers, but what matters most is that a writer, at any level of professionalism, requires assistance to ever be any good.

SOLICITATION

Querying and submitting work, and publishing options.

"Never put the keys to your happiness in someone else's pocket." - Unknown

What will happen with this polished and near-but-never-flawless manuscript? That is a big question, and every writer wants the same answer: a big publisher. Not to kill hope, but there is a miniscule chance of that ever happening. Odds suggest getting struck by lighting a few times is more feasible. A better answer: the book to be in print.

A book should never be created with the intention of finding fortune or fame. As already covered, the first question every writer should ask themselves: "Do I *want* to be a writer, or do I *need* to be a writer?" The answer should always be the latter. To land a book deal with a traditional publisher, a literary agent is required, and finding one is a strenuous process and takes time. Some successful writers take years to land an agent, or decades, often having already published a decent amount of work from smaller presses or independently.

LITERARY AGENTS

Literary Agents represent writers. They have connections to editors of presses (typically on a first-name basis), and they have experience and know "the market" and *what* sells, and likewise *how* to sell. They focus on the selling so the creator can focus on the creating. Having an agent involves establishing a long-lasting relationship with continuous communication. A good literary agent will quickly become an intimate friend.

In the article "The Life of a Literary Agent" by Johnny Geller, literary agent for the Curtis Brown Creative says that an agent "is a negotiator, editor, manager, mentor, friend, psychologist, fan, critic, marketeer, and impresario. Most of all a connector. Someone who takes huge pleasure connecting talented people with creative collaborators and seeing them flourish." [71]

Agents work for a percentage of sales, usually 15%, and so they have to sell books to make money. The odds of landing a literary agent, however, is also about as likely as getting struck by lightning (only once instead of twice), and it all starts with the all-important query.

QUERIES

Query letters, more commonly query *emails*, are correspondences sent from the writer to an agent, editor, or publisher (rarely). They also happen to be the most crucial representation of a writer because they act as the first impression.

If physically printed, a query should span no more than a single page. They should be short and professional and to the point. They should be no more than a few paragraphs, follow standard etiquette, and include the following:

Salutation - Like all letters and emails, a formal yet personalized greeting is required to acknowledge the recipient by name. Never send blindly, unless requested, in which case "To Whom It May Concern" might be needed; otherwise, "To Whom It May Concern" is a tell-all that the recipient is one of many and not so important. Queries start writer-agent relationships, or writer-editor or writer-publisher relationships, so imagine inviting someone on a first date and addressing them as "Whoever you may be . . ."

Paragraph 1 - This is the hook. An interesting query is intriguing from the first line. Include the title, genre, and word count, but keep the length of this paragraph short. If a connection exists between writer and recipient, include that as well. Has the manuscript been professionally edited? Mention that, especially since agents, editors, and publishers would rather work with writers willing to put in the effort and who already have polished manuscripts.

Paragraph 2 - Briefly summarize the book by way of an elevator pitch, although do not give too much away. Include character information (real or fictional) and the plot or purpose but leave them wanting more. This should be the longest paragraph out of the three, selling the book.

Paragraph 3 - Sell the author by way of a short biography, if what is included is book-relevant. Mention prior publications, awards, or at a minimum experience in the subject matter or reasoning behind the book's creation. This part of the query should only run a few sentences.

Valediction - Derived from the Latin *vale dicere*, or "to say farewell," a formal send-off is an effective way to show professionalism. *Sincerely* is enough.

Paragraphs should be on the smaller side and the words meaningful. Concise sentences and paragraphs. The writing should be in similar style and tone as the manuscript. The query is the introduction to the writer, so make an impression. Sell the book. Sell the writer.

What not to do:

Span more than a page - Efficiency highlights writer talent. The recipient reads hundreds of queries per day, so they appreciate conciseness. They are looking more for reasons to reject a query rather than to accept one (like editors with manuscripts). The single-page approach also applies to resumes, and a query letter serves the same function.

Oversell - Never include lines like "What you are about to read is the next best-seller" or "Much like David Sedaris, my writing is . . ." or "You won't want to pass on this opportunity." They will not care and have heard it all before. Let the writing (both query and manuscript) reveal the pride of the writer by way of professionalism.

Undersell - "I don't want to waste your time" and similar phrases is a means of self-deprecation. If the writer does not have faith in their work, or in themselves, why should an agent, editor, or publisher? Do not oversell, and do not undersell; just sell.

Fancify - Like the manuscript, industry standard font styles and sizes and colors and formatting should always be used. Whatever the word processor or email program uses as default is good enough.

An example query letter intended for a literary agent for *Righting Writing:*

Formal Name [spelling verified],

Tired of reading unprofessional manuscripts? *Righting Writing*, 80,000 words, is a nonfiction survival guide to help both novice and experienced writers draft and polish professional manuscripts. I had the pleasure of meeting you at [writing conference] last year and I have since collaborated with a developmental editor and a copyeditor to put this manuscript through multiple rounds of revisions. I am now seeking literary representation.

Righting Writing walks creators through building a manuscript from concept to final draft. The straight-to-the-point and sometimes witty narrative pushes writers past impostor syndrome, establishes the writer routine, and explores crucial elements of what makes books extraordinary: character, dialogue, voice, plot, conflict, theme, and setting. The journey continues with the evolution of the manuscript, educating writers about the importance of improving upon and tightening prose, pace, tense, point of view, show vs. tell, imagery, and finally manuscript framework and structure. By the end, writers will be ready to handle solicitation, rejection, and acceptance.

> Past publications include Novel Name, winner of the Book Award, as well as short stories and poetry published in *Magazine* and *Online Journal*. I am a book doctor and have a deep passion for motivating and helping writers right their writing. If interested, I can send the completed manuscript, sample chapters, and/or a synopsis.
>
> Sincerely,
>
> Author Name
> Mailing Address
> Phone Number
> Email [if sending a physical letter]

The example is under 250 words, so it would fit on a single page if printed. It is about as long as a query letter ever needs to be: *salutation; three paragraph structure; valediction.* And, of course, the all-important contact information.

Before sending a query letter, and a manuscript, which is the end goal, spend time researching and then following submission guidelines. Not adhering to the rules or being "cute" with queries and manuscripts could mean a quick rejection. Also, put the query through a few drafts.

SUBMISSION GUIDELINES

Submission guidelines exist, and for a reason. Although they are called "guidelines," which implies looseness of rule-following, guidelines need to be followed to specificity. Consider them submission "rules." They often include a minimum and/or maximum word count, accepted genres, content restrictions, and a multitude of other important items. Not following guidelines is often an instant rejection.

Those accepting submissions might not even want writers to submit manuscripts at all but instead sample chapters or pages and/or an outline and/or a synopsis.

SAMPLE CHAPTERS / PAGES

Always start at the beginning. Those considering submissions want to know if there is an initial hook and if the writing holds interest in the pages that follow. They want to be wowed as any reader should be when picking up the finished book and flipping through those opening pages.

Sometimes the first three chapters are requested, or the first thirty pages. This varies by agent, editor, or publisher. If the book has a prologue, feel free to skip that, but do not choose the "best" writing from a favorite chapter. The entire book needs to be a representation of the writer, including those crucial first pages.

OUTLINES

These manuscript "skeletons" are summarized versions of the story broken down chapter-by-chapter, and sometimes requested in place of manuscripts to save time. And like a skeleton, every bone must hold the book together, although only the major bones need mentioning; all those smaller pieces are not needed at this point.

The writer may have completed an outline before writing the book, but, just as multiple revisions are required for manuscripts, the outline also needs a few rounds to polish before it's submission-ready.

SYNOPSES

Book summaries come in various sizes: single-page, three-page, five-page, seven-page, etc. They are also outlines, in a way. If asked for a synopsis, the page length will be requested or at least mentioned in the submission guidelines.

A book synopsis can be more difficult to write than the book, the writer condensing tens or hundreds of thousands of words into a matter of thousands. It is challenging to compress a book without making it sound cheesy, and it will, even when ready to send. Which bones need to be there to recognize what kind of a body it represents?

Never send something that is not requested, and do not query until the manuscript is finished. Agents, editors, and publishers rarely want to see partials.

Despite how a writer finds a home for their manuscript, agented or not, they must first understand the types of publishers, primarily *traditional*, *independent*, *self-*, *vanity*, and *hybrid*. Each constantly evolve as technology in the book industry advances, each absorbing traits of the others.

TRADITIONAL PUBLISHING

Bookstores consist of traditionally published books. Seldom do physical stores carry independent or self-published books, or hybrid or vanity, for that matter. Most bookstores can order such titles, depending on distributors, but that takes someone contacting individual stores to order copies.

Upon writing and later revising *Righting Writing*, it was the "Big-5": HarperCollins, Hachette, Macmillan, Penguin Random House, and Simon & Schuster. Not so long ago it was the Big-6, and soon it will most likely be the Big-4 (if/when others merge). These giants produce 80% of all books ever published. If books do not fall under these brands, they fall under one of their many imprints.

The main advantage of traditional publishing is money —such as advances against royalty—and exposure. These publishing "houses" (or "mansions," might be a better term) are sought after first because they have the largest resources for marketing, publicity, ability to move books, and quality of editors and other professionals they readily keep on staff.

But there are more than the "Big-X." There are a handful of other major book publishers that do not fall under the giant umbrellas, as well as mid-level and small press.

Mid-level book publishers, for example, offer similar benefits as traditional publishing, yet lean toward smaller advances and publish books not as common or trendy, yet can still end up on bestseller lists now and again.

Few mid-size presses remain. Most have been "picked off," per *Publishers Weekly* in an article appropriately named "Where Have All the Midsize Book Publishers Gone?" Jim Milliot states, "All the Big Five companies became the size they are through series of acquisitions that began years ago." And most small-size presses are comfortable in their small sizes but "don't have the interest, time, or resources to engage in major expansions." [72]

There is no shortage of micro- and small-size presses,

which are significantly smaller publishers with a very limited number of titles released each year (ten or fewer in some cases). "Independent press" or "indie" is often used in place of small press and focus on limited-edition books or niche markets, such as with sub-genre fiction and poetry.

Independent publishing and self-publishing are terms often used interchangeably, although there are differences that set them apart and similarities that blur the line.

INDEPENDENT PUBLISHING

Smaller presses offer similar services as traditional publishers, yet at a reduced level. Most produce books using printers that offer smaller print runs or use Print on Demand / Publish on Demand (POD) and have access to limited distribution networks to make titles available.

While the POD model is highly effective for online distribution through places such as Amazon or Lightning-Source and have expanded distribution channels for many countries outside the United States, POD is unfortunately not as profitable for independent publishers and difficult for distribution into traditional brick and mortar bookstores.

Independent publishers do not have room for risk, nor funds like larger publishers, and so they rely heavily on their authors to handle much of the promotion. Contracts are typically looser and offer more compensation and rights to compensate. Contracts should thus be well-dissected before signing to assure and protect the writer and their work.

According to Polylyric Press in their article "What Is Independent Publishing, and How Does It Differ from Traditional Publishing and Self Publishing?" it describes that "Independent publishers are free to structure royalty arrangements in any way they and authors doing business with them see fit. This can mean that an author ends up with a much larger percentage of sale proceeds. [73]

The catch with independent publishing is that even though a company may have been used to publish the book, the author of the work is still considered "self-published" compared to traditionally published.

SELF-PUBLISHING

Similar to independent publishing, self-publishing relies on the author to publish the book and handle everything with production, marketing, etc. Some self-publishing services include Kindle Direct Publishing (KDP, previously CreateSpace), Xlibris, AuthorHouse, and Lulu, all of which provide tools to help writers with POD distribution.

Much higher profit margins for books are available with self-publishing, and expanded distribution to many countries, but the number of copies sold depends heavily on the motivation and effort of solely the author. All costs must be privately funded, which can be minimal if the writer is cable of design, self-editing, and everything else that goes into a professional quality book, or can be extensive if outsourcing editing, copyediting, proofreading, or any other service.

VANITY PUBLISHING

Also referred to as subsidy publishing, vanity publishing requires writers to pay for all or most of the cost to have their books published, similar to self-publishing, but outsourced.

Pay-to-play. "Vanity" has taken on negative connotations, and such presses are thought of as a last resort. If no one will take the book, why not publish it out of vanity?

There is a place for vanity publishing, but not in a traditional publishing sense. Some writers may not necessarily want their books to become bestsellers, or have the time to learn the ins and outs of self-publishing, or even desire to attempt publishing their books through more traditional means; or maybe they only want to publish a set amount of copies or don't intend for the book to generate income.

Avoid vanity publishing unless justified, in other words.

HYBRID PUBLISHING

There's a huge gap between self- or independent publishing and traditional publishing, an option that borderlines vanity but is commonly referred to as "author-assisted publishing" or "co-publishing" or "partnership publishing" or sometimes "entrepreneurial publishing": *hybrid.*

In Brooke Warners article "What Is Hybrid Publishing? Here Are 4 Things All Writers Should Know" for *Writer's Digest*, hybrid publishing is described as "an emerging area that occupies the middle ground between traditional and self-publishing and therefore includes many different publishing models—basically anything that is not self-publishing or traditional publishing." [74]

The hybrid model is somewhat controversial but doesn't have to be. The adage "never pay for your work" is good advice, in general, but consider the verb 'pay' and whether the hybrid option explored dips too much into vanity.

Is it wrong to *pay* for a manuscript to be professionally

edited, or copyedited, or proofread, or to have a beautiful book cover designed, or to pay for interior artwork / illustrations, or to hire an artist to design the interior for physical and/or eBook editions? Not at all, especially since designing a book takes other talents.

All self-published and independently published authors pay for their work at one time or another, and so do writers who manage to break through the traditional publishing wall. What matters is whether the money exchanged is an investment of the self.

A writer could spend up to ten thousand dollars or more improving their craft and perfecting their work before ever publishing. It adds up over years of dedication: workshops, conferences, lodging, flights, meals, and so on . . . most of which could be written off for taxes if handled correctly.

Some hybrid publishers rely on the author to pay for some or all services in exchange for higher royalty, and some work more like assisted self- or independent publishing and do not expect *any* royalties in return, pending whether or not those funds can be raised by way of crowdsource funding. Such campaigns are typically designed more like "pre-order" endeavors that offer perks such as autographed books or additional swag.

What sets apart hybrid publishers from vanity publishers is that they tend to care about both the author and the book, and they run more like traditional publishers, with professional staff on hand to help with editing, interior / exterior layout, and also distribution.

Is there a submission process? Do they have in-house editors (of all types) or artists and designers? Are potential hybrid-published books curated, or do they simply get published no matter what?

These are all good questions to consider when deciding if the hybrid model is the right choice for a book.

In the same *Writer's Digest* article, Brooke breaks down hybrid publishing into four distinct models:

1. "Traditional publishers that have been brokering hybrid publishing deals for years" - authors take on some upfront cost and to compensate for offered higher royalty rates.

2. "Partnership publishing models" - authors take on financial risk in trade for high royalties, and access to review sites and assistance selling books by way of publisher-bookseller partnerships.

3. "Agent-assisted publishing models" - authors are published under an agent's imprint, albeit with limited distribution but with a passion for producing quality books.

4. "Other assisted publishing models" - authors have more of a self-publishing experience, but with help throughout that journey.

What is the best publishing model? It depends on the purpose of the book, the condition / quality of the manuscript, and how much time the writer has already invested in righting their writing.

For first-timers who want to rush their book into the world, the hybrid approach is the emerging choice, since much of the experience in book publishing will be offered to them (for either a fee or crowdsourcing to pay for fees). But spend a great deal of time researching before committing. There are a lot of scams out there, and one good sign is when a "publisher" (in quotes for a reason) quickly sends an acceptance with a caveat that the writer must use paid service of a partner or third-party company.

Also consider that self-publishing takes a lot of experience and knowledge of book design, distribution, and marketing, and assumes the writer has already spent years bringing their writing and their brand up to professional standards; if not, there's risk of publishing a book that is not ready, causing embarrassment or shame.

If the book will be the second or later in the author's eventual bibliography, independent or even self-publishing is another good option, and also traditional publishing, but first consider spending time and even *paying* to bring the writing up to the highest quality possible.

No matter the book, why not start at the top? If not in a rush (and a writer never should be), why not focus on landing a literary agent after first polishing a query, a synopsis, and a book outline—depending on submission guidelines? This process can take years, though, and years more for a book to find a home at either a Big-X (not so likely) or mid- or small-size publisher (more than likely) *through* that agent, but worth a shot.

Books, especially debuts, need to make an impression. Once published, the book is a permanent representation of the writer. Books need to be done right. Books needs to be as professional as they can be and hold up to all the others out there, not as competition, but allies. Will the book be a bestseller? It should at least be capable.

REJECTION

A part of the journey.

"You have to know how to accept rejection and reject acceptance."
- Ray Bradbury

All writers must learn to embrace rejection, which is a part of becoming a better writer. A limited number of creators who finish a manuscript will publish traditionally; their work will instead end up at smaller presses or be self-published or released through independent or hybrid publishers. But one thing all successful writers have in common—which has nothing to do with fortune or fame—is that they learned to accept rejection and reject acceptance.

Am I good enough? Why am I doing this? Should I give up?

Not only do such questions haunt a writer early on in their endeavors, but indefinitely. Impostor syndrome rears its ugly head from concept to completion and beyond. Out of the multi-billions of people in the world, there are only a handful of creatives who have learned to hide their sense of fraudulence (it is always there) through perseverance.

It is well known that Stephen King threw *Carrie* in the trash. His debut novel, the first pages of which his wife Tabitha dug out and made him finish, would later spark one of the most successful writing careers of all time. He pushed through that self-rejection (with help) only to face another type of rejection. Once finished, the epistolary novel received a hard "no" from over thirty publishers, one stating, "We are not interested in science fiction which deals with negative utopias. They do not sell." [75]

In his nonfiction book *On Writing: A Memoir of the Craft*, King discusses experiencing and dealing with rejection letters at an early age: "By the time I was fourteen the nail in my wall would no longer support the weight of the rejection slips impaled upon it. I replaced the nail with a spike and went on writing." [76]

That is the type of attitude to have if ever wanting to become a "successful" writer. A writer needs to write, and rejection should never get in the way; it should be accepted as part of the journey. Success is a mindset the same way failure is a mindset.

Chicken Soup for the Soul by Jack Canfield was rejected 114 times. F. Scott Fitzgerald collected 122 rejections before ever publishing. The first *Harry Potter* novel was rejected by twelve different publishing houses, one editor offering J.K. Rowling a warning: "You do realize, you will never make a fortune out of writing children's books?"

Long after finding fortune and fame, Rowling attempted soliciting a new novel called *The Cuckoo's Calling* under the pseudonym Robert Galbraith. He (she) received a rejection letter with novice advice a first-time writer might expect, along with, "I regret that we have reluctantly come to the conclusion that we could not publish it with commercial success." The nail in the coffin was the dreaded, "I wish you every success in placing your work elsewhere."

Thank you, but no thank you.

Before his suicide in 1969, John Kennedy Toole went through five years of rejection for *A Confederacy of Dunces*. He was posthumously awarded the Pulitzer Prize.

Even Jack London, who went on to publish over fifty books in his short span as a writer and considered one of the most prolific and commercially successful writers, received 664 rejection letters in his first five years before his novella

The Call of the Wild launched his career and took him out of poverty. In his writing room, he kept a spindle on which he impaled his rejections with both a sense of pride and defeat, which at one point climbed four feet tall.

What if any of those writers had given up?

Without embracing rejection, consider the literary world today. How many future readers and writers would *not* be influenced because of a single agent's, editor's, or publisher's decision regarding commerciality (ability to produce a profit)? Imagine having sent those initial rejection letters to such now-prestigious names, and watching them flourish through another agent, editor, or publisher. Imagine being responsible for rejecting Stephen King.

Joseph Hillström King, who goes by the pseudonym Joe Hill, refused to emerge from his father's shadow. He hid for many years that he was the son of the "Master of Terror." It took a decade of collecting rejection letters before a small press published *20th Century Ghosts* in 2005, a collection of short fiction published under the pen name. Neither his agent nor his publisher knew about the connection.

His father had sold over 350 million books, and Joe was fearful his debut would only get published because he was the son of a living legend. "I was afraid a publisher would publish it regardless of whether it was good or not, because they saw a chance to make money on the connection. People would say, 'He only got published because of who his dad is.'" [77]

He could have chosen to ride the coattails of his father, but instead put in the challenging work to make a name for himself and create his own brand. It may have taken him ten years or more, but his story is a prime example of what it takes to become a successful bestselling author. He embraced rejection and rejected what would have been an easy acceptance.

The first rejection letter a writer receives is an accomplishment. It says, "I tried." And the second rejection letter says, "I tried, again, but harder." And the third, the 100th? With each letter pierced by nail or spindle or electronically foldered, a writer becomes stronger and learns what works and what doesn't, both in terms of solicitation and talent.

In rare occasions, an agent, editor, or publisher will offer useful feedback, such as specific reasons why the writing did not work for them specifically. They may not handle the genre or sub-genre of the submission or didn't connect with a main character as much as they would have liked, or found a theme too triggering, or maybe found the book not currently marketable. Personalized responses should be taken to heart, especially since they took the time to personalize what could have been a form response, and more so if what they offer mirrors feedback from other rejections.

> "Remember: when people tell you something's wrong or doesn't work for them, they are almost always right. When they tell you exactly what they think is wrong and how to fix it, they are almost always wrong."
> – Neil Gaiman

A writer needs to spend years investing in the self: writing out the bad until it becomes good, editing their work until it no longer needs editing, constantly righting their writing until ready. To become successful, they need to fail and then try again, and again, for as long as it takes.

It is common for writers to hold onto physical rejection letters or emails from traditional publishers or "bucket list" magazines or literary journals, and then shoving them in a box, a drawer, cataloged digitally; they are badges of honor. Having work rejected is tough, especially after so much time is spent perfecting it, but all prolific writers have wise words to say about the importance of rejection.

After receiving a rejection letter, there is no sense replying, not even a quick "thank you for considering my work" response. This is also not the time to retaliate for not being accepted. Every so often, those responsible for sending rejections receive responses from unhappy writers. No need to kill the messenger; those rejecting work are simply doing their job, whether or not they made the right decision.

Form letter responses are standard, containing phrases like "while we enjoyed your writing" and "we regret to inform you" and the dreaded "not the right fit at this time." Canned responses are not a reflection of the writer. They are often short and to the point because of the vast number of rejections sent out regularly by agents, editors, and publishers. Some contain personalized notes on what works or what does not for a particular piece, but most do not.

An example of a form response for a short story sent to an anthology:

> Thank you submitting "Story Title" to *Book Title*. We have received an incredible response from this open call and read every submission with careful consider-

```
ation. While your work is not the right
fit for this anthology, we wish you the
best in placing it elsewhere.
```

While the example is suited to handle multiple rejections, the phrasing at least includes the story title and would hopefully go after a salutation that includes the author's name. That is not always the case. Most rejections consist of a few lines that translate to an informal "Thank you, but no thank you." Again, this is not a reflection of the writer.

An example of a form response from a query letter for a book-length work sent to an agent:

> Dear AuthorName,
>
> Thank you for sending *Book Title*. After review of your query and sample pages, I found that I didn't connect with your work, and this will be a pass for me.
>
> Publishing is a subjective industry and what may not work for me may be exactly what another agent is looking for. Thank you so much for the opportunity of reviewing your query and I wish you the best of luck in your writing career.
>
> Sincerely,
>
> AgentName
> Literary Agency

One less informal and more positive:

Dear AuthorName,

It may not seem this way, but saying no is tough for me. I'm sure hearing it is tough for you, but it's really important for me to fall in love with a project and that just did not happen in this case. Please know that I really appreciate your patience during this process, and I truly wish you the best of luck in finding the right agent! I'll be rooting for you!

AgentName

Another type of rejection, most often sent as a form response, results from a writer failing to meet submission guidelines. In seldom cases, those handling rejections will send a nice message stating what guidelines were missed or instructions on how to submit properly, but this is not their job. It is always the submitter's responsibility to adhere to submission guidelines.

Submission windows must be observed, the submitter responsible for checking beforehand to make sure an agent, editor, or publisher is actively reading new material. If not, this may result in a quick informal message about the appropriate window, or an auto-response stating something like:

We are not currently accepting submissions.

Waiting for acceptance or rejection is a time-suck and an unhealthy habit. Anticipating a response (good or bad) without filling that void with new creations can be damaging and heighten impostor syndrome. Once a solicitation is sent, and to whomever, it is time to move on to the next project, not to think about the fate of the previous.

Always look forward, never back. Whenever a rejection arrives, collect it somewhere (or don't), submit elsewhere (or don't), and consider the response a writer-defining scar. How many rejection letters is too many, and when should a writer toss in the towel? Never. Consider the rejection history of the successful writers mentioned earlier.

A finished manuscript seems important to writers, but it is *not* for the person reading submissions. In fact, it is simply another potential manuscript to sell in a forever-growing pile of manuscripts to sell. It is work—a few hundred pages (digital or not) among millions of pages. And the person reading submissions is primarily looking for a reason to *reject* the manuscript, not accept it, and so long spans without a response can be a good thing.

Tips for coping with the stress of waiting:

1. Stop expecting a response. Let the rejection or acceptance come as a surprise.

2. Move on to something else. Read. Write. Revise.

3. Accept that the manuscript may never sell.

A response can arrive instantly (as an auto-response if not accepting submissions) or in a few hours, or months, or years, or never. Traditional publishers take the longest or do not respond at all, perhaps with an "if you don't hear from us in six months, we're not interested" cautionary message somewhere near submission guidelines.

Novice writers tend to submit and then wait, and wait, and wait, not realizing the importance of starting the next project, letting all the weight of their future writing career rely on that first book, or second, or third. Responses (good or bad) can take as much time as it would for the writer to complete another novel-length manuscript, so why not keep the words flowing in the meantime? A million words or more might need to be be written before a writer's debut.

Rejection is proof that the writer tried, and that must be good enough. A writer *needs* to write, and although they may *want* to sell their book to a publisher (major or otherwise), it cannot be the sole reason a writer writes.

Writers have stories to *tell*, not *sell.*

And there are a multitude of places a writer can publish outside of major publishing houses. Aim high, but consider the options. A writer can self-publish, use an independent publisher, small- or mid-size press, or they can work with a hybrid publisher, or as a last resort a vanity publisher, depending on the scope of the book.

Rejecting acceptance, as Bradbury states in that opening quote, is likewise as important as accepting rejection. Also keep in mind that the author of *Fahrenheit 451* had collected over eight hundred rejection letters in his time. Imagine Bradbury setting each of his rejection letters aflame and moving on.

ACCEPTANCE

Embracing “yes” and understanding contracts.

"If you persistently seek validation from others, you will inadvertently invalidate your own self-worth."
- Auliq Ice

There is no greater joy for a writer than the excitement of an acceptance letter, to read the words "On behalf of *Literary Agency / Publisher*, we are proud to accept *Title of Work* for representation / publication" or however it may be phrased.

Waiting for so long to read those words after countless rejections—or non-responses—gets the adrenaline rushing, the heart pounding. Finally, validation for all the suffering it takes to be a writer. Suddenly there's a contract and the first tendency is to quickly read through and then sign and date and return and announce the acceptance.

Through that excitement, the writer once again needs to put on the editor hat, this time reading through the contract meticulously, looking for verbiage that requests unnecessary rights or unrealistic expectations, or unfair compensation.

The first thing to do when receiving a contract is to look for anything that might warrant rejecting it, for along with accepting rejection, a writer must be comfortable rejecting acceptance. And it is okay to request changes to a contract because they are flexible until signed.

CONTRACTS

Contracts are agreements made between two or more parties, so everyone part of that contract needs to be in complete agreement before signing. Reputable literary agencies and publishers offer solid contracts, but newer agencies and smaller lesser-known publishers may offer contracts that need adjustments to protect the writer and their creation.

Prolific writer Brian Keene was full of excitement when receiving a contract for his debut novel *The Rising*, published by Leisure Books in 2003, which specialized in the horror and thriller genres until they dissolved in 2010. Keene has made it public that at a bar at a convention he handed the only copy of his contract to fellow writer and once-agent Dallas Mayr and asked, "You mind looking at this?"

Mayr pulled out a pen and skimmed the pages, editing on the fly, saying things like, "No, this needs to go" and "Let's change this" and made the pages bleed. Keene had planned to sign and turn in that very contract to the publisher later at the convention, shocked at all the requested changes—especially to an offered contract for his first book. "If they give you any grief," Mayr said, or something similar, "tell 'em I looked through this with you."

He eventually met with a representative of that publisher to review the changes and ultimately both parties agreed to the red-lined contract, Keene getting more of an advance, higher royalties, and able to hold onto additional rights.

Author rights or *literary rights* for certain intellectual property are interchangeable with the term *copyrights*. Per the Cornell University Library, "Copyrights are granted under federal law to authors of creative works at the time of the work's creation in a fixed, tangible form. Authors do not have to apply for or file a copyright." [78]

Copyright for written work begins when words are put onto a physical or digital platform, with all rights belonging to the creator at that moment. Writers tend to unnecessarily worry about protection. The Copyright Act of the United States (section 106) states, "only the owner of a copyright has the authority to use the work, and in one of six ways:

- To reproduce the work
- To prepare derivative works based upon the work
- To distribute copies of the work
- To publicly perform the work
- To publicly display the work
- To publicly perform sound recordings via a digital audio transmission" [79]

Only the current owner of the copyright can engage in any of the options above, and either *statutorily* or *contractually*. The most common statutory limits are *fair use:* permitting unlicensed use of copyright-protected words through freedom of creative expression, not for profit; and the *libraries exception:* allowing libraries or archives, on a limited basis, to reproduce and/or distribute copyright-protected works without permission to preserve, replace, or for research.

When limits are applied, the copyright owner continues to own the work, but others can use it, depending on the situation. When a copyright expires—seventy years following the author's death, typically—then a copyright dissolves and the public can use the work however desired. F. Scott Fitzgerald's *The Great Gatsby*, for instance, published April 10, 1925, entered the public domain January 1, 2021. The public domain is a space where intellectual property rights do not exist, whether expired, forfeited, or inapplicable.

Contractual rights, on the other hand, can be transfered from one party to another by way of a private agreement, in which case an author relinquishes rights by signed contract.

The six exclusive rights above are sometimes referred to as a "bundle of rights" since the copyright owner controls each right individually, and is able to transfer or license *none*, *some*, or *all*, depending on the contract.

Most author agreements unfortunately hand over *all* copyrights, which is why contracts need special attention. Once rights are relinquished, the previous owner becomes powerless of the work until the contract expires.

When *all* copyrights are "signed over" to another party, the author (previous copyright owner) loses the ability to control how or where their work appears, and the publisher (or new owner, whoever that may be) can reuse the author's work without permission and/or notice.

Read contracts and understand them before signing.

A quick acceptance can sometimes mean a scam, or a publisher willing to "accept and publish" a book on condition that the author pays for editing or other such services through a partner of that publisher. This is where "pay to play" is most dangerous, with money-hungry "publishers" (in quotes for a reason) preying on the all-too-excited novice writer eager for their work to find print. These types of publishers rarely care about the product or the author.

Part of deciding whether a contract is worthwhile is to research who is offering representation. Include "scam" in an online search and spend time on their website to see what other books and writers they have published or currently represent and the quality of the books.

Reading a contract can seem like translating a foreign language, everything in legal jargon.

A few contract definitions:

Agreement or **Author's Agreement** - Denotes the parties involved and crucial contact information.

Author's Grant - Also known as the "grant of rights," this is the clause in a contract relinquishing rights from author to publisher or another party.

Rights - Detailed information on what rights are relinquished in the contract (see "Common rights" section).

Terms of License - Length of the contract and end clause.

Payment and Royalties - Specifics on the agreed upon payment to relinquish rights, sometimes including contributor / author copies, a flat sum, royalties (a percentage of money paid for the work based on sales), or an advance against royalties (money received in advance of sales, after which royalties commence when profitable), or any combination thereof. Payment schedule may also be included.

Author's Warranties and Indemnities - A contractually enforceable promise of the contract, sometimes including how a contract may be breached and damages for breaches.

Changes in Text - What the new copyright owner can alter in terms of the text, layout, etc. for the purpose of publication and company standards.

Publishing Formats - The medium(s) in which the work will be published (trade paperback, hardcover, eBook, audio book, online, etc.)

Copyright - Further information on rights retained.

Reversion of Rights / Withdrawal of Offer to Publish - Detailed information on dissolving (ending) the contract and returning rights.

Author's Credit - How the author will be credited for the work (also known as the author "by-line"), either by legal name, shortened name, or pseudonym.

Venue - Where the agreement will be executed and applicable laws.

PUBLISHING RIGHTS

Common rights include: *First Rights, One-time Rights, Reprint Rights* (or *Second Serial Rights*), *Anthology Rights* (for works appearing in collections from multiple authors), *First World English, Foreign Rights, Translation Rights, Excerpt Rights, Electronic Rights, Archival Rights . . .*

Research rights before signing them over. *First World English* rights, for instance, means the entire English-speaking world; *First American, First Australian, First British,* and *First Canadian*, then, would be unavailable. *First North American Serial Rights (FNASR)* would be another option, allowing for the work to be published only in North America, and only *once*, with all copyright reverting back to the author.

All Rights, as the name implies, relinquishes all rights to the work, and so the author would no longer be able to use that writing again in its current form. And the copyright owner would have the opportunity to reprint, sell to another publication / publisher, or display on the internet however they please, all without the author receiving compensation.

Once work appears online (website, blog, social media, etc.), it is considered "published" and publishers may not consider it, or *First Electronic Rights* may be requested to keep the work from appearing on the internet.

All rights can be separated into two categories: *exclusive*, and *nonexclusive*. Exclusive means the work will not appear anywhere else, typically within an agreed-upon span of time (months, years). Nonexclusive is the opposite, allowing the work to appear in multiple places simultaneously.

Every contract is different, requesting varying rights, and this can be dangerous. Does a publisher need 10 years exclusivity? Do they need audio rights, or film rights? Why? Understand what rights are worth retaining as a writer.

The following is an example of some potential contract language. This is for a small press seeking rights for a novel, offering a low advance but high royalties, and designed (which is not always the case) to protect the writer and their work. The bold sections are typical, although the wording may read differently; the underlined / italicized sections change depending on what is offered and who is involved.

AGREEMENT

This contract is made between Publisher Name, hereinafter referred to as the PUBLISHER (physical address and/or e-mail), and Legal Name (physical address and/or e-mail), hereinafter referred to as the AUTHOR. The parties agree as follows:

AUTHOR'S GRANT

The AUTHOR grants permission to publish *Title of Work*, a novel of approximately XX,XXX words, hereinafter referred to as the WORK.

The AUTHOR grants permission to have the work illustrated by Illustrator Name, who will provide Number of Illustrations (numerical value) original Size of Illustrations (full-page, half-page, quarter-page, etc.) illustrations to be agreed upon by both the AUTHOR and PUBLISHER.

RIGHTS

This use of the WORK by the PUBLISHER entails the assignment of Print Rights (first world print rights, reprint rights, etc.) in Format (hardcover, trade paperback, etc.) for publication in the Language (English, German, etc.) language.

Rights revert back to the AUTHOR immediately upon publication, although the PUBLISHER requests twelve (12) months exclusivity before AUTHOR publishes the WORK elsewhere.

The AUTHOR has the right to include the WORK in a "best of" anthology or "personal collection" during the time of exclusivity listed above.

The AUTHOR retains all rights not specified.

TERMS OF LICENSE

The AUTHOR agrees to grant the PUBLISHER the right to keep the WORK in print for as long as there is a demand. After two (2) years following publication, the AUTHOR may request the work to be taken out of print by the PUBLISHER with a 60-day notice via email or in writing.

PAYMENT AND ROYALTIES

The AUTHOR will receive payment of Payment Rate ($0,000.00 US), as well as X (numerical value) contributor's copies (author copies) mailed to the address listed above for the AUTHOR.

The above payment will act as an advance against royalties. Once advances are met, and publication costs are reimbursed to the PUBLISHER, royalty payments will commence.

Royalty payments will be distributed as follows: 50% of profit from sales of the WORK distributed to the AUTHOR, and 50% to the PUBLISHER.

AUTHOR'S WARRANTIES AND INDEMNITIES

The AUTHOR represents and warrants that he/she is the sole author of the WORK. The AUTHOR also represents, to the best of knowledge, that the WORK does not contain libelous material.

CHANGES IN TEXT

The PUBLISHER reserves the right to make alterations to the WORK text, including, but not limited to, copyediting changes to conform the style / design of the text to its customary form and usage.

This does not mean that the editor will change the story, only that the editor will correct mistakes and make sure the story is consistent in format for print.

No deletions from, additions to, or changes in the text may be made without the prior written approval of the author except for corrections to spelling, grammar, and punctuation. No additions or corrections can be made post-publication.

PUBLISHING FORMATS

The PUBLISHER will prepare the book for distribution in hardcover, trade paperback, and e-book. Other formats will require a contract addendum.

The PUBLISHER agrees to secure a unique ISBN (Internatinoal Standard Book Number) and submit the WORK to distributors including Ingram Book Group, Amazon, Barnes and Noble, and other channels, so that it may be available for purchase through these systems.

COPYRIGHT

The AUTHOR retains copyright to the WORK.

The PUBLISHER retains copyright to the TITLE.

Copyright credit will be listed to the AUTHOR for the WORK on the copyright page.

REVERSION OF RIGHTS / WITHDRAWAL OF OFFER TO PUBLISH

In the event that the WORK is not published within 12 months of signing this agreement, all rights revert to the AUTHOR, and the AUTHOR has the right to sell or arrange for publication of the above-named WORK elsewhere. The AUTHOR shall keep any payments made by the PUBLISHER.

The PUBLISHER may withdraw offer to publish at any time, for any reason, prior to publication of the WORK with a written notice, at which point all licenses herein shall revert to the AUTHOR.

AUTHOR'S CREDIT

The AUTHOR will be credited on the table of contents page and at the beginning of the story as Author Name (by-line / pseudonym, not necessarily the author's legal name).

VENUE

This agreement shall be deemed executed under the laws of the state of State, which shall be the applicable law of this agreement.

Author's Signature (legal name) ________

AUTHOR DATE

Representative's Signature____ ________

PUBLISHER REPRESENTATIVE DATE

Title of Representative

If a work is submitted to more than one market (those accepting what is referred to as *simultaneous submissions*), it is common courtesy for the writer to inform other agents, editors, or publishers they have accepted an offer. It is equally important as agents, editors, or publishers to inform the writer whether their work is accepted or rejected.

And if a work is accepted for representation or publication, and a contract agreed-upon and signed, what then?

PROMOTION

The importance of branding.

"Too many people overvalue what they are not and undervalue what they are."
- Malcolm Forbes

BRANDING

After acceptance, whether that is a writer finding an agent or publisher and signing a contract, or accepting the fact that their work would be better off self-published or hybrid-published, it is time to build the brand. Writers need to make a name for themselves—by their real name, nickname, or pseudonym—and create an online presence.

One free place to start is social media, snagging handles and making them consistent: facebook.com/AuthorName, twitter.com/AuthorName (@AuthorName), and LinkedIn, Instagram, TikTok, or any other platform that may eventually be used. If a new social media app trends, why not snag a handle before someone else takes it?

Search engines can be utilized to check if the author's name is already taken or similar to other published writers, as well as searched for similar book titles. If using a common name like John Doe, it may be worthwhile to add a middle name or initial to distinguish from another John Doe or use a new name altogether. If the book title is simply a character name, such as *Daphne*, see if another writer recently used that title.

And while searching the name (everyone self-Googles), what might be found online that is worth taking down? What else is "published" about the author? How should a writer represent themselves to the public? How are they represented currently? What is their *brand?* Agents and editors and publishers research who they consider representing.

Consider one's profession prior to becoming known as an "author." Does a Human Resources Manager in the non-literary world want to be linked to erotic fiction? Does an accountant want to be recognized for a crime novel series involving embezzlement and espionage? Should a therapist publish a nonfiction self-help book about real-world case studies, despite protecting clientele identities?

Multiple brands might be needed if spanning genres. Someone writing psychological thrillers may run into issues selling mid-grade children's books, or when switching from western to romance, or nonfiction to fiction.

Securing a domain name is also not a bad idea and not expensive: AuthorName.com, or .whatever. Novice writers often feel a need to secure BookTitle.com or .whatever, but it does not make sense to grab a unique domain name for each title ever released, the same way Nike does not build a website for every shoe designed.

There are a lot of services that streamline the process of building and hosting a website, but the most important thing at the beginning (or end if starting late) is to snag everything that can be snagged before they are snagged.

Cross-platform branding is essential. The profile image used on Twitter should match Facebook, and LinkedIn, and all other platforms, making it easier for future readers and fans to find the writer, especially since it is not always possible to obtain identical handles across social media. What *theme* might a writer span across their web presence, and what *tone*, and *mood?* There are also services available that make cross-posting simpler. A blog post on a site hosted by WordPress, for example, can easily be shared across the internet, saving time.

Social media is not the place to sell books. Spammy posts with links to titles and "where to buy" information gets filtered through most algorithms and if done too often will drive readers away. Instead, the focus should be on articles that mention the writer or their work, or interviews, or book reviews, or updates on the manuscript or editing progress or cover design. An initial book-launch announcement, sure, but how much more is needed?

Readers want to know writers personally: their pets, what they eat, what they do recreationally, what they thought about the latest movie or book or song or fad. Consider all the "stuff" quickly scrolled through on social media—those microseconds are tracked—and what might cause the scroller to pause and enjoy what is on their screen for a moment. Save business for websites and let people land on domains naturally.

Future "fans" can be stalky, so avoid harassment by protecting the identity. What is visible to the public? Pictures of children, a school, a house? Imagine posting a photo of a fun time at home in Wherever, USA (home pictured in the background), then soon after sharing a location or getting tagged at a nearby establishment, then soon after leaving a message on social media stating, "Vacation! I can't wait to spend the next few weeks away from home!" In other words: *Here's where I live, and a close reference point, and, by the way, I'm going to be gone for a while, so have at it.* Geo-tagged locations let people know location real-time, and any information given adds to the threat.

Fan is short for *fanatic*, meaning someone who is enthusiast or an aficionado of one thing or another; in this case, a level of obsession with the writer and on varying levels. People might love one's writing, or hate their words with a passion, so avoid potential invitations to getting robbed, vandalized, stalked, threatened, or even killed.

Also assess what information is available to the public and privatize what should not be. Revisit security settings. Hide phone numbers, mailing / physical / email addresses; such information only needs to be shared with family and close friends. Find what is out there and take it down. And why not revisit those "friends" lists and cull occasionally?

When sharing online, a good general rule is to not bring up or debate any of the big four that should not be discussed among family and close friends: *money, politics, religion, sex*. Those four topics can be relationship- and career-ending.

In the United States, a democratic or republican writer can lose nearly half their readership by publicly badgering the opposite political party. A well-established and proudly straight author can destroy an entire legacy by promoting or supporting sexual phobias. In a world mostly comprised of the religious, what negative effects might readers take against religion?

A personal brand requires professionalism, a constant state of think-before-you-post.

SALES RANKINGS

A dream for many writers is to become a bestselling author, or to at least one day walk into a bookstore—if they still exist in the near future—and see their book on the shelves alongside so many others. But it is just a dream.

Traditionally published books make the bestseller lists, such as *Publisher's Weekly*, *The New York Times*, *The Wall Street Journal*, the *USA Today*, and others that deem books highly successful based on sales figures or what is popular.

According to Tucker Max, a four-time *New York Times* bestselling author and co-founder of Scribe, "No bestseller list measures the actual best selling books." He argues that every single list is measured on sales from few, specific places, or "far worse, it's a curated list and a small group of people are deciding what to put on their list." The books listed are thought of as "'important' books, not based on what is actually selling" and all have admitted to this at one point or another. [80]

William Blatty's novel *The Exorcist* sold over ten million copies worldwide since first published but did not appear on the *New York Times Bestseller* list until after Blatty lost a lawsuit filed against them. At the time, the highly controversial novel had sold more than 84,000 copies, enough to make the list, but was excluded for "editorial reasons."

He sued for nine million dollars, claiming "the newspaper has damaged sales of his new book by negligently leaving it off its best-seller list." His prior novel *Legion* had sold a similar number and made the list. According to *The New York Times* during that specific lawsuit, their bestseller list was "based on weekly sales reports obtained from a scientifically selected sample of bookstores throughout the United States." That lone statement forever admitted that their sales numbers were selectively sourced. [81]

Independently published books, hybrid, and vanity—even if they sell enough copies to make bestseller lists—are often not recognized or are refused to be recognized because they are not published by major publishing houses. Another thing to note is that hitting a bestseller list could require anywhere between 3,000 and 5,000 books sold per week, minimum, and only from specific sources, and that excludes Amazon completely.

Amazon, excluded for eBook and promotional sales for the main bestseller lists, have their own "best seller list," which anyone can get with narrowly-specific BISAC categories (Book Industry Standards and Communications) and temporary sales rankings. According to their Amazon Bestsellers page: "Our best selling products. Updated Hourly."

What does it take to make the Amazon top 100? In general, around 500 sales in a day. The top 10 takes around 2,000. And for exceedingly specific categories, as little as 10. How important, then, is the "bestseller" status?

Bestseller means as much to a writer as a writer wants it to mean. Is it cool to have *New York Times Bestselling Author* on the cover of a book, or *USA Today Bestselling Author?* Is it cool to mention online that a book is an *Amazon Bestseller*? It matters what the writer thinks is cool.

PROTECTION

Trending and temporary sales aside, a question many writers have is whether they need to protect the work they have created, often asking about obtaining trademarks and copyrights and whatnot.

"Book titles do not need to be copyrighted." © Just like song and movie titles, the short lengths of book titles make them not fall under copyright protection, so do not waste the time. While a writer's *work* is copyrighted to the author the moment it is written, their title can be used by any other writer. The shorter the book title, the easier the chance that it might be the title of another writer's work because such titles are too generic.

"Book titles do not need to be trademarked." ™ That is not really a protected phrase, but an example of how that little logo appears next to something that is trademarked. Many first-time authors think they need to trademark their debut book so no one else can steal the title, but book titles *cannot* be trademarked; however, a series of books under one similar name can be. For example, the *Harry Potter* series.

Trademarks exist to protect the consumer as much as the writer to help avoid confusion over similar titles. If the *Harry Potter* series had not received its trademark, for example, who could stop a disgruntled writer from creating *Harry Potter and the Transphobic Author* (and later receiving a copyright infringement notice)? Fans could arguably see the new title and insta-buy if the design were similar enough, or the logo ripped-off, and if they didn't get past the all-too-familiar *Harry Potter* name and typeface and read the rest of the jab at Rowling's personal beliefs on sexuality.

A similar issue with Stephen King and a certain Stephen R. King surfaced online, the second "author" (definitely in quotes) listing numerous titles of similar name choice, and a nearly-identical font and style choice used for the "author" name and book titles. Originally, the hack-writer, piggybacking on already-established fortune and fame, published his books as "Stephen King" and was much later forced to at least include the middle initial after a cease and desist.

Books and other creations "inspired by" popular books, on the other hand, are considered fan art, which are easy enough to pick out from the originals but create a problem. Fan art, while not legally permitted, can be "published" (online or handed out) if no money is transacted. Fan *fiction*, specifically, inspired by popular culture, is an extremely controversial, complex, and continuing issue.

Creating art too close in form to another is plagiarism, such as if a writer highly enjoyed the *Star Wars* series and wrote a book featuring a gun-toting hero wearing a vest, a squeaky-voiced blond boy wielding a "light sword," a princess they rescue who happens to have a unique hairdo, and a pair of annoyingly-cute robots, all battling a great empire in space and their planet-destroying satellite. If even remotely close, it is infringement. Then there is *Spaceballs* . . .

Parodies are allowed under copyright law and sometimes argued under the fair use law as "for purposes such as criticism [or] comment," which can be difficult waters to tread. Those who have made their careers from parodying works (Weird "Al" Yankovic for his music, *South Park* for their cartoons) are constantly under scrutiny and often facing legal action.

To be considered "fair use," each work needs to fit within the four-factor analysis codified in Section 107 of the U.S. Copyright Act:

> First, the purpose and character of the use. This factor considers whether the use is for commercial or nonprofit educational purposes and whether the use is "transformative," or whether the use adds something new to the original creative work or presents it in a different light.

> Second, the nature of the copyrighted work, which asks whether the copyrighted work is creative or factual, and if it has been previously published.
>
> Third, the amount or substantiality of the new use in relation to the original work.
>
> Fourth, whether the new work affects the market for the original work. This factor considers the degree of market harm caused by the new work and the potential market harm that may arise.

According to the Copyright Alliance, "Both parody and satire use humor as a tool to convey a message, but each serves a different purpose. Parody imitates the style of a particular creator with deliberate exaggerations for comedic effect. Satire uses humor to comment on the world-at-large, particularly in the context of politics." [82]

The U.S. Patent and Trademark Office will not consider a title (or brand) a distinctive mark if it cannot be indisputably distinguishable from others, and so they will deny trademark protection.

Every writer might dream of their work becoming "the next big thing," but there is no rush to go out and protect it right away. Focus on finishing the book first, spending time *really* finishing it, and getting it published.

And once the book is in print, ignore the reviews. Do not read them. Do not respond to them.

> "Be yourself; everyone else is already taken." - Oscar Wilde

PERFORMANCE

The art of reading aloud.

"A half-read book is a half-finished love affair." - David Mitchell [83]

Writers must become performers. This is difficult for most to grasp, but those who author books eventually need to read their work aloud. In front of the mirror. In front of family and friends. In front of complete strangers. In front of crowds. All successful writers will be required to do this, so as soon as the uncomfortableness can be made comfortable the better.

Standing in front of people and/or behind a stand to perform can be terrifying. It causes knees and hands to shake, the eyes to burn, the voice to waver and crack. The unfortunate soul adds additional words not on the page, *uh* and *um*, and uncomfortable pauses when re-finding where they are on the page or when happening upon writing that should have been smoothed more during revisions.

Just about everyone has sat in a chair on the opposite side of this scenario, thinking, *I'm sure glad that's not me up there*, while listening through the struggle.

Reading aloud creates "narrative transportation," an imaginative state in which listeners are disconnected from reality and absorbed into narrative flow, temporarily forgetting their surroundings with a sense of time distortion when the story ends; meanwhile, auditory, visual, emotional, and kinesthetic senses are stimulated.

In Storytelling.NYC's *The Science of Storytelling*, they state that stories "take listeners on a journey, immersing them in the world of the narrative and creating intrigue and curiosity. Storytelling is a highly effective communication strategy because stories captivate attention, elicit thoughts and emotions, and ignite curiosity, so listeners are always tugging on the rope, eager to hear more."[84]

And isn't the point of storytelling to do one of three things: educate, inform, or entertain?

Good story*telling*, as in "telling story" by reading aloud, requires constantly-provided intrigue. There needs to be an initial *hook*, but also a tug that keeps pulling the listener out of the real world and into the imaginary; if done right, once released, those fully immersed realize they've experienced a nearly hypnotic state of wonderment.

The Storytelling article expands on the science behind this: "When a speaker induces a flow state in listeners, it triggers a cascade of potent neurochemicals, including *norepinephrine, dopamine, anandamide, serotonin*, and *endorphins*. These neurochemicals are potent 'feel good' drugs, triggering pleasure and excitement in listeners."

Similar to exercise releasing endorphins and sparking creativity, being read to aloud allows for another's creativity to invade the mind. Those who attend author readings never go to simply listen, they want to be entertained.

Reading aloud is a good practice in general. Well before one's writing is published, reading aloud irons out awkward writing. Sentences might be too long, not allowing room for breaths. This is why sentence and paragraph structure are important. When read aloud, paragraphs might seem to go on and on instead of creating beats for pause and reflection. The work might even be bland, which is why it is so important during the editing process to cut every unnecessary word, leaving behind only what is entertaining, informative, or educational.

What makes a successful reading? How can one rid the shakes and jitters and tell a damn good story and entertain an audience, causing laughter, pleasure, disgust, etc.? How are butterflies in the stomach settled? Like some phobias, fears can be addressed with exposure therapy. Practice. Trial and error. Reading in front of the mirror, then in front of family and friends, then in front of small crowds, then larger crowds.

Don't read aloud; perform the work.

Look around during a boring reading and one might find others distracted with cellphones or reading other books, or an occasional dedicated listener struggling through it thinking, *I'm sure glad that's not me up there.*

Readings are pleasant or painful, so below is advice from a wonderful performer sharing secrets after years of storytelling. He started the same: shaking knees and hands, burning eyes, and a wavering, cracking voice. He got through it, though, eventually realizing that reading the written word aloud requires more than *telling* a story but *performing* a story.

ON READINGS

by Jack Ketchum

So, they've asked you to read, have they? Well, what makes a good reading?

First, rehearse. Don't go in cold. We writers are accused of arrogance often enough as it is. So do your homework. You're an actor now. Do what all good actors do. Know your lines. You don't have to memorize. But know your lines.

Respect your own text. For petesakes, don't rush it.

And *remember* it.

Remember what the text was when you wrote the thing. Exactly what word in a sentence, what line in a paragraph, did you want to emphasize back then? Emphasize those things now as you read them. Come down hard on them. Slow down for effect. Break for effect. You're trying to communicate here. Emphasis is meaning. There is nothing in a reading as important as this.

Make eye-contact with your audience. If you know your text, it shouldn't be too difficult to raise your head from the page every so often. If your audience is lit, it's easy. Hell, you can stare them down if you want to. If the audience is in darkness, take the measure of the room's seating and sweep it now and then with your eyes. Chances are Betsy in row nine is going to think you're reading that line for her.

Have fun. Your audience wants to like you, wants to like what you've written. Or else they wouldn't be here.

Relax. Breathe deep. Enjoy your moment in the light.

Jack Ketchum is the author of *The Girl Next Door*, *Red*, *The Secret Life of Souls*, and others. 1946 - 2018. Pseudonym for Dallas Mayr. Most of his books have been adapted to film. This was one of the last things he wrote before he died.

AUTHOR'S NOTE

Final thoughts on righting writing.

"It is good to have an end to journey towards; but it is the journey that matters, in the end."
- Ursula Le Guin [85]

Books need endings, so consider these final words the conclusion. Short and to the point. *Righting Writing* required three acts: *the beginning*, *the middle*, and *the end*, and since the book was designed as such to serve structural purpose, it did not leave much room for a summary chapter. But is one needed?

What is this book I'm holding?

Why read it?

What's the purpose?

All three important questions should be addressed in Introductions and Author's Notes, as mentioned earlier. The title itself is the answer to all three. *Righting Writing*; that is the book, why it should be read, and its purpose.

This also makes the title a conclusion, in a way. Those two words summarize a present-tense narrative that includes a beginning, middle, and end: writing needs to be righted, an unstated but assumed "inside are tools to help," and finally a message that writing can always be improved upon but never perfected, otherwise the title would be *Writing Righted.*

Writing is a cureless disease; the only option is to write with an understanding that a book (or whatever creative project it may be) is never finished, only abandoned. As much time or longer needs to be spent bettering—not worsening—what will later become the finished product than it took to complete the original draft.

While books require dissection, revision, endless edits, and rewrites, at some point a writer needs to set their work aside and move on to the next project to avoid an endless loop of tinkering. Insanity is doing the same thing over and over and expecting different results, so to avoid insanity, writers must eventually reach "The End."

It is the end of this book, after all, and the combined reader / writer / editor, *you* (this part written in second-person because this section is supposed to address the reader directly) are hopefully inspired to start writing or return to writing something already started. And now you have the help of a little editor-devil on one shoulder poking you with his red pen every time a bad habit surfaces, and a little editor-angel smiling every so often on the other.

Consider the core components of the Author's Note:

1. Hook the reader
2. Address the subject matter(s) / topic(s)
3. Address issue(s) to which the book relates
4. Create credibility / trust for the author
5. Present a hypothesis / theory
6. Address the intended audience
7. Provide reasoning why the book is worth reading

Is everything covered in these final pages; so far, everything but number four. Who am *I* to offer this advice (now switching to first-person because Author's Notes and Introductions are often written by the author)? It does not really matter, but there is eventually an About the Author page.

The end is only the beginning, and so now it is time to close this book and begin another. Write, but do it right.

ENDNOTES

Cited material.

1. Nash, Jennie. "5 Steps to Writing a Killer Elevator Pitch for Your Book." BookBub Partners Blog, October 19, 2020. https://insights.bookbub.com/steps-to-writing-a-killer-elevator-pitch-for-your-book.

2. Clance, P. R., & Imes, S. A. (1978). The imposter phenomenon in high achieving women: Dynamics and therapeutic intervention. *Psychotherapy: Theory, Research & Practice*, 15(3), 241–247.

3. Weir, Kirsten. "Feel like a Fraud?" American Psychological Association, November 2013. https://www.apa.org/gradpsych/2013/11/fraud.

4. Young, Valerie. *The Secret Thoughts of Successful Women Why Capable People Suffer from the Impostor Syndrome and How to Thrive in Spite of It.* Three Rivers Pr, 2012.

5. Cherry, Kendra. "The Importance of Maintaining Structure and Routine During Stressful Times." Verywell Mind, April 21, 2020. https://www.verywellmind.com/the-importance-of-keeping-a-routine-during-stressful-times-4802638.

6. Vidal, Juan. "100 Years After Jack London's Death, Hearing His Call." NPR, November 26, 2016. https://www.npr.org/2016/11/26/502608299/ 100-years-after-jack-londons-death-hearing-his-call.

7. Roorback, Bill, and Kristen Keckler. "Craft True-to-Life Nonfiction Characters." *Writer's Digest*, August 6, 2009. https://www.writersdigest.com/improve-my-writing/craft-true-to-life-nonfiction-characters.

8. MasterClass. "Writing 101: All the Different Types of Characters in Literature - 2020." MasterClass, October 2, 2020. https://www.masterclass.com/articles/guide-to-all-the-types-of-characters-in-literature.

9. Jung, C. G. *The Archetypes and the Collective Unconscious*. London: Routledge, 2014.

10. Ball, Jonathan. "Don't Attribute Dialogue." Jonathan Ball, PhD, May 2, 2019. https://www.jonathanball.com/dont-attribute-dialogue.

11. Wiehardt, Ginny. "An Explanation of the Term 'Voice' in Fiction Writing." The Balance Careers, August 9, 2019. https://www.thebalancecareers.com/what-is-voice-in-fiction-writing-1277142.

12. Humphrey, Robert. *Stream of Consciousness in the Modern Novel*. Berkeley, CA: University of California Press, 1995.

13. Potter, Daniel. "4 Essential Types of Writing Styles." Grammarly, December 20, 2019. https://www.grammarly.com/blog/writing-styles.

14. Hill, Beth, ed. "Tone, Mood, & Style-The Feel of Fiction." The Editor's Blog, April 20, 2013. https://theeditorsblog.net/2013/04/19/tone-mood-style-the-feel-of-fiction.

15. O'Connor, Timothy, and Christopher Franklin. "Free Will." Stanford Encyclopedia of Philosophy. Stanford University, August 21, 2018. https://plato.stanford.edu/entries/freewill.

16. Reid, Ruthanne. "What Is Plot? The 5 Elements of Plot and How to Use Them." The Write Practice, January 4, 2020. https://thewritepractice.com/plot.

17. Freytag, Gustav, and Elias J. MacEwan. *Freytag's Technique of the Drama: an Exposition of Dramatic Composition and Art by Gustav Freytag*. New York, NY: B. Blom, 1968.

18. Booker, Christopher. *The Seven Basic Plots: Why We Tell Stories.* London, England: Bloomsbury Continuum, 2015.

19. Strathy, Glen C. "The Nine Basic Plots." How to Write a Book Now, 2014. https://www.how-to-write-a-book-now.com/basic-plots.html.

20. Turner-Francis, Mahogany. "Book Genres That Make the Most Money." Bookstr, November 20, 2018. https://bookstr.com/article/book-genres-that-make-the-most-money.

21. Alonso, Eva Collins. "Kurt Vonnegut, Shape of Stories." The Case College Scholars Program. Recorded on February 4, 2014, posted July 14, 2018. YouTube video, 17:36. https://youtu.be/GOGru_4z1Vc.

22. Bell, James Scott. *The Art of War for Writers: Fiction Writing Strategies, Tactics, and Exercises.* New York, NY: F+W Media (Penguin Random House), 2011.

23. Trettenero, Scott. "My Way Versus Your Way: How to Handle Conflict." Psychreg, July 20, 2020. https://www.psychreg.org/how-to-handle-conflict.

24. Campbell, Sherrie. "The 10 Benefits of Conflict." *Entrepreneur*, July 28, 2016. https://www.entrepreneur.com/article/279778.

25. Vonnegut, Kurt. *Palm Sunday an Autobiographical Collage.* London, England: Grafton Books, 1987.

26. Griffith, Jeremy. "Video 10: What exactly is the human condition?" World Transformation Movement. Streamed live on November 23, 2018. YouTube video, 28:04. youtube.com/pGQpBx2Lj9I.

27. MasterClass. "Complete Guide to Literary Themes: Definition, Examples, and How to Create Literary Themes in Your Writing - 2020." Master Class, November 8, 2020. https://www.masterclass.com/articles/the- complete-guide-to-narrative-theme-in-literature-definition-examples-and-writing-how-to.

28. Hauge, Michael. *Writing Screenplays That Sell.* London: Methuen Drama, 2011.

29. Maass, Donald. *The Breakout Novelist: How to Craft Novels That Stand Out and Sell.* Cincinnati, OH: Writer's Digest Books, 2014.

30. Munro, Alice. *Hateship, Friendship, Courtship, Loveship, Marriage: Stories.* New York, NY: Vintage Books, 2008.

31. Maltz, Maxwell, and Melvin Powers. *Psycho-Cybernetics: a New Way to Get More Living out of Life.* Chatsworth, CA: Wilshire Book Co., 2010.

32. Fassler, Joe. "Why Stephen King Spends 'Months and Even Years' Writing Opening Sentences." *The Atlantic.* Atlantic Media Company, June 11, 2015. https://www.theatlantic.com/entertainment/archive/2013/07/why-stephen-king-spends-months-and-even-years-writing-opening-sentences/278043.

33. O'Chee, Katherine, Paige Riddiford, and Elaine Mead. "7 Clever Steps To Hook Your Reader Into Your Narrative." Writer's Edit, September 8, 2018. https://writersedit.com/fiction-writing/7-steps-hook-reader-narrative.

34. Oates, Joyce Carol. *I Lock My Door upon Myself.* New York, NY: Ecco Press, 1990.

35. Ingermanson, Randy. "Defining the Target Audience for Your Novel." Advanced Fiction Writing, November 8, 2012. https://www.advancedfictionwriting.com/blog/2012/07/11/defining-the-target-audience-for-your-novel.

36. Lexico Dictionaries. "Prose: Definition of Prose by Oxford Dictionary on Lexico.com Also Meaning of Prose," Lexico Dictionaries | English (Lexico Dictionaries), accessed October 28, 2020, https://www.lexico.com/en/definition/prose.

37. Gross, John. "The New Oxford Book of English Prose," in *The New Oxford Book of English Prose* (Oxford: Oxford University Press, 1999).

38. Lasky, Dorothea. "What Poetry Teaches Us About the Power of Persuasion," *The Atlantic* (Atlantic Media Company, October 13, 2012), https://www.theatlantic.com/national/archive/2012/10/what-poetry-teaches-us-about-the-power-of-persuasion/263551.

39. DiYanni, Robert. *Literature: Reading Fiction, Poetry, Drama, and the Essay.* Boston, MA: McGraw-Hill, 1998.

40. Carpenter, Courtney. "7 Tools For Pacing A Novel & Keeping Your Story Moving At The Right Pace." *Writer's Digest*, April 24, 2012. https://www.writersdigest.com/improve-my-writing/7-tools-for-pacing-a-novel-keeping-your-story-moving-at-the-right-pace.

41. Naillon, Buffy. "What Is Narrative Pace?" Pen and the Pad, July 3, 2021. https://penandthepad.com/narrative-pace-3907.html.

42. Agarwal, Prateek. "Importance of Tense in English Language." Medium, February 2, 2016. https://medium.com/@hdi.prateek/importance-of-tense-in-english-language-1ea7b9720634.

43. Chitty, David. "The Benefits and Drawbacks of Past Tense." Thanet Writers, October 20, 2016. https://thanetwriters.com/essay/setting/the-benefits-and-drawbacks-of-past-tense.

44. Bunting, Joe. "The Ultimate Point of View Guide: Third Person Omniscient vs. Third Person Limited vs. First Person." The Write Practice, July 24, 2020, https://thewritepractice.com/point-of-view-guide.

45. Biederman, Roseann. "Showing vs. Telling in Your Writing." *Writer's Digest*, June 13, 2012. https://www.writersdigest.com/whats-new/showing-vs-telling-in-your-writing.

46. Gerke, Jeff. *The First 50 Pages: Engage Agents, Editors and Readers and Set up Your Novel for Success.* Cincinnati, OH: *Writer's Digest*, 2011.

47. Bureau of Labor Statistics. "American Time Use Survey - May to December 2019 and 2020 Results". U.S. Department of Labor, July 22, 2021. https://www.bls.gov/news.release/pdf/atus.pdf.

48. *The Merriam-Webster Dictionary*. Springfield, MA: Merriam-Webster, Incorporated, 2019.

49. Gaiman, Neil. "Writing 101: What Is Figurative Language? Learn About 10 Types of Figurative Language with Examples - 2020." MasterClass, October 2, 2020. https://www.masterclass.com/articles/writing-101-what-is-figurative-language-learn-about-10-types-of-figurative-language-with-examples.

50. Lexico Dictionaries. "Figurative: Definition of Figurative by Oxford Dictionary on Lexico.com Also Meaning of Figurative," Lexico Dictionaries | English (Lexico Dictionaries), accessed October 29, 2020, https://www.lexico.com/en/definition/prose.

51. Watson, Amy. "U.S. Daily Reading Time by Age 2020." Statista, July 26, 2021. https://www.statista.com/statistics/412454/average-daily-time-reading-us-by-age.

52. Nowak, Paul. "What Is the Average Reading Speed?" Iris Reading, May 29, 2018. https://irisreading.com/what-is-the-average-reading-speed.

53. McSpadden, Kevin. "Science: You Now Have a Shorter Attention Span than a Goldfish." *Time*, May 14, 2015. https://time.com/3858309/attention-spans-goldfish.

54. Alioto, Daisy. "Ode to the Dinkus." *The Paris Review*, June 8, 2018. https://www.theparisreview.org/blog/2018/06/08/ode-to-the-dinkus.

55. Atwood, Blake. "How Many Words in a Novel? Word Counts for All Book Genres." The Write Life, June 8, 2021. https://thewritelife.com/how-many-words-in-a-novel.

56. Sambuchino, Chuck. "Word Count for Novels and Children's Books: The Definitive Post: How Long Should a Book Be?" *Writer's Digest*, October 25, 2016. https://www.writersdigest.com/whats-new/word-count-for-novels-and-childrens-books-the-definitive-post.

57. The Royal Literary Fund Editors. "What Is a Writing Block?" The Royal Literary Fund. Accessed August 10, 2021. https://www.rlf.org.uk/resources/what-is-a-writing-block.

58. Summers, Scott. "8 Tools and Tips to Use When Self-Editing Your Work." Business 2 Community, May 8, 2020, https://www.business2community.com/communications/8-tools-and-tips-to-use-when-self-editing-your-work-02308430.

59. King, Stephen. *On Writing: A Memoir of the Craft.* New York, NY: Scribner, 2000.

60. Merriam-Webster.com Dictionary, s.v. "manuscript," accessed September 10, 2021, https://www.merriam-webster.com/dictionary/manuscript.

61. Mann, Meredith. "Where Did Times New Roman Come from?" The New York Public Library, August 23, 2021. https://www.nypl.org/blog/2014/12/09/times-new-roman.

62. Felici, James, and Frank J. Romano. *The Complete Manual of Typography: A Guide to Setting Perfect Type.* Berkeley, CA: Peachpit Press, 2012.

63. Betts, Jennifer. "Using Endnotes and a Bibliography." Bibliography.com, October 7, 2020. https://www.bibliography.com/chicago/using-endnotes-and-a-bibliography.

64. Goldman, William. *Marathon Man.* New York: Ballantine Books, 2001.

65. Max, Tucker. "How to Write an Author Bio & Why." Scribe Media, February 9, 2021. https://scribemedia.com/write-author-bio.

66. BusinessTerms.org Editors. "Economic Contraction" BusinessTerms.org, 2018. https://businessterms.org/economic-contraction.

67. Pierce, Leigh. "Alpha and Beta Readers: What Are They and Why Bother?" IngramSpark, June 11, 2020. https://www.ingramspark.com/blog/alpha-and-beta-readers-what-are-they-and-why-bother.

68. Norton, Scott. *Developmental Editing: A Handbook for Freelancers, Authors, and Publishers.* Chicago, IL: University of Chicago Press, 2019.

69. University of Chicago Press Editors. "Developmental Editing." University of Chicago Press, March 1, 2009. https://press.uchicago.edu/ucp/books/book/chicago/D/bo5604692.html.

70. FreelanceWriting Editors. "What Is a Ghost Writer?" Freelance-Writing, December 4, 2020. https://www.freelancewriting.com/ghostwriting/what-is-a-ghostwriter.

71. Geller, Jonny. "The Life of a Literary Agent." Curtis Brown Creative, December 11, 2019. https://www.curtisbrowncreative.co.uk/jonny-geller-the-life-of-a-literary-agent.

72. Milliot, Jim. "Where Have All the Midsize Book Publishers Gone?" PublishersWeekly.com, October 1, 2021. https://www.publishersweekly.com/pw/by-topic/industry-news/publisher-news/article/87526-where-have-all-the-midsize-book-publishers-gone.html.

73. Borgerson, Eric. "What Is Independent Publishing, and How Does It Differ from Traditional Publishing and Self Publishing?" Polylyric Press, November 8, 2018. https://polylyric.com/what-is-independent-publishing.

74. Warner, Brooke. "What Is Hybrid Publishing? Here Are 4 Things All Writers Should Know." *Writer's Digest*, August 11, 2016. https://www.writersdigest.com/self-publishing-by-writing-goal/what-is-hybrid-publishing-here-are-4-things-you-should-know.

75. Temple, Emily. "'Perhaps We're Being Dense.' Rejection Letters Sent to Famous Writers." Literary Hub, June 20, 2019. https://lithub.com/perhaps-were-being-dense-rejection-letters-sent-to-famous-writers.

76. King, Stephen. *On Writing: A Memoir of the Craft.* New York, NY: Scribner, 2000.

77. Moreton, Cole. "Joe Hill on Following in the Footsteps of Father Stephen King." Daily Mail Online. Associated Newspapers, May 14, 2016. https://www.dailymail.co.uk/home/event/article-3586818/Joe-Hill-following-footsteps-father-Stephen-King.html.

78. Cornell University. "Author Rights Resources: Home." Author Rights Resources: Understanding Author Rights. Cornell University Library, May 12, 2021. https://guides.library.cornell.edu/authorrights.

79. Copyright Office. *Copyright Law of the United States and Related Laws Contained in Title 17 of the United States Code*. Washington, D.C.: Library of Congress, 2016.

80. Max, Tucker. "How to Get on the NY Times & Other Bestseller Book Lists." Scribe Media, October 12, 2021. https://scribemedia.com/get-best-seller-list.

81. The New York Times. "Blatty Sue Times on Best-Seller List." The New York Times, August 29, 1983. https://www.nytimes.com/1983/08/29/arts/blatty-sue-times-on-best-seller-list.html.

82. Williamson, Erin. "Is My Parody Fair Use?" Copyright Alliance, October 22, 2021. https://copyrightalliance.org/is-my-parody-fair-use.

83. Mitchell, David. *Cloud Atlas: A Novel.* New York, NY: Random House Trade Paperbacks Modern Library, 2004.

84. Dixit, Jay. "Narrative Transportation." Storytelling.NYC, 2019. https://storytelling.nyc/narrative-transportation.

85. Le Guin, Ursula. *The Left Hand of Darkness*. London: Orbit, 1997.

ABOUT THE AUTHOR

Who wrote this thing?

Michael Bailey is a recipient of the Bram Stoker Award (and eight-time nominee), a multiple recipient of the Benjamin Franklin Award, a four-time Shirley Jackson Award nominee, and a few dozen independent publishing accolades. He has authored numerous novels, novellas, novelettes, and fiction & poetry collections. Recent work includes *Agatha's Barn*, a tie-in novella to Josh Malerman's *Carpenter's Farm*, a collaborative novella with Erinn L. Kemper called *The Call of the Void*, and *Sifting the Ashes*, a collaborative and lengthy poetry collection with Marge Simon. He runs the small press Written Backwards and has edited and published twelve anthologies, such as *The Library of the Dead*, the *Chiral Mad* series, and *Miscreations: Gods, Monstrosities & Other Horrors*. He lives in Costa Rica where he is rebuilding his life after surviving one of the most catastrophic wildfires in California history, which is explored in his memoir *Seven Minutes*. Find him online at nettirw.com, or @nettirw in most places.

ALSO AVAILABLE

Other books written / edited by the author.

NOVELS

Palindrome Hannah

Phoenix Rose

Psychotropic Dragon

NOVELLAS

Agatha's Barn

The Call of the Void
(with Erinn L. Kemper)

NOVELETTES

Our Children, Our Teachers

COLLECTIONS

Scales and Petals

Inkblots and Blood Spots

Oversight

The Impossible Weight of Life

Sifting the Ashes
(poetry with Marge Simon)

ANTHOLOGIES

Pellucid Lunacy

Chiral Mad

Chiral Mad 2

Qualia Nous

The Library of the Dead

Chiral Mad 3

You, Human

Adam's Ladder
(with Darren Speegle)

Chiral Mad 4: An Anthology of Collaborations
(with Lucy A. Snyder)

Miscreations: Gods, Monstrosities & Other Horrors
(with Doug Murano)

Prisms
(with Darren Speegle)

Chiral Mad 5

Made in the USA
Coppell, TX
17 March 2023